Lyle R Trueblood

Y0-BRW-354

# CORPORATE
# POWER AND
# SOCIAL
# RESPONSIBILITY

# CORPORATE POWER AND SOCIAL RESPONSIBILITY

*Studies of the Modern Corporation*
*Columbia University*
*Graduate School of Business*

# A Blueprint for the Future

## NEIL H. JACOBY

Foreword by *Arthur F. Burns*
Chairman of The Board of Governors
Federal Reserve System

DISCARDED
UNIVERSITY OF TULSA

MACMILLAN PUBLISHING CO., INC.
New York

COLLIER MACMILLAN PUBLISHERS
London

UNIVERSITY OF TULSA - McFARLIN LIBRARY

*Copyright © 1973 by Trustees of Columbia University in the City of New York*

Printed in the United States of America
All rights reserved. No part of this book may be
reproduced or transmitted in any form or by any means,
electronic or mechanical, including photocopying, recording,
or by any information storage and retrieval system,
without permission in writing from the Publisher.

Macmillan Publishing Co., Inc.
866 Third Avenue, New York, N.Y. 10022

Collier–Macmillan Canada Ltd., Toronto, Ontario

Library of Congress Catalog Card Number: 72–14073

*printing number*
1   2   3   4   5   6   7   8   9   10

HD2791
.J33
1973

## STUDIES OF THE MODERN CORPORATION
*Columbia University Graduate School of Business*

The Program for Studies of the Modern Corporation is devoted to the advancement and dissemination of knowledge about the corporation. Its publications are designed to stimulate inquiry, research, criticism, and reflection. They fall into three categories: works by outstanding businessmen, scholars, and professional men from a variety of backgrounds and academic disciplines; annotated and edited selections of business literature; and business classics that merit republication. The studies are supported by outside grants from private business, professional, and philanthropic institutions interested in the program's objectives.

RICHARD EELLS
*Editor of the Studies*

To Pat and Chris
*Who will inherit and help to shape
our emerging society*

# CONTENTS

*Foreword*                                                          xiii
*Preface*                                                             xv
*Introduction*                                                      xvii

PART I    CRITICISM AND REALITY

CHAPTER 1. *The Criticism of Corporate Business*                      3

The Evolution of American Business Criticism / A Typology of Corporate Criticism / Five Major Theses of the
Corporate Critics / Standards for Judging Corporate Performance

CHAPTER 2. *The Corporate Economy: Myths and Realities*             20

The Growth of Corporate and Human Populations / The
Growth of Corporate, Enterprise, and Self-Employed Pop-
ulations / Enterprise Entries, Exits, and Life Expectancies
/ Trends in Corporate Size / Trends in Corporate Con-
centration / Corporations as Generators of Income /
Corporations as Employers of People / Corporations as
Owners of Tangible Wealth / Corporations as Earners of
Income / Changes in the Corporate Shareowner Popu-
lation / The Concentration of Corporate Share Owner-
ship / The Actual Role of the Corporation

PART II    POSTWAR DEVELOPMENTS IN
ORGANIZATION AND OPERATIONS

CHAPTER 3. *Corporate Management: Adding Science to Art*            55

Postwar Innovations in Management Practices / Management Education Before World War II / Postwar
Changes in Management Education / The Rising Status
of Schools of Management / The Future of Management
Education / The Global Tasks of Managers

CHAPTER 4. *The Conglomerate Corporation: Monstrosity or
Model?*                                                             72

The Conglomerate Corporation Defined / Lessons from
Three Merger Waves / A Merger Wave Hypothesis /
Foundations of the Early Merger Waves / Foundations

of the Conglomerate Merger Wave / Private Gains from Conglomeration / Social Gains from Conglomeration / Conglomeration and Competition / Potential Financial Effects / Public Policy for Conglomerates / Perspective

CHAPTER 5. *The Multinational Corporation: Imperialist or Pacifist?*      94

The Multinational Corporation Defined / The Rise of Corporate Multinationalism / The Extent of Foreign Economic Penetration / Motives to Multinationalize / Management Patterns and Processes / Effects on Less Developed Host Countries / Effects on Developed Host Countries / Effects on the Socialist Countries / Effects on Investing Countries / Effects on International Relations / Effects on International and Transnational Institutions / A World Corporation Authority / Policies to Expand Multinational Business / The Future of the Multinational Company

PART III    LEADING ECONOMIC AND POLITICAL ISSUES

CHAPTER 6. *Corporate Economic Power: Concentration or Fragmentation?*      129

Two Perspectives on Concentration and Competition / Corporate Growth: Attitudes and Actualities / Postwar Changes in Concentration / Barriers to Entry into Business / Economies of Scale / A Multi-Vectored Dynamic Model of Competition / Corporate Discretionary Power under the Model / The Economic Balance Sheet of Large-Scale Enterprise

CHAPTER 7. *Corporate Political Power: Involvement or Detachment?*      148

Politicization and Social Pluralism / Instruments of Corporate Political Action / The Decline of Corporate Political Power / Present Corporate Political Power / Corporate versus Union Political Power / Postwar Shifts in Political Alignments / Toward a Consumer-Oriented Politics

CHAPTER 8. *Corporate Government: Autocratic or Democratic?*      165

Contemporary Corporate Government / Constraints on Corporate Government / Restrictions on the Corporate Charter / The Multi-Interest Board of Directors / The European Corporation Board / The Yugoslavian Enterprise Board / Strengthening the American Corporate Board / The New "Managerial" Stockholder / Steps Toward Better Corporate Government

## Part IV  Critical Social Roles

CHAPTER 9. *The Corporation as Social Activist*  185

Social Problems as Expectation-Reality Gaps / Political and Economic Interactions in the Social System / Social Responsibility in Three Models of the Enterprise / The Rise of Political Influence on Business Behavior / Corporate Social Action and Self-Interest / The Rationale for Corporate Giving / Public Policies to Trigger Corporate Social Action / Corporate Policies to Respond to Social Needs

CHAPTER 10. *The Corporation as Environmentalist*  206

Focus on the Urban Physical Environment / Roots of the Environmental Problem / The Swift Rise of the Problem / Aspects of Environmental Deterioration / Illusory Approaches to a Solution / Basic Environmental Economics / Assessing the Costs / Instruments of Policy / Improving Political and Corporate Behavior

CHAPTER 11. *The Corporation as Arms Maker*  225

The Military Hardware Industry / The Myth of the "Military-Industrial Complex" / The Foreign Threat to National Security / The Value of Civilian Expenditure Programs / The Cost of Military Hardware / Profits in the Military Hardware Business / Alternative Sources of Defense Products / A New Structure of Procurement / Improving the Reward/Risk Ratio / Toward an Efficient Corporate Role in Defense

## Part V  The Future

CHAPTER 12. *The Future of the Corporation in Society*  249

Perspectives on Social Prediction / The Global Business Environment in the 1990's / American Society of the 1990's / The Emerging American Business System / New Thrusts of Corporate Management / Multinational Business Prospects / Corporations in a Supranational Ocean Regime / The Continuing Decline of Corporate Power / The Restoration of Shareowner Control / The New Partnership Between Government and Business / Systems Analysis—A Fresh Approach to Public Policy / The Corporation—An Enduring Social Institution

ADDENDUM  *The World Monetary Crisis of Early 1973*  273

*Index*  275

# FOREWORD

THIS BOOK does not fall into a conventional mode. The author's objective is neither to laud nor condemn, but to evaluate dispassionately the performance of the corporation—not only in its economic function, but also as an institution vitally affecting the nation's social and political life. He sets forth constructive suggestions for reform where performance is found wanting.

A lifelong student of business enterprise, Professor Jacoby is well aware that the governmental structure of the typical American corporation needs improvement. He knows that controls are needed to avoid abuses of power by large businesses as well as by other economic and social groups. But he argues, and I think correctly, that the business corporation has contributed powerfully to meeting the evolving needs of our economy. Public policy should, therefore, aim to preserve the positive values of corporations operating in free markets, while at the same time ensuring that the activities of corporate business foster widely held social objectives.

Jacoby develops a "social environment model" to explain corporate behavior as a response to both market and nonmarket forces that influence costs, revenues, and profits. The model is considerably closer in spirit to the classical theory of the firm than to the managerial model of corporate behavior elaborated by Berle and Means. Within the framework of the Jacoby model, corporate concern with social responsibility is viewed as consistent with enlightened self-interest. He recognizes, however, that profit-seeking corporations cannot be expected to absorb all the costs to society that are incidental to their productive activities unless government regulations or fiscal policies encourage them to do so.

Jacoby considers in a forthright manner the principal criticisms of large corporate business that have been voiced in recent years. He argues persuasively that industrial concentration has not increased over the postwar period; that governmental regulatory agencies are not captives of big business; that manufacturers of defense goods have little influence over the aggregate of military outlays; that direct investment by multinational firms in less developed countries is generally beneficial to the host country; and that the political power of businesses is often exaggerated, and in any case is on the wane.

This book, as any other of large importance, will provoke questions on numerous issues. For that reason, as well as because of its authoritative findings, both academic students and men of practical affairs will be rewarded by Professor Jacoby's scholarly analysis of the role and promise of the modern corporation.

Arthur F. Burns

# PREFACE

This work is the product of research, reflection, and—not the least—personal experience. The ideas it contains have evolved over the many years of my life spent as an economist specializing in public policy, as an academic administrator, as a governmental adviser, and as an organizer and director of corporations.

The immediate occasion to undertake this social assessment of the business corporation was the teaching of a course on Business and Society in the Graduate School of Management of the University of California, Los Angeles. A sabbatical year spent as a Visiting Fellow at the Center for the Study of Democratic Institutions during the 1968–1969 academic year provided me the opportunity to review the literature in the field and to outline the book. I am grateful to the Fellows of the Center for their criticisms, from which I have derived a number of new insights. I have also benefited from discussions with my students and with my colleagues at UCLA, especially Professors Harold D. Koontz, George A. Steiner, and J. Fred Weston.

My greatest debt for inspiration and encouragement is due to Richard Eells, Adjunct Professor in the Graduate School of Business of Columbia University and Director of the Program for Studies of the Modern Corporation. A leading American authority on the theory of the corporation, his published works on many facets of the institution set a high standard for other authors to emulate.

I owe an equally heavy debt to Chauncey G. Olinger, Jr., who was on leave from teaching philosophy at Rutgers University, during the spring of 1972, to serve as the editor of this book as well as on the staff of the Secretary of State's Advisory Committee on the United Nations Conference on the Human Environment. He has gone over the entire manuscript, helping me to smooth the flow of the argument and to translate technical economic concepts into language which, I hope, will be clear to the general reader.

Extensive foreign travel on economic missions undertaken for the President and the Department of State have enabled me to observe the interface between business and government in many cultures. Service as a member of the Council of Economic Advisers, as a public member of the

Pay Board, and as the United States Representative in the Economic and Social Council of the United Nations have provided me with a knowledge of governmental operations. In addition, I have had the advantage of much contact with the world of business. This experience has included organizing corporations, serving as a director of several companies, and acting as the chairman of the executive committee of one of the largest multinational corporations. In these capacities I have had to deal with many types of organizations and managerial methods. This experience has involved weighing the risks of investments in foreign countries, as well as in the United States. It has included the burdens of assessing the performance of executives. An actor as well as an observer in the world of business, my ideas about the corporation have been tested in the crucible of experience.

The reader may rightfully conclude that the roots of this book lie deep in activities carried on over many years and that the author's obligations are numerous. I am grateful to Dr. Armand Hammer, whose Professorship Award has provided me with the necessary secretarial, statistical, and editorial assistance. Dean Harold Williams of the Graduate School of Management at UCLA kindly granted me leave to complete the work. Mrs. Lynn Hickman, my secretary, patiently typed successive drafts of many chapters. Earle Birdzell, Jr., Neil H. Jacoby, Jr., and Irving Michelman read the entire manuscript and contributed many perceptive comments that have strengthened the book. The names of contributors to individual chapters are noted at the beginning of each chapter. Above all, I thank my wife, Clair, whose substantive contributions have been numerous. While expressing gratitude to all who contributed to it, I, of course, assume full responsibility for the product.

Neil H. Jacoby
*Los Angeles, California*
*Spring, 1973*

# INTRODUCTION

I N THIS book, we present a social assessment of the American business corporation. We have endeavored to make a thorough and, it is hoped, objective examination and assessment of the performance of this much-praised—and much-maligned—institution of our pluralistic society. As a basis for this appraisal, many of the salient changes in corporate business during the past quarter-century are examined. Building on this examination of these changes and our appraisal of them, we attempt to identify trends pointing to the future role of the corporation both in the United States and in the world. Finally, we propose many reforms of corporate and public policies, which, we believe, will enable the corporation to serve better the goal of a just, efficient, creative, and democratic society.

This comprehensive examination of the corporation builds upon a formidable body of specialized literatures, each of which deals with a particular corporate issue from the standpoint of its related discipline. Thus, corporate law treats of the corporate constitution; economics of corporate pricing, production, and finance; political theory of corporate government; psychology of organizational behavior; sociology of the interaction between corporations and other social bodies; and history of the development of corporate enterprise in the nation. Each of these specialized studies throws light on a significant facet of corporate structure and behavior; each has been taken into account in our effort to achieve a comprehensive view of the corporate institution.

The corporation is viewed here as a central institution within a dynamic economy and a transforming society, in which it is both a vital agent of change and a leading outcome of change. Indeed, an important test of corporate performance, we believe, is the sensitivity with which it has adapted to societal changes and the degree to which it has either facilitated or obstructed the process. To assess an institution in a static framework is to apply a false test, from which irrelevant or erroneous conclusions are drawn. Only with an understanding of its dynamic social context can the true strengths and weaknesses of corporate business be appraised.

Institutions remain the dominant forces in contemporary society. The lives of people are profoundly shaped by their relationships to the family, the church, the school and university, to the trade union and the business corporation, and to the government and the state. Because of their pervasive influence, institutions should be examined continuously, critically, and comprehensively, to determine how well they are meeting individual and social needs and to provide guidance for public and private policies. Studies of the evolution of institutions, of their functions and modes of operation, of their benefits and costs to society, of their rise and decline, can lead to insights of both philosophical and practical value.

To attempt a social audit of the corporate institution as it exists within the vast and complex matrix of American society is an audacious undertaking, as the author is well aware. Besides a grasp of the fields indicated above, a broad experience with both corporate and governmental operations is needed to keep academic insight tied to practical realities. Such requirements make it clear why comprehensive, multidisciplinary studies of major social institutions are comparatively rare. Although the author is an economist, he fortunately has had the opportunity to study other social disciplines and also to participate in many aspects of corporate and governmental activity.

The privately-owned, profit-seeking corporation is the primary actor in the capitalist economy. As such, it is both the devil of the socialist theorists and the hero of the capitalist ideologues. We have sought to examine corporate enterprise with the objective eye of the scholar, hoping to avoid both the extremism of the Right and of the Left. Our studies assume that the business corporation will continue to function within the socioeconomic assumptions of Western liberalism. They take for granted the continued existence of private property, freedom of entry into business, and market competition as the primary regulatory force in the economy. Accordingly, this work does not enter into the ideological debate between socialism and capitalism as alternative systems for satisfying man's economic demands. In another work, the author examined the real-life, practical operation of state socialism and concluded that American capitalism, despite its faults, is more than holding its own.*

This work is basically policy-oriented. Most of the chapters begin with a formulation of the primary issues and end with proposals for the reform of private and public policies. In today's skeptical world, negative criticism of people and institutions is in oversupply, while viable and constructive ideas for improving our society are lamentably wanting. It is hoped our proposals will help to redress the imbalance.

The book is divided into five parts. Part I describes the status of

---

* Neil H. Jacoby and James E. Howell, *European Economics, East and West: Convergence of Five European Countries and the United States* (New York: World Publishing Company, 1967).

corporate business, both in American social thought and as a leading actor in the American economy. It reveals the strange paradox of a dominant mood of adverse criticism of corporate behavior alongside an impressive record of achievement.

Part II analyzes the three most important developments in the internal structure and methods of operating corporations that have taken place since World War II. These are the revolution in the science and practice of management, the great expansion of conglomerate enterprise, and the burgeoning of multinational business.

Part III deals with the principal economic and political issues that have arisen as a result of corporate interaction with its social environment. They include the problems of concentration and competition, the political role of business, and the design of corporate government.

Part IV examines the critical social roles played by the corporation in helping to solve social problems, in improving the physical environment, and in supplying military hardware.

Part V explores the future of corporate business and speculates upon new corporate tasks. Based upon plausible models of American and of world society in the 1990's, forecasts are made of probable changes in corporate relationships with governments and with other social institutions.

A fundamental conclusion of this work is that *public understanding of the business-government relationship must be developed and clarified, if our pluralistic society is to function at its best in the future.* People need to understand what the respective roles and responsibilities of government and of the corporation are, and how they should interact to serve the commonwealth, in order to judge their performance fairly. Otherwise corporate business will be wrongly blamed for the failures of government, and *vice versa,* with the inevitable consequence of frustration and confusion. But we do take the position that improvements in the American political system are even more urgently needed than reforms of the corporate system, if we are to attain the Good Society.

Finally, it seems clear that *the American people are in the process of writing a new "social contract" to govern corporate-societal relationships.* A fresh wind of public opinion about corporate business is blowing, and corporation shareowners and managers would be wise to heed its force and direction. The people of our highly interrelated society expect more of the corporation than they did in the past. While the new "social contract" does not call for revolutionary changes in corporate structures and policies, it does require the many incremental reforms set forth in the pages that follow.

# PART I

## CRITICISM AND REALITY

# CHAPTER I

# The Criticism of Corporate Business

A N INSTITUTION is likely to be more searchingly appraised if attention is focused at the outset upon its faults rather than its virtues. Thus, an assessment of the social role of the business corporation, which has become a central institution of American society, is best begun by an effort to set forth and evaluate the many criticisms that are made of it. In this opening chapter, we present a systematic account of the various schools of such criticism and identify the flaws that each finds in it. In this way, we uncover those issues that are basic to the business corporation's social role, issues which we will examine and appraise in succeeding chapters.

We shall use "corporation" to mean the profit-seeking company of the business system. While there are many corporations not-for-profit and the number of business partnerships and proprietorships outnumbers incorporated enterprises two-to-one, the significant fact is that profit-seeking corporations dominate the corporate population and conduct over four-fifths of the private business of the United States economy. One is not far wrong, therefore, in following the general practice of identifying the corporation with business.

Many social critics, however, go further and identify corporate business with American society. Eminent scholars and able journalists contend that large business corporations dominate the polity and the society, as well as the economy, of the United States to such a degree that it may be called a "corporate state." [1] In their view, corporate business has made all social institutions—governments, unions, consumers, even the educational system—subservient to its purposes. It has attained a near-monopoly of social purpose, wielding virtually untrammeled political and economic power. Standing astride the entire social structure, the giant business corporation is seen as its most basic prototype. For these critics, it follows naturally that the errors and shortcomings of society are those of corporate business: their social criticism coincides with their corporate criticism. But should not their strictures, in fairness, be brought against government, unions, and other institutions, as well as corporate business? Are not many really applicable to the weaknesses of human nature?

# THE EVOLUTION OF AMERICAN BUSINESS CRITICISM

The enormous diversity of grounds on which American business is condemned and denounced almost defies analysis. Consider the following statements which typify criticisms of American business in recent literature:

- The United States is dominated by two hundred giant corporations.
- Giant corporations control, rather than are controlled by, their markets.
- Big corporations are operated for the benefit of their managers rather than their stockholders.
- Corporations control the government agencies that are supposed to regulate them.
- The "military-industrial complex" inflates arms expenditures for private power and profit.
- The multinational corporation is the modern instrument of imperialism and neocolonialism.
- Business corporations exploit workers, cheat consumers, and degrade the environment.
- Businesses conspire to raise prices and to suppress improved products.
- Corporate lobbying and campaign contributions corrupt public officials.
- Corporations are ruled by self-perpetuating managements, responsible to no one.
- The "corporate state" has made Americans corrupt, disorderly, distrustful, militaristic, and unjust.
- In the "corporate state" material values always take precedence over moral, intellectual, and cultural values.

The list could be extended indefinitely. Anyone seeking a recent, encyclopedic listing of all the indictments of the American business system voiced by the Radical Left can reach for Charles Reich's *The Greening of America*. This polemic against the "corporate state" offers a virtual bouillabaisse of criticisms on economic, political, sociological, psychological, legal, and moral grounds. At the heart of Reich's argument is the idea mentioned above that giant corporations dominate and corrupt all the institutions of American society. Reich concludes that the human condition has been getting steadily worse in the "corporate state." He forecasts a bloodless revolution of American youth that will sweep away the present iniquitous social order and, in some miraculous—and unexplained—manner, replace it with a Garden of Eden in which everyone will freely pursue happiness, unrestrained by the disciplines of work and organization, corporate or otherwise!

Reich's obsession with the evils of the "corporate state" and his total disregard of the strengths and achievements of American society make his assessment a fantastic caricature of reality. The facts show that the "corporate state" model of American society is a gross distortion, and a misleading guide to an understanding of that society and of policies to improve it. The economy of the United States is *pluralistic* in the nature and sizes of its enterprises, just as the society of the United States is pluralistic in its institutions. Yet Reich's call for revolutionary social change should not be the occasion for launching a counter-revolution against all reforms. Rather, reasonable men will welcome many elements of Consciousness III—Reich's label for a set of individual values that stress brotherhood, community, tolerance, and equality—as a motive force for salutary reforms in the economy and in society. Reforms are needed in *all* of our institutions in order to improve the quality of life in our society.

As economic historian Theodore Saloutos has pointed out, businessmen and business institutions have been a target for critics and reformers in Western societies for a long time. "Peace between piety and profit has rarely been made." [2] In our history, the post-Civil War era was marked by freewheeling private enterprise, unrestrained by governmental regulation. The reaction to its excesses was the Farmers' Cooperative movement, the Populist movement, the Interstate Commerce Act of 1887, and the Sherman Act of 1890. In addition to critics who sought and gained regulation of business, there were also radical theorists who advocated the replacement of capitalism by socialism and radical activists who used violence as a means to accomplish change.

The public image of business improved somewhat during the first thirty years of the twentieth century as a result of the philanthropies of Rockefeller, Carnegie, Mellon, and others, as well as of the rising prosperity of the people, and the greater social sensitivity and increasing public regulation of business. The onset of the Great Depression of the 1930's, however, brought American business into a new "valley of despair." Business was seen as having failed in its responsibility to provide employment and a rising standard of living for the people. The Great Depression spawned a new wave of social critics and reformers, of which the more spectacular were the Technocrats, the Townsendites, and the Coughlinites. The main stream of reform was, of course, Franklin D. Roosevelt's New Deal. It installed the Federal government in unquestioned leadership of the economy of the United States and established a host of agencies to monitor and regulate the private sector: the Securities and Exchange Commission (SEC), the Federal Power Commission (FPC), the Federal Communications Commission (FCC), the National Labor Relations Board (NLRB), Social Security Administration (SSA), and the ill-fated National Industrial Recovery Administration (NIRA) and Agricultural Adjustment Administration (AAA).[3]

The public reputation of business was at least partially restored during the early 1940's because of the extraordinary productivity of business, "the arsenal of democracy" in World War II. And the problem of "jobs after victory" for returning servicemen was resolved with unexpected celerity. Partly as a result of such progressive businessmen's organizations as the Committee for Economic Development, corporate business made peace with government and labor unions. The Eisenhower era of the 1950's was, by and large, an era of good feeling between business and the American public.

But beginning in the 1960's, an adverse tide of public opinion began to rise against business. A more affluent, better-educated, more critical public began to question the value of ever-increasing production, the resulting pollution and environmental decay, and the defective products and services being produced; and they began to protest the public's seeming inability to influence the behavior of the business system. Frustration over the Vietnam War added fuel to the fires of discontent. Suddenly, consumerism, stockholderism, racial equalitarianism, antimilitarism, environmentalism, and feminism became forces to be reckoned with by corporate managements. For the most part, they replaced the classical "isms"—socialism, communism, syndicalism, fascism—as the main driving forces seeking the reform of the American business system. Classical Marxists, nevertheless, continued to voice their familiar allegations against "monopoly capitalism," "imperialism," "neocolonialism," and "the exploitation of the dispossessed."

As the 1970's began, it could be said that at no time in history had American business been subjected to a more widespread criticism. Paradoxically, this faultfinding mounted to a crescendo at the end of a decade of unparalleled social progress. Moreover, it was also true that at no time in history have American businessmen been more sensitive to criticism or more motivated to respond to it. In his best-remembered remark, the taciturn Calvin Coolidge had said in 1928 that "the business of America is business." The critics are now saying that the business of America is to build a good society and business is only a means to that end. Progressive business leaders have understood this message, as the public policy statement of the Committee for Economic Development (CED), *Social Responsibilities of Business Corporations,* attests.[4]

## A TYPOLOGY OF CORPORATE CRITICISM

The foregoing sketch of the evolution of the criticism of American business suggests the formulation of a typology of such criticism which might be useful for identifying corporate issues that need examination. It suggests a grouping of business critics into three categories, according to the depth of their criticism and the radicalism of their proposed reforms of the system.

### Level 1. The Reformist Critics

*First are the reformist critics, who accept the basic institutional framework of the contemporary American economy and society.* They support the institutions of private property, freedom of enterprise, open markets, competition, limited government enterprise, and public regulation of the private sector. However, they call for reforms of market mechanisms, increasing governmental regulation of business, and restrictions on the use of private property to enhance the well-being of society. Reformist groups include those who support consumerism, environmentalism, antiracism, and stockholderism, as well as those seeking to make corporate business active in the solution of such social problems as urban decay, hard-core unemployment, the development of black capitalism, the abatement of crime and pollution. The "new wave" of business critics that arose during the 1960's is composed primarily of those who identify with the contemporary social order, but who are increasingly concerned with changing corporate behavior through political as well as through market action.

Reformist critics comprise the majority of contemporary critics of American business. To a considerable extent, their demand is not for new or stricter governmental controls, but for attitudes and policies on the part of corporate leaders that are more responsive to public needs. Our society needs reformist critics and the author counts himself among them.

### Level 2. The Leftist Critics

*Leftist critics seek to substitute authoritarian socialism for the capitalistic system of competitive private enterprise.* Their criticism goes to a deeper level than that of the reformers; they reject the institutional framework of the present economy and call for the complete ownership and operation of the means of production by the state. Orthodox socialists of the Marxist-Leninist persuasion advocate a high degree of authoritarian discipline of the individual, by the state and the Communist party elite, in the interest of material progress. Classical Marxists also demand the substitution of centrally determined (i.e., planned) prices, production schedules, and resource allocations for those that are produced impersonally by market competition. Libermanian revisionists, however, advocate the introduction of the "market socialism" of Oscar Lange instead. Market competition between government enterprises would then substitute for much central planning.[5]

Although the Marxist antithesis to the capitalist thesis has been vigorously advanced for more than a century, it has never gained significant support in the United States. Marxist voices have, during recent years, been drowned out by the complaints of the Reformers, on the one hand, and of the Utopian critics, on the other.

## Level 3. The Utopian Critics

*Utopian critics reject both capitalism and authoritarian socialism and seek to establish new social orders based upon different human values.* They believe that human nature can be radically changed. Individualistic striving for material gain is to be replaced by cooperative efforts to elevate the moral and cultural character of society. Wealth and income are to be shared according to need rather than according to productivity—an ideal not yet realized in any of the socialist countries. American-style capitalism and Soviet-style socialism equally err, they contend, in having hierarchical structures and in stressing material rewards; the differences between them are not significant.

Professor Martin Bronfenbrenner has observed that recent Utopians can be divided into three quite different schools: the Hippies, the Yippies, and the Humanist Marxists including the Maoists, Castroists, and Allendists.[6] The Hippies and the Yippies are both anarchistic in philosophy and differ primarily in their attitude toward the use of violence as an instrument of social change.

The Hippies are nonviolent anarchists who withdraw from the mainstream of society into their own communes. They are apolitical, libertarian, anti-industrialist, and essentially parasitic upon society. They have a nostalgic yearning for the smaller, simpler social orders of the past. Communal living, handicraft workshops, and a boycott on machine-made products are their "bag." Feeling and intuition are claimed as the sources of their attitudes rather than reason and intellect. The Hippie counter-culture appeals only to a minor fringe of anti-Establishment youth, who feel equally repelled by what they see as the "repressive and exploitative" character of Soviet socialism and American capitalism. Marxist ideas about class structure they consider outmoded. The Hippie attitude is one of resignation from a system they feel powerless to change. This brand of student radicalism arises mainly from the exposure of youth to grandiose but impractical ideas for social change, ideas which they find appealing, but which cannot be turned into social reality.

The activist anarchists are the Yippies, who call for the destruction of the present social order as an essential first step in building a new one. To them there is no real economic problem—scarcity is "artificial." People should be freed from the drudgery of work because "the machines can do it." They have embraced the dubious idea, advanced by Theobald and others, that technological progress will make work obsolete.[7] They offer no blueprint for the future; the necessary steps will somehow become clear after the present iniquitous order has been swept away. While professing anarchism, their stance is basically one of unthinking activism.[8]

Humanistic Marxism is the third branch of modern Utopianism. It must be taken more seriously than the other branches because it is the basis of actual experiments in Yugoslavia and Chile.[9] The attempt of Czechoslovakian revisionists to introduce it in 1968 was brutally suppressed by Soviet tank divisions. The central theme of Humanistic Marxism is *the replacement, in the economy, of authoritarian penalties and material incentives with democratic processes and moral incentives.* "Moral incentives," however, are reinforced by massive propaganda campaigns by the state. Great stress is laid upon an egalitarian distribution of income and wealth. Everyone is expected to perform some physical work. (To seek credibility as Humanist Marxists, Castro's executives occasionally cut sugar cane and Mao's managers sometimes sweep factory floors.) The inefficiencies of unspecialization are offset, it is believed, by higher morale and less worker alienation. Corporations are maintained as state-owned facilities under joint government-worker control. Market competition and profit motivation are blunted or obliterated. Authoritarian political methods, officially shunned, are used in some degree to stifle dissent and to enforce the industrial discipline provided by market competition in the United States.

Humanistic Marxism appeals to those who believe—including not a few intellectuals—that *radical* changes in human nature are possible.[10] Whether the new "Humanist Marxist man" will ever appear in sufficient numbers to make voluntary, democratic socialism operate efficiently remains in doubt. We do know that, after more than half a century, the "new Communist man" has not emerged in the Soviet Union. Russians continue to live under the dictatorship of the Communist party in a totalitarian state that has defied Marx's prediction of "withering away." The Soviet Union has, to be sure, made sustained material progress with an authoritarian socialist regime. Whether Yugoslavia or Chile will ever achieve it with truly democratized and humanistic socialism remains to be demonstrated.

## FIVE MAJOR THESES OF THE CORPORATE CRITICS

Having before us a portrait of the three major groups of critics of American corporate business, we now examine their substantive charges in more detail. While the three groups differ sharply in their remedies for corporate faults, there is much overlapping of their indictments. A review of the very extensive literature indicates that contemporary criticism of corporate business may be organized into five master theses. Big business corporations are alleged to:

1. Exercise concentrated *economic* power contrary to the public interest.
2. Exercise concentrated *political* power contrary to the public interest.
3. Be controlled by a self-perpetuating, irresponsible "power elite."
4. Exploit and dehumanize workers and consumers.
5. Degrade the environment and the quality of life.

This classification presents *the salient issues* more sharply than does that of John D. Glover, who grouped criticisms of American big business into: (1) economic (monopoly and inefficiency); (2) political and social (oligarchy, antidemocracy, antipluralism); and (3) ethical and moral (materialism, egotism, perversion of human values).[11]

We will examine these five theses in turn.

THESIS 1. *Big business corporations exercise concentrated economic power contrary to the public interest.* This thesis alleges that they:

(a) Dominate and control the private sector.
(b) Shape national economic policies to their will.
(c) Impede the entry of new firms and stifle free enterprise.
(d) Enrich the private and starve the government sector.
(e) Are less efficient than small enterprises.
(f) Enlarge military spending for private profit.
(g) Generate monopolies.

The antisocial use of concentrated economic power is a key indictment brought against big corporate enterprise by critics of all schools. By "economic power" is meant the capability to shape the structure and performance of the entire economy. The fear of, or belief in, the excessive concentration of the output of major industries in the hands of giant corporations leading to oligopolistic behavior and a blunting of competitive discipline has been a recurrent theme in American economic literature since the late nineteenth century. Contemporary reformist critics, such as Walter Adams, John M. Blair, and Representative Emanuel Celler, advocate breaking up the giants into smaller components through antitrust action. Leftist critics, like American Marxists Paul Sweezy and Paul Baran, describe the economy of the United States in the standard Communist party cliché, "monopoly capitalism." Their solution is not the disintegration of the giants, but rather the nationalization of their ownership and control.[12] The remedies of Utopian critics range from "democratic" management of big companies by worker's councils to the destruction of all such "repressive" structures.

Scholarly critics of corporate size and concentration often refer to studies by the Federal Trade Commission purporting to show that the "hundred largest" American manufacturing companies have increased their share of total manufacturing assets during the past decade or two. They draw mournful conclusions about the "decline of competition" and the "foreclosure of opportunity" for small enterprises.

There are observers who argue, to the contrary, that both the economic and political power of corporate business has declined, relatively, during the last forty or fifty years. In the 1930's, Roosevelt's New Deal, they contend, elevated the federal government to preeminence as the source of power and transferred the nation's effective capital from Wall Street to Pennsylvania Avenue. The New Deal created the labor union and the farm lobby as countervailing power centers against big business. As a result of these developments, corporate business has lost its strategic influence over national affairs.

Before one can pass judgment on the allegations of this first Thesis, several subjects require careful and objective analysis. Among them are: the meaning to be assigned to "industrial concentration," changes in the form and effectiveness of competition, and alterations in the structure of the American enterprise population. The meaning of business "efficiency" needs clarification, and its relationship to changing economies of scale in marketing, finance, and management, as well as in production. Finally, a judicious assessment must be made of the influence of business upon the policies of the nation, including defense, the performance of the economy, and—beyond that—upon international relations and the development of world order.[13]

THESIS 2. *Big business corporations exercise concentrated political power contrary to the public interest.* Contributory elements to this thesis are that they:

(a) Make campaign contributions to gain political power.
(b) Destroy social pluralism by subjugating other institutions.
(c) Subvert and corrupt democratic government to serve their own interests.
(d) Have replaced democracy with a corporate oligarchy.
(e) Control public agencies established to regulate them.
(f) Are heavily subsidized by government franchises, licenses, loans, and contracts.
(g) Have "bought" the support of the universities by gifts, grants, and contracts.
(h) Have influenced the judicial system to treat corporate crimes less severely than the crimes of persons.
(i) Generate ill-will abroad and exploit poor countries when they become multinational.

We have already noted that the central indictment of big business by the New Left and many academic critics is that it has captured the whole society and manipulates it for its selfish ends. The American political system, they contend, has been unable to tame the political power of business. The state, which originally delegated authority to the profit-seeking business corporation, has been overwhelmed and rendered powerless by the monster it created. This common theme is played, with minor variations, by critics as diverse as James Burnham, C. Wright Mills, Paul Sweezy, Michael Harrington, and Andrew Hacker.[14]

If giant corporate business does indeed dominate and control governments, unions, churches, and the educational system, it would follow that it should be blamed for all the imperfections and failures of contemporary society. If the charge were true, what other institution could be censured for unemployment, inflation, racism, crime, poverty, urban slums, and the war in Vietnam? Reformist critics cry for more "social responsibility" from business. Leftist critics contend that, because of its failures to resolve social problems, American "monopoly capitalism" is moribund and ripe for replacement by state socialism. Utopians press for radically changing the system, or for tearing it down and starting over.

Thesis 2 also requires careful and dispassionate examination. Its advocates must answer such troubling questions as the following: How can the idea of untrammeled corporate power be reconciled with the facts of rising consumerism and stockholderism? With the ability of labor unions to wring huge wage increases from business? With a thickening network of governmental regulation of business? With continued, high corporate profits taxation? With the shrinking share of corporate profits in the national income? How can the statement that business interests dominate the foreign policy of the United States be squared with American support of Israel, in which our *economic* stake is negligible, in its conflict with Arab nations, where American corporations have billions in oil investments at risk? Would a business-dominated foreign policy remain quiescent, and even continue foreign economic aid, when Latin American countries seize American corporate property without paying just compensation? If American business has, indeed, "purchased" the support of academia with gifts and grants, why do universities remain focal centers of corporate criticism? How can one reconcile the realities of widely diffused social progress since World War II with the critics' vision of a stagnant and problem-laden society? [15] Doesn't the evidence indicate that American society continues to be institutionally pluralistic, socially progressive, and politically more democratic than ever? Isn't the political influence of corporate business circumscribed by governments, unions, consumers, interest groups, and—above all—competitors? In studying these matters, special attention should be given to the corporate role in politics, including candidates, issues, elections, legislation and its administration.[16]

THESIS 3. *Big businesses are controlled by a self-perpetuating, irresponsible "power elite."* This major indictment can be factored into the propositions that their:

(a) Policies are controlled by managers rather than by stockholders.
(b) Operation is designed to optimize managerial interests in power, security, and prestige, rather than profitability.
(c) Government is oligarchic because management controls the board of directors that appoints the corporate officers.
(d) Government is not responsible to any constituency and its power is "illegitimate."
(e) Boards of directors are facades with only ceremonial functions.
(f) Management systems tend to become inefficient bureaucracies.

Ever since Berle and Means drew sweeping conclusions from what they perceived to be a separation of the ownership and management of big American business corporations, the government of the profit-seeking corporation has been under attack.[17] Critics who had formerly charged that monopoly was the major sin of business, enabling it to ignore the interests of consumers, now added the charge that it was irresponsible to its shareholders as well. Manifestly, the critics pose profound issues of corporate government which need analysis in the light of recent social trends.[18]

Among these trends are the institutionalization of equity investment in business corporations, the rise of the "managerial stockholder," the gearing of executive compensation to corporate earnings, and the great expansion in the legal liabilities of the corporate director.

THESIS 4. *Big corporate businesses exploit and dehumanize workers and consumers.* This comprehensive indictment contains the specific points that corporations:

(a) "Repress" individual expression by means of their hierarchical structures.
(b) Strip the employee of his individuality through their management processes.
(c) Offer little psychological satisfaction to workers.
(d) Emphasize status and material gain, ignoring other human values.
(e) Rule employees autocratically, without democratic participation.
(f) Make decisions that are scientific and rationalistic rather than humanistic.
(g) Impair the sense of community and the quality of working life.
(h) Care little for employees' civil rights, which are not protected by the Constitution of the United States.

Those corporate critics who focus on Thesis 4 range from behavioral scientists in the universities, who call for reforms in management, to the Utopian anarchists, who reject hierarchical structures of any kind. Clearly, the serious issues posed in this context have to do with those changes in the philosophy and style of business management that are desirable in a society growing more affluent and better educated. Because any task-oriented organization confronts the imperatives of economy and efficiency in the use of limited resources, only the most dreamy Utopian will deny the need for *some* structuring of authority and responsibility, and *some* submission of the individual to organizational discipline. The fundamental problem is to find the optimum balance between individual freedom and organizational order, between anarchy and hierarchy, between material and nonmaterial incentives, and between authoritarian and democratic processes. Is contemporary American business management responsive to changes in the values, beliefs, and motives of employees? Are there untapped reservoirs of psychological energy in corporate employees that could be released by more intelligent leadership? Are large gains possible in both productivity and worker satisfaction? [19]

THESIS 5. *Big corporate businesses degrade the environment and the quality of life.* The components of this denunciation are that corporations:

(a) Overproduce and prematurely exhaust natural resources, robbing future generations.

(b) "Exploit" the resources of the poor nations.

(c) Seek only to maximize output, with no regard to long-run or to side effects.

(d) Thrust heavy external costs on the public in pollution, noise, and ugliness.

(e) Frustrate and pervert good urban and regional planning.

(f) Stress economic values to the neglect of moral, social, and aesthetic values.

While charges of wasteful overproduction of domestic natural resources and inequitable "exploitation" of them in less developed nations are longstanding accusations, the condemnation of external costs and of environmental degradation is a product of the 1960's. Environmentalists raise basic questions about the respective roles of governments and business enterprises in environmental improvement. The principles upon which these issues can be resolved also have application to the wider questions of business's role in resolving such social problems as slums, hard-core unemployment, crime, poverty, and other conditions that lessen the quality of life.[20]

## STANDARDS FOR JUDGING CORPORATE PERFORMANCE

A review of this rich panoply of criticism of American corporate business leads one to ask: By what standards are the critics judging the performance of the business corporation? By what standards *should* they judge this—or any other—social institution? Clearly, each faultfinder must have in mind some standard of behavior which he holds to be superior to that which is being followed in practice. Probably, these standards are as numerous as the critics, each being based upon a different ordering of fundamental human values. Some place heavy emphasis upon equality of income and wealth, some upon individual freedom and opportunity, others upon security or material standards of living, still others upon aesthetics, justice, morality, or social harmony. Given this great diversity of criteria, no one mode of corporate performance will satisfy all critics. The value-sets of environmental reformers, classical Marxists, and violent anarchists, for example, are utterly irreconcilable. The best that can be done in a democratic society is to seek a mean between the extremes, a mean which approximates the standards of the majority.

Thus, *we propose that the performance of corporate business be judged by the degree to which it has fostered progress toward the consensual goals of the American people.* The proper measure of its success as a social institution is its actual contribution to the Good Society, as most Americans envision it, compared with its potential contribution. What, then, are the goals of Americans?

American presidents each January describe the "state of the Union," set forth national goals, and propose policies to advance toward them. Yet, the most recent *comprehensive* effort to "set up a series of goals in various areas of national activity" was made in 1960 by President Eisenhower's Commission on National Goals.[21] A nonpartisan panel of ten distinguished citizens from the principal walks of life identified eleven "goals at home" and four "goals abroad." The goals at home were: maximum individual freedom, equality of opportunity, perfection of the democratic process, strengthening of education, advancement of the arts and sciences, diffusion of economic power, fostering economic growth, planning for technological change, reestablishing free markets for agriculture, improving urban planning and housing, and extending health services. The goals abroad were: building an open and peaceful world, defending the Free World, working for disarmament, and strengthening the United Nations. The Commission did not rate these goals in order of importance, nor did it identify conflicts and measure trade-offs among them. It clearly accepted the existing framework of the polity, economy, and society of the United States as the proper starting point for progress toward these goals.

We will assess the contributions of corporate business to relevant goals identified by the President's Commission. The salient issue in respect to each goal is this: How does the actual contribution of corporate business compare with its full potential? This requires, of course, that business be judged not only as an economic agency, producing to meet market demand in hope of profit for its shareholders, but also as a "political" agency governing the working lives of its employees, and as a social institution offering psychological and social satisfactions to those with whom it deals. Today, it is not enough to show that corporate enterprise has been the major generator of an unprecedented material welfare for Americans. It is also necessary to assess its effect upon equality of opportunity, racial and sexual discrimination, opportunities for self-fulfillment, justice and equity, social mobility, the physical environment, and the individual's sense of community.

In assessing business performance, we must keep in mind that ours is a pluralistic society. Indeed, the maintenance of pluralism by the diffusion of power among diverse institutions is itself a national goal. In such a society, each institution tends to specialize in the performance of those tasks in which it has a comparative advantage. The society is a highly complex system of interacting subsystems and institutions, in which the performance of each is affected by that of others.[22] Hence, *the business corporation should be assessed primarily with reference to the performance of its unique function of production,* taking into account the effects of other institutions, such as governments and labor unions, upon its performance; no institution in a pluralistic society should be evaluated in isolation.

But, none should be expected to perform all of society's tasks. There are two schools of thought about corporate business. One holds that the corporation should expand its role to satisfy man's needs for education, recreation, self-esteem, social status, and other values, and should involve itself deeply in the solution of social problems. The other school maintains that each institution in a pluralistic society should specialize and that none should try to be all things to all men. A society of specialized institutions is more productive, efficient, and coherent.[23]

American society may be viewed as a set of interacting subsystems, political, social, economic, religious, military, and so forth.[24] Each subsystem has its characteristic institutions, a dynamic of its own, and each may fortify or hamper the operation of the others. We see corporate business as a powerful subsystem, which is generally supportive of the other subsystems, but which comes into conflict with some of them at various points of intersection. The art of social policy is to find ways of reconciling the conflicts and of mutualizing support of the different social subsystems and their institutions.[25]

Beyond doubt, American corporate enterprise suffers from a generally unfavorable public "image." This is due, in no small degree, to unceasing fault-finding by the intellectual community, which is now many times larger than it ever was before. Intellectuals are, in the main, "viewers with alarm." Criticism is their stock in trade. But isn't it possible that many intellectuals, out of touch with the fast-changing facts, are the victims of a "cultural lag" in their knowledge of corporate structures and processes? Max Ways has written:

> Many American intellectuals are still so trapped in the values and patterns of the pre-industrial society that they have refused to believe that individuality and voluntary cooperation have flowered within large organizations. When freedom increased, these intellectuals saw slavery. When power became more widely spread, they said it was concentrating. When higher standards of social morality appeared, they diagnosed hypocrisy. These intellectuals, rather than the leaders of the "corporate state," have been manipulating the present American consciousness.[26]

We propose to evaluate the critics' charges against corporate business by analyzing the available evidence. The ultimate purpose of these studies is to identify reforms in the corporate institution and in its political-economic matrix that will enhance its service to American society.

## NOTES

1. John Kenneth Galbraith, *The New Industrial State* (Boston: Houghton Mifflin, 1967); Charles Reich, *The Greening of America* (New York: Random House, 1970); Morton Mintz and Jerry S. Cohen, *America, Inc.: Who Owns and Operates the United States* (New York: Dial Press, 1971); Robin Marris, "Is the Corporate Economy a Corporate State?," *American Economic Review*, Vol. 62, No. 2 (May 1972), pp. 103–115.

2. Theodore Saloutos, "Historical Protest Movements and Their Consequences for Business" (Lecture, University of California, Los Angeles, August 4, 1971.)

3. See Irving Michelman, *Business at Bay: Critics and Heretics of American Business* (New York: Augustus M. Kelley, 1969), for an authoritative and lively account of the ideas of so variegated a group of twentieth-century business critics as Thorstein Veblen, Sinclair Lewis, Marriner Eccles, T. K. Quinn, Cyrus Eaton, Adolph Berle, Michael Harrington, and Herbert Marcuse.

4. Research and Policy Committee, Committee for Economic Deveolpment, *Social Responsibilities of Business Corporations*, A Statement on National Policy (New York: Committee for Economic Development, 1971).

5. See Oscar Lange and Fred M. Taylor, *On the Economic Theory of Socialism* (Minneapolis: University of Minnesota Press, 1938). Also, E. G. Liberman, N. K. Baibakov, and L. Gatovskii, "Reform of Soviet Economic Management and Planning," *Problems of Economics* (*Voprosy Ekonomiki*), Vol. 8, No. 9 (January 1966).

6. Martin Bronfenbrenner, "Radical Economics in America, A 1970 Survey," *Journal of Economic Literature*, Vol. 8, No. 3 (September 1970). Also his lecture, "New Left Economic Ideologies," University of California, Los Angeles, August 2, 1971. We have not listed the "modernized Marxism" school distinguished by Bronfenbrenner because it does not appear to be significantly different from Soviet-style authoritarian Marxism, which we have identified in Level 2.

7. Robert Theobald, *Free Men and Free Markets* (New York: Doubleday, 1965).

8. Abbie Hoffman, *Revolution for the Hell of It* (New York: Dial Press, 1968). Also, Assar Lindbeck, *The Political Economy of the New Left: An Outsider's View* (New York: Harper and Row, 1971).

9. Some would add Cuba and the Peoples Republic of China, but in the author's opinion these are authoritarian regimes rather than examples of Humanistic Marxism.

10. An example is the American economist John Gurley. See his "Man and the Chinese Economic Development" (Stanford: mimeo., 1969); also his "Economic Conversion and Beyond," *Sloan Management Review*, Vol. 11, No. 3 (Spring 1970); and this author's reply, "Capitalism and the Solution of Social Problems," *Sloan Management Review*, Vol. 12, No. 2 (Winter 1971).

11. John D. Glover, *The Attack on Big Business* (Boston: Graduate School of Business Administration, Harvard University, 1954).

12. See Paul M. Sweezy, *The Theory of Capitalist Development* (New York: Oxford University Press, 1942); Paul A. Baran, *The Political Economy of Growth* (New York: Monthly Review Press, 1957).

13. These subjects are explored in Chapters 2, 4, 6, and 11.

14. See James Burnham, *The Managerial Revolution* (New York: John Day

Company, 1941); C. Wright Mills, *The Power Elite* (New York: Oxford University Press, 1959); Paul M. Sweezy, *Monopoly Capital: An Essay on the American Economic and Social Order* (New York: Monthly Review Press, 1966); Michael Harrington, *The Other America* (New York: Macmillan, 1962); Andrew Hacker, ed., *The Corporation Takeover* (New York: Harper and Row, 1964).

15. See U.S. Department of Health, Education, and Welfare, *Toward a Social Report* (Washington, D.C.: U.S. Government Printing Office, January 1969).

16. These matters are assessed in Chapters 5, 7, and 9. See also Neil H. Jacoby, "Capitalism and the Solution of Social Problems," *op. cit.*

17. Adolf A. Berle, Jr., and Gardiner C. Means, *The Modern Corporation and Private Property* (New York: Macmillan, 1932).

18. See Adolf A. Berle, Jr., *The 20th Century Capitalist Revolution* (New York: Harcourt, Brace and World, 1954). See also his *Power without Property* (Harcourt, Brace and World, 1959).

19. These matters are examined in Chapters 3, 8, and 12.

20. These issues are analyzed in Chapters 9 and 10.

21. See *Goals for Americans: The Report of the President's Commission on National Goals* (New York: Prentice-Hall, Inc., 1960).

22. See Richard Bellman and Goran Borg, *Mathematics, Systems and Society: An Informal Essay* (Washington, D.C.: NIH Technical Report No. 70-58, December 1970). Also, Kenneth Boulding, *A Primer on Social Dynamics* (New York: Free Press, 1970), Ch. 1.

23. The issue of institutional specialization versus generalization has been actively debated in connection with the American university. After World War II, the academy increasingly became a vocational trainer, extension educator of the middle-aged, adviser to government and industry, and seat of political activism and social revolution. Some observers have held this trend desirable. Others have argued that the salvation of the university lies in a return to its original tasks of general education and the discovery of knowledge for its own sake. See Clark Kerr, *The Uses of the University* (Cambridge: Harvard University Press, 1964); Robert M. Hutchins, *The Learning Society* (New York: Praeger, 1968); Robert A. Nisbet, *The Degradation of Academic Dogma* (New York: Basic Books, 1971).

24. Boulding, *A Primer on Social Dynamics.*

25. Frank Tannenbaum gives an elegant statement of this principle in *The Balance of Power in Society* (New York: Macmillan, 1969).

26. Max Ways, Editorial, *Fortune,* Vol. 82, No. 5 (November 1970).

# CHAPTER 2

# The Corporate Economy: Myths and Realities

S OCIAL critics have formulated a model of American society, now widely accepted, called the "corporate state." [1] The central *economic* concept of this model is that giant corporations increasingly dominate and engross American economic life, and employ a rising fraction of all workers. Corporate managers effectively control government, employees, customers, and stockholders, and are able to manipulate the behavior of all groups in order to serve their own ends. Further, giant corporations are held to be the model and prototype of the future; medium and small firms are considered a transitional phenomenon, destined to play a shrinking role in the American economy.

The model of the "corporate state" raises many significant questions: Is the profit-seeking corporation really becoming more important as a producer of products, an employer of people, a holder of wealth, and a recipient of income? Is corporate business becoming more concentrated in giant firms and more uniform in its mode of operation? Is the number of small firms losing ground proportionately to the total number of enter-

An earlier version of this chapter was published in the *Conference Board Record*, Vol. 8, No. 6 (June 1971), under the title, "The Myth of the Corporate Economy." I gratefully acknowledge the helpful comments of Miss Betty Bock of the Conference Board staff and of my colleague, Professor J. Fred Weston, as well as the statistical research assistance of Neil H. Jacoby, Jr., and Steven Lustgarten. Professor George Katona of the University of Michigan, Professor Raymond Goldsmith of Yale University, and Assistant Secretary of Commerce Harold Passer kindly provided data which were used in this chapter.

prises? Is there more or less dispersion of the ownership of business corporations? How is the structural configuration of corporate business changing? Responses to these questions, grounded on statistical evidence, enable one to determine whether the notion of the "corporate state" conforms to reality or whether some other model might be truer and a better guide for public policy.

But first let us say summarily what we take the essence of the corporation to be. The corporation is a task-oriented institution whose valuable attributes include: a standardized form of organization, policy control of resources in the board of directors, and operating control in the officers; joint stock-ownership with easily transferable ownership interests; perpetual succession, common funds, and a permanent capital; protection from claims based on a shareowner's private debts; legal personality and a capability to sue and be sued in its own name; limited liability; the right to petition legislative bodies as a person; anonymity of the owners; and the ability to shelter income from high taxation.

Since corporations are "intangible persons" [2] in American law, the population of corporations can usefully be studied by demographic methods analogous to those used in studying human populations. Like natural persons, corporations are born (chartered), grow (enlarge assets, sales, or profits), marry (merge), divorce (spin off), have children (organize subsidiaries), become healthy or ill (incur profits or losses), migrate (are licensed to conduct business in new jurisdictions), become parts of hierarchical structures (become components in a holding company complex), and die (dissolve and surrender their charters). Less like natural persons, corporations can become citizens of many nations (multinationalize through subsidiaries). And unlike natural persons, corporations are not independent political entities, but are owned and managed by changing groups of natural persons. [3]

The business corporation has been described as the *central* economic institution of American society. [4] It is timely, therefore, to provide a quantitative picture of its changing role in the economy of the United States over the past half century.

## THE GROWTH OF CORPORATE AND HUMAN POPULATIONS

At the end of 1968, the United States contained about 1.6 million active, profit-seeking corporations and about 200 million people—one corporation for each 126 persons. The estimate of 1.6 million includes financial as well as industrial, commercial, service, and other corporations, plus such corporation-like enterprises as joint stock companies, trusts, associations, and limited partnerships. It excludes nonprofit corporations and farmers' cooperatives. Because all corporations in existence in any part of a year are required to file Federal income tax returns, the number of returns filed is the best available approximation of the population of active profit-seeking companies in the nation.[5] Reliable information about their number is available back to 1910. (See Table 1; tables are grouped at the end of this Chapter.)

Looking at the comparative growth of the corporate and human populations over the fifty-eight-year period from 1910 to 1968, three points stand out:

1. Over the past half century, the corporate population grew at an average compound rate of more than two and one-half times that of the human population—3.5 percent a year against 1.4 percent a year.[6] Whereas in 1910 there were 342 people per corporation, in 1968 the corresponding figure was 126 people.

2. Prior to World War II, the active corporate population did not grow consistently, and even declined for extended periods. It grew rapidly up to World War I, then receded. It grew again up to the beginning of the Great Depression in 1930, then stabilized and contracted during World War II.

3. A great burst of corporate fecundity began with the coming of peace in 1945. During the postwar years, the corporate population nearly quadrupled from 447,000 to 1,600,000, exhibiting an average compound growth rate of well over 6 percent a year versus an average of 1.5 percent for the human population. (See Table 1.)

The relationships between the corporate and human populations over the period from 1935 to 1968 were generally similar in the United States and in the United Kingdom. The human population of Britain grew at a compound rate of 0.7 percent a year, whereas the company population rose about 5.0 percent a year—more than seven times as rapidly. The growth of the British company population was not interrupted, as it was in the United States, by the economic depression of the 1930's and World War II. By the middle 1960's, the United Kingdom was *more* densely populated with companies in relation to its human population than was the United States, although the reverse had been true in 1935. (See Table 1.)

Nor was the growth of the corporate populations of Britain and the United States related directly to the growth of their real gross national products.[7] Evidently, these growth rates were determined by a complex set of factors. In both countries there was a shift after World War II in the preferences of businessmen toward the corporate form of business organization. In both countries, corporate-human population ratios remained close enough to suggest that common historical, legal, and economic traditions were the determinants. The vitality of the corporate populations of both countries demonstrates the high utility of this institution in advanced market economies.

## THE GROWTH OF CORPORATE, ENTERPRISE, AND SELF-EMPLOYED POPULATIONS

The profit-seeking corporation is the principal legal form of enterprise in a market economy, the others being the individual proprietorship and the partnership. The latter forms are found mainly in small owner-managed firms, whose principals carry unlimited personal liability for the debts of the enterprise. The number of "business enterprises," of all legal forms, in operation in the United States during 1968 has been estimated at 5.1 million.[8] This count includes all business firms under one management, having either an established place of business or at least one paid employee. It excludes agricultural and professional services as "non-business" activities.

In 1968, on the other hand, there was one "business enterprise" for every forty persons in the nation, a relationship that has held almost constant over many years. Evidently, the business enterprise continues to be a sturdy human institution in our urbanizing and technologizing society. The postwar growth of very large firms has been accompanied by an unflagging expansion of the number of small firms. This expansion has been associated with the postwar transformation of the United States from an industrial to a service economy.

The corporation has nevertheless come to form a steadily rising proportion of all business enterprises. Incorporated enterprises rose from 14 percent in 1945, to 32 percent in 1968, of the respective totals. The shift in the preferences of entrepreneurs for the corporate form presumably reflected the rising valuation of corporate charters because of potential tax reduction, limited liability and a greater assurance of enterprise continuity, as well as other factors. Much higher personal income tax rates endowed the corporate charter with higher value. The rising level of business risk made limitation of liability for losses more desirable. A corporate form also opened up more sophisticated channels of finance.

*For at least a century, a rising proportion of all American business has been done by corporations.* According to Doane, corporations accounted for one-fifth of business expenditures in 1870, about one-third by 1890, and more than half by 1920.[9] In 1963, corporations accounted for

90 percent and 96 percent, respectively, of all payrolls in mining and manufacturing, and for 75 percent and 71 percent, respectively, of all payrolls in retailing and services.[10] Relatively more business was done in the retailing and service sectors by small proprietorships and partnerships. Nevertheless, corporations made incursions even into these strongholds of noncorporate enterprise during the postwar years.

Even the population of business enterprises does not provide a comprehensive measure of "entrepreneurship" in the United States because it excludes farmers, professionals, and other persons devoting at least part-time to selling their services in markets and who have neither an established place of business nor employees. A conservative estimate of the "entrepreneurial" population is given by the number of individual income tax returns filed reporting income from self-employment.[11] An estimated 11.1 million persons did so for 1968, one for each 18 persons in the United States. The proportion of the human population engaging in entrepreneurship has not changed significantly over the past quarter-century, and the proportion of the employed civilian labor force which works for itself has risen.[12] (See Table 2 and Chart 1.)

These facts contradict the notion that individual enterprise is waning in American society, that we are steadily becoming a nation of hired employees. On the contrary, *as large a proportion of working Americans now work for themselves as in 1945.* Even high income taxation, rising governmental regulation, and labor unionism—the classic triple threats to new and small business—have not dampened individual enterprise.

## ENTERPRISE ENTRIES, EXITS, AND LIFE EXPECTANCIES

The formation, life expectancy, and dissolution of corporations are fundamental properties of a private-enterprise market economy. The act of incorporation requires some effort and investment by an entrepreneur, and is presumably taken with a definite intention to launch or expand a venture. The annual number of incorporations is an index of entrepreneurial activity, a forecast of investments to be made.[13] The annual number of corporate dissolutions (exits) measures ventures completed, successfully or unsuccessfully. The net annual change in the corporate population is an index of the vitality of the corporate institution. The ratio of companies discontinued annually to the total corporate population— the exit rate—enables one to measure average corporate life expectancy.

Although annual numbers of incorporations and operating companies

CHART 1

*Corporation, Enterprise, and Entrepreneurial Populations of the*
*U.S., 1954-1968*

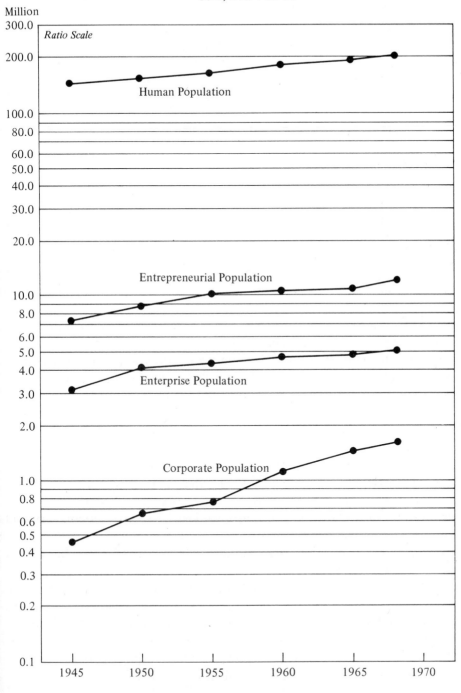

are published currently, the annual number of corporate exits must be inferred from other data. We assume that corporate exits account for the difference between the number of new incorporations and the (smaller) net addition to those filing returns. Table 3 presents annual entry and exit rates of American corporations calculated on these assumptions, and it compares them with similar rates for all operating business enterprises over the postwar period from 1946 to 1968.

Corporate entry and exit rates are so surprisingly high that *the annual turnover of the corporate population has been higher than that of unincorporated enterprises.* Thus, after World War II, the corporate entry rate averaged about 14 percent a year and the exit rate averaged about 9 percent a year. This implies that the average life expectancy of a corporation at the date of chartering was approximately eleven years. As in the human population, mortality rates are much higher in the early years of corporate life. A company may even be chartered in the morning, accomplish its purpose in the afternoon, and file dissolution papers by the close of the business day! A study of the life spans of Maryland corporations showed that half of them lived less than two years, 70 percent less than ten years, and 85 percent did not survive their twenty-fifth year.[14] These findings are consistent with an *average* life expectancy of about a decade. (See Chart 2.)

It is a surprising but undeniable fact that the *unincorporated business has a longer life expectancy than does the corporation.* The average postwar entry rate of *all* business enterprises was about 9 percent a year, while the average exit rate was about 7.5 percent a year, and the average life expectancy was fifteen years. The shorter life expectancy of the business corporation is probably due to the fact that a large proportion of incorporations are made for specific ventures of limited duration. Many are formed either to take advantage of contingencies that do not arise, or for specific purposes that are soon achieved. Examples are joint-venture construction companies, which dissolve after the completion of a project, or special companies formed to hold title to property for a short time, pending permanent ownership arrangements. The lives of proprietorships and partnerships, on the other hand, are usually determined by the active working lives of the owners. However, unincorporated firms also suffer a high mortality during their early years.

Bearing in mind that the annual increment of the human population of the United States has fluctuated between 1.0 percent and 2.5 percent a year since World War II, and that the life expectancies at birth of human males and females were, respectively, sixty-seven and seventy-four in 1967, it is apparent that both the corporate and the enterprise populations have been much shorter-lived than the human population.[15]

CHART 2

*Annual Entry and Exit Rates of U.S. Corporations, 1948-1968*

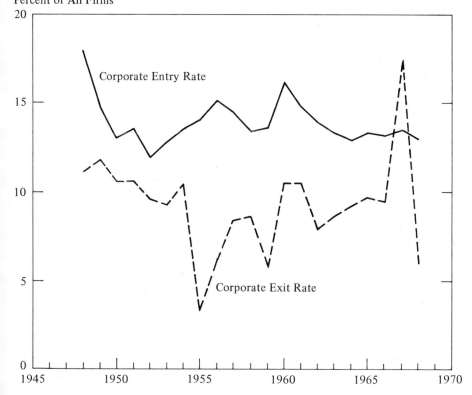

Percent of All Firms

## TRENDS IN CORPORATE SIZE

Long-term changes in the size-distribution of business corporations are important because of the possible implications for our competitive economic order and for our political pluralism. The American credo is one of faith in institutional pluralism and of mistrust of large size and concentrated power, political or economic. The growth of giant institutions has always been viewed with apprehension, even though it has been for the most part the natural product of rising population and income, and of technological changes that created economies of larger scale.[16]

The widespread belief that American business is becoming ever more concentrated in a few giant enterprises may be attributed partly to the fact that many agencies of the Federal government focus attention upon *manufacturing* industries, in which concentration has been alleged to have increased significantly since World War II.[17] Even if this allegation were true—which is not obvious—it is important to recall that manufacturing originates only 30 percent of national income. Hence, postwar trends in the size-distribution of *all* business corporations are more significant.

The corporate population of the United States contains a vast number of small firms and relatively few giant firms. Of the 1,424,000 corporations which filed tax returns for 1965, no less than 42.7 percent possessed assets under $50,000 and 94 percent had assets under $1 million. At the other end of the size spectrum, 1,900 companies, comprising 0.13 percent of the corporate population, each had assets of $100 million or more. Concentration of the *number* of corporations was clearly very high among the smallest size-classes.

When the corporate population is arrayed according to the percentage of aggregate assets held by companies in each size-class, concentration is high at the upper end of the scale. The 608,000 companies in the smallest group—those having assets under $50,000—collectively accounted for a picayune 0.65 percent of all corporate assets; whereas the giants, each with $100 million or more of assets, jointly held 59.6 percent. The 608,000 companies in the under-$50,000 class collectively owned only $11 billion of assets in 1965, whereas the 1,900 giants, each with assets over $100 million, jointly held $1,028 billion.

## TRENDS IN CORPORATE CONCENTRATION

When the percentages of the total number of companies in each size-class are computed for each year in the period from 1946 to 1965, *a high degree of stability is found.* The proportion of companies in each size-class—large, medium, and small—expanded at approximately equal rates, so that the ratio of each size-class to the corporate population was about the same at the end as at the beginning of the period. However, the growth rate in numbers of the largest group was somewhat higher than that of the smallest class. Whereas the number of companies with assets under $50,000 expanded from 199,000 to 608,000, a compound rate of about 6 percent a year, the number of firms with assets over $100 million rose from 541 to 1,900, a compound rate of nearly 7 percent a year. The overall picture is, nevertheless, one of remarkable stability. (See Chart 3.)

Changes in the degree of concentration of the number of corporations are best measured by the Gini Coefficient.[18] It shows no significant postwar change in the concentration of the American corporate population. (Gini Coefficients were 0.628 in 1946, and 0.622 in 1965.) (See Chart 4.)

This postwar stability in the size-distribution of the corporate population is remarkable in view of the 60 percent rise in the price level between

CHART 3

*Percentages of the Number of U.S. Corporations in Each Asset
Size-Class, 1946-1965*

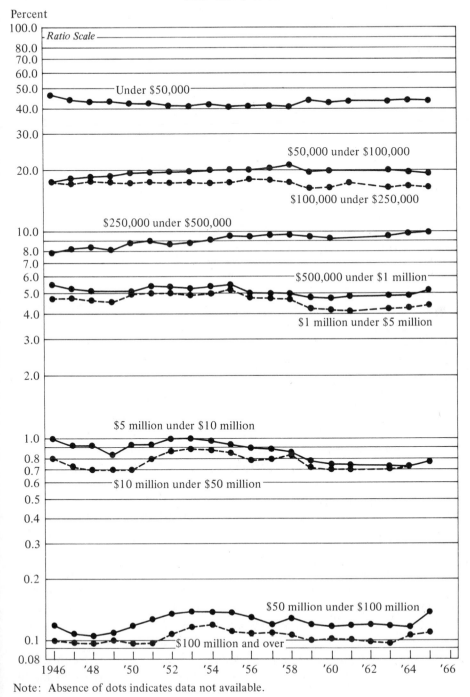

Note: Absence of dots indicates data not available.

CHART 4

*Cumulative Percentage Distributions of Number of U.S. Corporation Tax Returns by Asset Size-Classes, 1946 and 1965*

Cumulative Percentages of Number of Corporate Returns

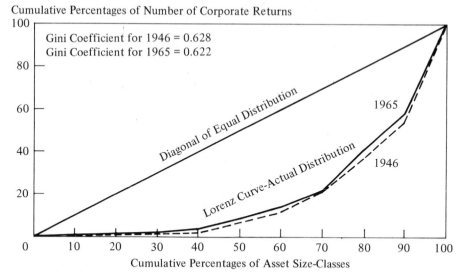

Cumulative Percentages of Asset Size-Classes

1946 and 1965. Price inflation tends to shift larger fractions of the corporate population into bigger size-classes. The fact that this did not occur shows that powerful forces were at work expanding the number of smaller companies.

Examination of changes in the percentages of corporate *assets* owned by companies of different sizes reveals that *during the postwar years the largest firms gained assets relative to medium and smaller companies.* The share of all corporate assets owned by the smallest companies (assets under $50,000) declined from 0.92 percent to 0.65 percent over the period, although their amount nearly tripled from $4.2 billion to $11.1 billion. In contrast, the share of the largest class (assets of $100 million and over) expanded from 49.0 percent to 59.6 percent of the total, while the value of assets in this class more than quadrupled from $223 billion to $1,028 billion. (The Gini Coefficient of *asset* concentration rose from 0.56 in 1946, to 0.63 in 1954, a gain of 12 percent or about 0.6 percent a year. There is evidence that Gini Coefficients of *value-added* concentration were lower and would have shown a slower rise.[19]) (See Charts 5 and 6.)

The slow postwar rise in the proportion of corporate assets held by the largest companies was probably due primarily to the efforts made by businessmen to realize expanding economies of scale. Scale economies now go far beyond the production plant and embrace the functions of marketing, financing, and general management. Postwar technological changes have enlarged these economies, which have been realized mainly

CHART 5
*Percentages of the Total Assets of U.S. Corporations in Each
Asset Size-Class, 1946-1965*

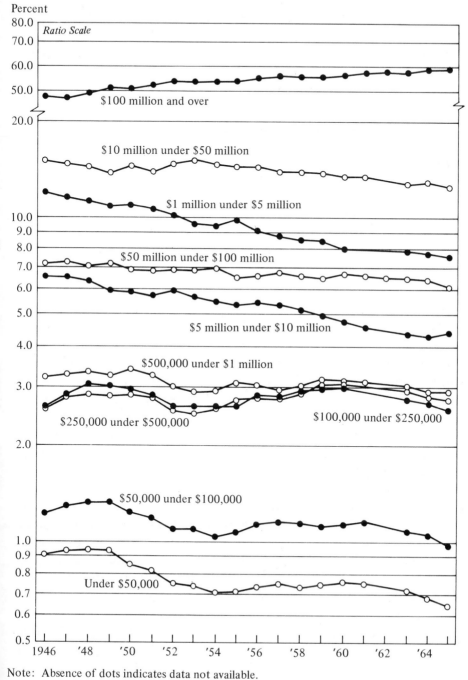

Note: Absence of dots indicates data not available.

CHART 6

*Cumulative Percentage Distributions of U.S. Corporation Assets,
by Asset Size-Classes, 1946 and 1965*

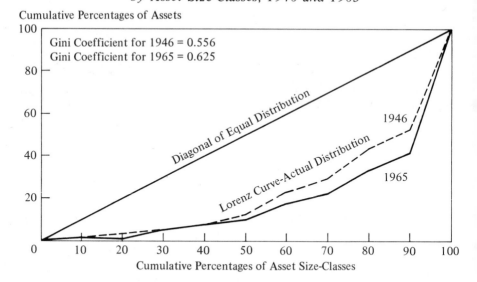

Cumulative Percentages of Assets

Gini Coefficient for 1946 = 0.556
Gini Coefficient for 1965 = 0.625

Diagonal of Equal Distribution

Lorenz Curve-Actual Distribution

1946

1965

Cumulative Percentages of Asset Size-Classes

by the internal growth of firms and only to a minor degree by mergers which have been mostly of the conglomerate form. Because of the rising importance of conglomeration among big companies, and the enormous increase in the number of small companies, the slow postwar rise in aggregate concentration of assets does not appear to have been accompanied by any important change in *market* concentration or in the effectiveness of competition in the economy.[20] Indeed, it is a striking fact that, *after correction for price inflation, the average real volume of business done per operating American corporation was less in 1968 than it was in 1950!*

The largest corporations, like companies of lesser size, are a changing rather than a static group. Their annual turnover rate reflects the rise or decline of management and the vagaries of business fortune. Of the hundred largest industrial corporations in 1909, only thirty-six remained on this list in 1948. And, of the top hundred companies in 1948, only sixty-five continued to hold this ranking in 1968.[21] These figures imply an annual turnover rate of about 1.6 percent a year. In every generation, striking changes have occurred in the industrial affiliations of the corporate giants. Thus, the period from 1948 to 1968 marked the emergence of large aerospace and conglomerate companies, and the disappearance from the top rank of many tobacco, motion picture, and merchandising firms. In a technologically dynamic economy with changing consumer preferences, commanding size does not continue automatically nor guarantee immortality.

The salient postwar trends in the size-structure of the corporate sector have been:

1. Moderate gains in the share of corporate assets held by the largest firms at the expense of medium and small companies.
2. An enormous increase in the number of small corporations.

Both trends derive largely from technological changes. Contemporary technology has created numerous economies of scale. At the same time it has opened up a myriad of opportunities for new and small companies.[22] And the rise of the service sector of the economy has also augmented the number of small firms. Small and large enterprises play complementary economic roles, each having comparative advantages in performing particular tasks. Thus, small companies account for many innovations in the American economy. With their lower overhead, closer contact with customers, and superior flexibility, they compete successfully with large companies in many markets, and outdo them in some. They manufacture and supply products, components, and services to big firms, and distribute and repair their products. *Small companies occupy an important and enduring position in the economy of the United States. It is a serious error to assert that they are transient institutions, destined to vanish.*

## CORPORATIONS AS GENERATORS OF INCOME

The most comprehensive measure of the role of the profit-seeking corporation in the economy of the United States is the proportion of the national income it originates. During the forty-year period from 1930 to 1969, the proportion of the national income originating in the business sector (corporate plus unincorporated) *declined* from 90 percent to 82 percent, while that originating in the general government sector rose, and the proportion coming from households and institutions did not change. The loss in the share of the business sector took place almost wholly in unincorporated business, whose fraction dropped from 38 percent to 28 percent. Corporate business expanded its share slowly from 52 percent to 56 percent over the whole period, but all of this gain was made prior to the mid-1950's; *during the past twenty years, the proportion of national income originating in corporations has been stable.* (See Table 4.)

The widely held notion that the business corporation increasingly dominates the American economy as a generator of income is not supported by the facts. Although its role as a generator of income is major, it has not grown for a generation. General government is the true "growth" sector of the economy. Nearly half of the national income comes from the noncorporate sector, which includes, in addition to general government, unincorporated firms, mutual insurance companies, certain savings and loan and other associations, cooperatives, professional and trade associations, governmental companies, and a host of nonprofit schools, hospitals, clubs, unions, and other institutions. Indeed, in our pluralistic economy, the nonprofit sector has been growing faster than the profit sector.[23]

# CORPORATIONS AS
# EMPLOYERS OF PEOPLE

The impression is widespread that most gainfully employed Americans work for big business corporations. It comes as a shock to many, therefore, to learn that the majority of the labor force in the United States works for government, unincorporated business, nonprofit institutions, or are self-employed. *Less than half of the total labor force was employed in the entire corporate sector in 1969. Less than one-quarter worked for "large companies,"* defined for present purposes as those employing more than two hundred people.[24]

Earning one's living as a member of a big corporate organization is by no means typical in American society. As Fuchs pointed out in 1968, after noting that the role of the corporate sector as a generator of national income had remained stable after 1957:

> As these and other facts become better known, we may see an end of the myth of the dominance of the large corporation in our society. Most people do not work and never have worked for large corporations; most production does not take place and never has taken place in large corporations. In the future, the large corporation is likely to be overshadowed by the hospitals, universities, research institutes, government agencies, and professional organizations that are the hallmarks of a service economy.[25]

It is true, however, that the corporate sector as a whole expanded its share of employment in the economy after World War II from 44 percent in 1950, to 49.5 percent in 1969. This came about because the corporate sector embraced a larger proportion of business enterprises, while the role of these enterprises in the whole economy remained stable.[26] The preponderance of the conversions of noncorporate to corporate business were, of course, among small firms formerly operating as partnership or proprietorships. Hence, most of the relative gain in corporate employment since World War II was in small rather than large companies. (See Table 5.)

# CORPORATIONS AS OWNERS OF TANGIBLE WEALTH

It is widely believed that big business firms collectively own the preponderance of America's wealth and are steadily expanding their share. The facts show the contrary. Corporate business owns about 28 percent of the tangible wealth of the United States, and its share has *not* changed much during the past fifty years. The bulk of the nation's tangible wealth is held by the household and government sectors of the economy and is not employed in profit-seeking enterprise, corporate or noncorporate. Goldsmith estimated that, in 1958, corporate business owned $349 billion of tangible assets, noncorporate business owned $76 billion, and households and governments owned $820 billion of the national total of $1,245 billion.[27] *If the character of a society were to be designated by its major wealth-holding institution, the United States could more appropriately be described as a "household state" than as a "corporate state."* However, all such simplistic designations are inadequate and misleading, the reality being at once more complex and less dramatic. (See Table 6.)

# CORPORATIONS AS EARNERS OF INCOME

Additional insight into the changing role of profit-seeking corporations in American society can be gained by comparing their aggregate rewards for productive services with those going to other economic groups. Specifically, we seek to compare changes during the past forty years in corporate profits with changes in the national income. If the hypothesis of the "corporate state" is correct, one would expect that the share of national income going to the corporate sector would have risen as a consequence of an expansion of corporate economic and political power.

Again, the facts refute the popular impression. *During the recent nineteen-year period from 1950 to 1969, corporate profits, both before and after taxes, formed a shrinking proportion of the national income.* After-tax profits declined from a peak of 10.3 percent of the national income in 1950, to 5.0 percent in 1969, whereas before-tax profits fell from 15.2 percent to 11.2 percent during the same years. Prior to 1950, profits before and after taxes formed a fluctuating share of the national income, reaching an all-time low point in the Great Depression of the 1930's and rising to a peak in the Korean War boom year of 1950. (See Table 7.)

This relative decline in corporate profits occurred despite the conversion of much business to the corporate form and despite stability in the proportion of national income *produced* in the corporate sector. Indeed, when corporate profits are combined with unincorporated enterprise income, the total rewards to the business sector of the economy fell from 30 percent to 20 percent of the national income between 1950 and 1969, while employees' compensation claimed an expanding fraction of national income. Insofar as one may infer relative changes in economic or political power from income shares, the corporate sector has been losing ground for at least a generation.

## CHANGES IN THE
## CORPORATE SHAREOWNER POPULATION

Social thinkers generally agree that a broad diffusion of corporate ownership is desirable in a market economy in which private enterprise plays a major role. If ownership is broadly based among the people, a fuller popular understanding and support of the enterprise system is likely to prevail than if the ownership base remains narrow. A diffused ownership can also add to equity in the distribution of income, as well as to efficiency in corporate operations.[28] What changes have occurred in the population of shareowners and in the concentration of shareownership?

Information about the population of direct shareowners in American public business corporations is provided by the *Census of Shareowners,* first taken by the New York Stock Exchange in 1952 and repeated intermittently thereafter. The 1970 census revealed that the number of direct shareowners in the United States was 30.9 million, 15 percent of the total population and more than 26 percent of the population twenty-one years or more. Of these shareowners, 20.1 million held shares listed on national securities exchanges, 6.7 million owned shares traded over the counter, and 4 million owned shares of investment companies. The typical stockholder had an above-average income and education, was likely to be aged forty-five or older, and was engaged in professional, technical, or managerial pursuits, or was a housewife or retired. There were about equal numbers of male and female stockholders. The estimated market value in that year was $1,065 billion, giving an average value of $31,300 per shareholder.

The fact that one out of four adult Americans was a direct corporate shareowner demonstrates that there is a relatively wide diffusion of corporate ownership, compared with other Western countries or with our own past.[29] This statement gains even greater force when it is recognized that the New York Stock Exchange census excluded owners of companies whose shares are not publicly traded, as well as millions of *indirect* owners of corporate equities who have interests in life insurance policies, variable annuities, and retirement funds.

*The population of direct shareowners nearly quintupled from 6.5 million in 1952 to 30.9 million in 1970, registering a compound growth of 9 percent a year.* (See Table 8.) The direct shareowner population grew more than six times as fast as the human population.

There is evidence that the rapid growth of the direct shareowner population after World War II was not characteristic of the late 1930's and the early 1940's. If we can give credibility to the estimates of Berle and Means that there were 4 to 6 million shareowners in 1927,[30] and to the estimates of the Temporary National Economic Committee that there were 8 to 9 million shareowners in 1937,[31] it appears that the direct shareowner population fluctuated during the Great Depression and World War II, and consistent growth did not appear until the 1950's. (See Chart 7.)

While *direct* ownership of corporate shares has special significance, *indirect* ownership also has burgeoned during recent years as a result of the "institutionalization" of stockholding. The Securities and Exchange Commission estimated that in 1965 investment companies, insurance companies, pension and retirement funds, and personal, college, and governmental trust funds owned $200.4 billion of shares in American corporations, nearly 30 percent of the total market value of $674.7 billion.[32] In that year, mutual investment companies had 6.7 million stockholder accounts.[33] (This count duplicated those shareowners who had accounts in more than one fund.) At the same time, 25.4 million employees were covered by private retirement systems, and 5.8 million employees were under public retirement systems.[34] Because most investment companies and retirement systems held corporate shares in their portfolios, their participants were indirect shareowners. Millions of policyholders of life, fire, and casualty insurance companies also owned equities indirectly. *Thus, in 1970, a majority of adult Americans probably were either direct or indirect investors in corporate business.*

These are gratifying developments to believers in a competitive private enterprise economy. Even in 1962, 58 percent of all American households had property income in the form of interest, rents, or corporate dividends.[35] The percentage was undoubtedly much larger by 1972.

## THE CONCENTRATION OF CORPORATE SHARE OWNERSHIP

A *lessened concentration* of the ownership of business corporations is as desirable as is a *wider dispersion* of share ownership. Unfortunately,

## CHART 7
### Direct Shareowner and Total U.S. Populations, 1952-1970

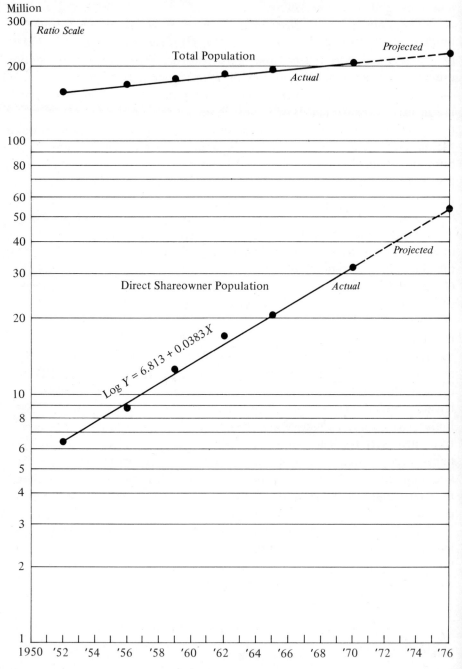

information by which to measure changes in concentration with much confidence is lacking. Available data indicate that, *up to the 1960's, the ownership of American business corporations continued to be highly concentrated among persons in the high income and wealth classes,* even though the distribution of personal wealth as a whole became significantly less unequal over the preceding forty years. Lampman found that over the period from 1922 to 1953 the top one percent of American adults owned between 60 and 70 percent of the total value of corporate stock. However, the share of personal wealth held by the wealthiest one percent of American adults declined from 31.6 percent to 26 percent over the same period. He also found that among top wealth holders—persons worth $60,000 or more—corporate stock was the most preferred type of asset and accounted for 39 percent of the total value of estates subject to the Federal estate tax.[36]

A high degree of concentration in the ownership of corporate stock among top wealth holders was confirmed by a study of the composition of the incomes of American consumers during 1962. It was found that dividends from public corporate stocks were the most concentrated type of income. The 10 percent of households with the highest incomes received 68 percent of all corporate dividends, and the next 10 percent received 14 percent of all dividends. Thus, the richest one-fifth of American households then accounted for 82 percent of all dividend income.[37]

Why has a high concentration of stock ownership among the rich persisted in the face of a falling concentration of wealth in general and an enormous increase in the shareowner population? The answer may be found in the dynamics of wealth distribution. The share of the top-income families in aggregate wealth has fallen over time because these families failed as a group to maintain a proportion of total personal saving equal to their share of total wealth. Hence, rates of saving from current income worked to *reduce* inequality in the distribution of wealth. On the other hand, economic growth and price inflation tended to increase such inequality. The rich held relatively large fractions of their assets in the form of stocks which appreciated in value over time, whereas middle- and low-income persons held proportionately more of their assets in savings deposits, life insurance, and other assets with fixed-dollar values.[38]

Although ownership of corporate equities continued up to the 1960's to be concentrated among the wealthiest families, the members of this group constantly changed. Entrepreneurial families tend to traverse cycles in their wealth. Typically, the founder of the family develops a business of great value, and then sells part of his stock to the public to diversify his assets and gain liquidity. Later, the executors of his estate distribute more stock to the public in exchange for cash, which is used to pay estate taxes. The balance of the holdings are broken up among the heirs of the founder; they tend to spend heavily on consumption, sell more stock to the public, and slip downward in wealth ranking. Meanwhile, new entrepreneurs build new enterprises and families, and the cycle begins anew. Perhaps the adage, "Shirtsleeves to shirtsleeves in three generations," is an overstatement; but it does contain a few grains of truth.

## THE ACTUAL ROLE OF THE CORPORATION

This study of the corporate sector of the American economy over the past half-century leads us to the conclusion that while the profit-seeking corporation is indeed a vital institution, the United States neither is, nor is becoming, a "corporate state." By most measures the corporate sector has maintained a stable relationship with the rest of the economy for at least a generation. To recapitulate:

1. The vitality of the corporate institution is shown by the 6 percent compound rate of growth of the corporate population since World War II, which resulted in some 1,600,000 corporations by 1968. In 1945, under 15 percent of all American business enterprises were corporations; in 1968, about 31 percent held corporate charters. But corporations made 80–85 percent of all business sales.

2. Surprisingly, corporations had higher entry and exit rates and a shorter average life than did unincorporated enterprises.

3. Throughout the postwar period, the vast majority of companies were small. In 1965, some 94 percent of all corporations had assets of less than $1 million, while only 0.13 percent had assets of $100 million or more.

4. Concentration of corporate assets among companies of the largest size apparently increased about 12 percent from 1946 to 1965. In 1946, the 531 companies with assets over $100 million collectively owned 49 percent of all corporate assets, whereas, in 1965, the 1,900 companies in this class held 59.6 percent.

5. The 1.6 percent a year postwar turnover rate of the one hundred largest industrial corporations was about the same as during the prewar era.

6. Direct shareownership in public corporations exploded during the postwar era, rising 9 percent a year after 1952. By 1970, nearly 31 million Americans—one out of every four adults—directly owned corporate stock. If indirect ownership of shares by beneficiaries of financial intermediaries are added, it appears that a majority of American adults owned an interest in corporate equities by 1970.

7. The economic role of the corporate sector of the economy of the United States has not expanded relatively during the past fifteen years, while that of government has expanded considerably. In 1968 corporations generated about 56 percent of the national income, nearly the same proportion as in 1950. The share of general government rose from 9 to 14 percent.

8. As an employer of people, the corporate sector was outweighed by the other sectors in 1969, when only about one-quarter of all gainfully employed Americans worked for large corporations. (See Chart 8.)

## CHART 8
### *The Corporate Sector in the U.S. Economy, 1929-1969*

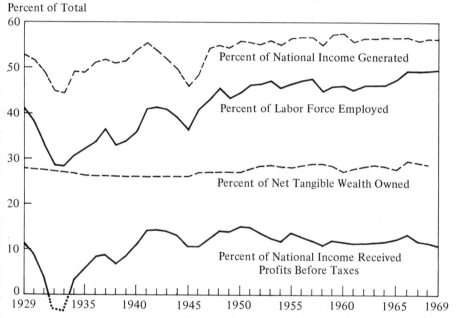

Percent of Total

Percent of National Income Generated

Percent of Labor Force Employed

Percent of Net Tangible Wealth Owned

Percent of National Income Received
Profits Before Taxes

9. During the past twenty years, the rewards going to the corporate sector in the form of profits declined as a percentage of national income, whereas the rewards to employees rose significantly.

10. The role of the corporation as an owner of the nation's tangible wealth remained stable at 28 percent during the past half-century, while the share of the government expanded.

To sum up: The main postwar trend has been toward a larger role for government. Although more business has become corporate in form, more of the economy has become socialized. *The contemporary American economy is pluralistic rather than dominantly corporate in character.*

TABLE 1

*Corporate and Human Populations of the U.S. and the U.K., 1910-1968*

| | United States[a] | | | | United Kingdom[b] | | | |
|---|---|---|---|---|---|---|---|---|
| Year | Corporate Returns Filed (Thousands) | Resident Population (Thousands) | Percent Corporate to Human Population | Number Humans per Corporation | Registered Companies (Thousands) | Human Population (Thousands) | Percent Companies to Human Population | Number Humans per Company |
| 1910 | 270 | 92,407 | 0.29 | 342 | | | | |
| 1915 | 366 | 100,549 | 0.36 | 275 | | | | |
| 1920 | 346 | 106,466 | 0.32 | 308 | | | | |
| 1925 | 430 | 115,832 | 0.37 | 269 | | | | |
| 1930 | 519 | 123,077 | 0.42 | 237 | | | | |
| 1935 | 534 | 127,250 | 0.42 | 238 | 152 | 46,861 | 0.32 | 308 |
| 1940 | 517 | 132,549 | 0.39 | 256 | 176 | 48,867 | 0.36 | 278 |
| 1945 | 454 | 140,468 | 0.32 | 309 | 201 | 49,150 | 0.41 | 245 |
| 1950 | 666 | 152,271 | 0.44 | 229 | 262 | 50,616 | 0.52 | 193 |
| 1955 | 754 | 165,931 | 0.45 | 220 | 308 | 50,947 | 0.60 | 166 |
| 1960 | 1,121 | 180,684 | 0.62 | 161 | 393 | 52,372 | 0.75 | 133 |
| 1965 | 1,490 | 194,592 | 0.77 | 131 | 539 | 54,744 | 0.99 | 101 |
| 1968 | 1,600 (est.) | 201,152 | 0.80 | 126 | 570[c] | 56,150* | 1.02 | 99 |

* Figures for 1967.

SOURCES: [a] Number of corporate returns from *Statistics of Income: Corporations*; resident population from *Statistical Abstract of the United States 1969*, p. 5.
[b] Number of Companies from Board of Trade, *General Annual Report on Companies*; population from *Abstract of Statistics* (Central Statistics Office, United Kingdom).

TABLE 2

Corporation, Business Enterprise, and Entrepreneurial Populations of the U.S., 1945-1968

| Year | Corporations | | Business Enterprises | | Entrepreneurs | |
|------|-------------|---|---------------------|---|---------------|---|
| | Returns Filed (Thousands) | Persons Per Company | Number Operating (Thousands) | Persons Per Enterprise | Individuals With Self-Employment Income (Thousands) | Persons Per Entrepreneur |
| 1945 | 454 | 309 | 3,114 | 46 | 7,377 | 19 |
| 1950 | 666 | 229 | 4,051 | 44 | 8,988 | 17 |
| 1955 | 754 | 220 | 4,286 | 39 | 10,200 | 16 |
| 1960 | 1,121 | 161 | 4,652 | 39 | 10,518 | 17 |
| 1965 | 1,490 | 131 | 4,900 (est.) | 40 | 10,751 | 18 |
| 1968 | 1,600 (est.) | 126 | 5,126 (est.) | 39 | 11,080 (est.) | 18 |

SOURCES: Corporation returns filed from *Statistics of Income: Corporations*. Operating business firms from U.S. Department of Commerce. Individual returns reporting self-employment income from *Statistics of Income: Individuals*. Population from *Statistical Abstract of the United States 1969*, p. 5.

TABLE 3

Annual Entries and Exits of Corporations and of all Business Enterprises in the U.S., 1946-1968

(Figures in thousands)

| Year | (1) Corporations Filing Returns | (2) Net Annual Change in (1) | Corporations (3) Corporate Entries in Preceding Year | (4) Entry Rate (3)/(1) (Percent) | (5) Implicit Exits (3)/(2) | (6) Implicit Exit Rate (5)/(1) (Percent) | (7) Number of Operating Business Enterprises | All Business Enterprises (8) Number of New Business Enterprises | (9) Entry Rate (3)/(7) (Percent) | (10) Number of Discontinued Businesses | (11) Exit Rate (10)/(7) (Percent) |
|---|---|---|---|---|---|---|---|---|---|---|---|
| 1946 | 526 | | | | | | 3,487 | 617 | 17.6 | 209 | 6.0 |
| 47 | 588 | 62 | 133 | 22.6 | 71 | 12.1 | 3,783 | 461 | 12.2 | 239 | 6.3 |
| 48 | 631 | 43 | 113 | 17.9 | 70 | 11.1 | 3,948 | 393 | 10.0 | 282 | 7.1 |
| 49 | 650 | 19 | 96 | 14.8 | 77 | 11.8 | 4,000 | 331 | 8.3 | 307 | 7.7 |
| 1950 | 666 | 16 | 86 | 12.9 | 70 | 10.5 | 4,051 | 348 | 8.6 | 280 | 6.9 |
| 51 | 687 | 21 | 93 | 13.5 | 72 | 10.5 | 4,067 | 327 | 8.0 | 276 | 6.8 |
| 52 | 705 | 18 | 84 | 11.9 | 66 | 9.4 | 4,118 | 345 | 8.4 | 276 | 6.7 |
| 53 | 731 | 26 | 93 | 12.7 | 67 | 9.2 | 4,188 | 352 | 8.4 | 299 | 7.1 |
| 54 | 754 | 23 | 103 | 13.6 | 80 | 10.6 | 4,239 | 366 | 8.6 | 319 | 7.5 |
| 1955 | 842 | 88 | 117 | 13.9 | 29 | 3.4 | 4,286 | 408 | 9.5 | 314 | 7.3 |
| 56 | 925 | 83 | 140 | 15.1 | 57 | 6.2 | 4,381 | 431 | 9.8 | 342 | 7.8 |
| 57 | 985 | 60 | 141 | 14.3 | 81 | 8.2 | 4,471 | 398 | 8.9 | 335 | 7.5 |
| 58 | 1,033 | 48 | 137 | 13.3 | 89 | 8.6 | 4,533 | 397 | 8.8 | 347 | 7.7 |
| 59 | 1,120 | 87 | 151 | 13.5 | 64 | 5.7 | 4,583 | 422 | 9.2 | 346 | 7.5 |
| 1960 | 1,188 | 68 | 193 | 16.2 | 125 | 10.5 | 4,652 | 438 | 9.4 | 384 | 8.3 |
| 61 | 1,241 | 53 | 183 | 14.7 | 130 | 10.5 | 4,713 | 431 | 9.1 | 389 | 8.3 |
| 62 | 1,319 | 78 | 182 | 13.8 | 104 | 7.9 | 4,755 | 430 | 9.0 | 387 | 8.1 |
| 63 | 1,382 | 63 | 182 | 13.2 | 119 | 8.6 | | | | | |
| 64 | 1,437 | 55 | 186 | 12.9 | 131 | 9.1 | | | | | |
| 1965 | 1,490 | 53 | 198 | 13.3 | 145 | 9.7 | | | | | |
| 66 | 1,545 | 55 | 204 | 13.2 | 149 | 9.5 | | | | | |
| 67* | 1,488 | 57 | 200 | 13.4 | 257 | 17.3 | | | | | |
| 68* | 1,600 | 112 | 207 | 12.9 | 95 | 5.9 | | | | | |
| Arith. Mean | | | | 14.7 | | 9.1 | | | 9.6 | | 7.3 |

*Estimated

SOURCES: Corporations filing tax returns from Statistics of Income: Corporations. Corporate entries (new incorporations) from Economic Report of the President to the Congress, 1970,

TABLE 4

Национ *National Income Originating in Corporate Business and Other Sectors of the U.S. Economy, 1930-1969*

(Amounts in billions of dollars)

| Year | Corporate Business | | Other Business[a] | | General Government | | Households and Institutions[b] | | Rest of the World | | Totals | |
|---|---|---|---|---|---|---|---|---|---|---|---|---|
| | Amount | Percent | Amount | Percent | Amount | Percent | Amount | Percent | Amount | Percent | Amount | Percent |
| 1930 | $39.2 | 52.1 | $28.2 | 37.5 | $4.5 | 6.0 | $2.7 | 3.6 | $0.7 | 0.9 | $75.3 | 100.0 |
| 1935 | 27.8 | 48.6 | 21.2 | 37.1 | 5.9 | 10.3 | 1.9 | 3.3 | 0.4 | 0.7 | 57.2 | 100.0 |
| 1940 | 43.3 | 53.3 | 27.3 | 33.6 | 7.8 | 9.6 | 2.4 | 3.0 | 0.4 | 0.5 | 81.2 | 100.0 |
| 1945 | 83.3 | 45.9 | 58.5 | 32.2 | 35.2 | 19.4 | 4.1 | 2.3 | 0.4 | 0.2 | 181.5 | 100.0 |
| 1950 | 134.0 | 55.6 | 78.6 | 32.6 | 20.9 | 8.7 | 6.4 | 2.7 | 1.2 | 0.5 | 241.1 | 100.0 |
| 1955 | 188.0 | 56.8 | 98.0 | 29.6 | 34.2 | 10.3 | 9.1 | 2.7 | 1.8 | 0.5 | 331.1 | 100.0 |
| 1960 | 234.1 | 56.5 | 117.3 | 28.3 | 47.5 | 11.5 | 13.2 | 3.2 | 2.4 | 0.6 | 414.5 | 100.0 |
| 1965 | 317.5 | 56.8 | 151.1 | 27.0 | 67.8 | 12.1 | 18.3 | 3.3 | 4.3 | 0.8 | 559.0 | 100.0 |
| 1969 | 432.9 | 56.3 | 200.6 | 26.1 | 103.6 | 13.5 | 28.1 | 3.7 | 4.3 | 0.6 | 769.5 | 100.0 |

[a] Includes proprietorships, partnerships, cooperatives, nonprofit and governmental corporations.
[b] Includes households, clubs, unions, nonprofit schools, hospitals and religious, charitable, and welfare organizations.

SOURCES: U.S. Dept. of Commerce, *The National Income and Product Accounts of the United States, 1929-65 Statistical Tables;* and *Survey of Current Business.*

TABLE 5

*Employment in the Corporate Sector and Other Sectors
of the U.S. Economy, 1929-1969*

| Year | (1) Corporate Employment (Millions) | (2) Total Labor Force (Millions) | (3) Percent (1) to (2) |
|---|---|---|---|
| 1929 | 20.5 | 49.4 | 41.5 |
| 1930 | 19.0 | 50.1 | 37.9 |
| 1935 | 17.0 | 53.1 | 32.0 |
| 1940 | 20.3 | 56.2 | 36.1 |
| 1945 | 23.7 | 65.3 | 36.3 |
| 1950 | 28.1 | 63.9 | 44.0 |
| 1955 | 31.7 | 68.1 | 46.5 |
| 1960 | 33.3 | 72.1 | 46.2 |
| 1965 | 36.7 | 77.2 | 47.5 |
| 1969 | 41.7 | 84.2 | 49.5 |

SOURCES: *Survey of Current Business,* November 1969, pp.18-23, and data supplied by U.S. Department of Commerce.

## TABLE 6
### Corporate and Other Ownership of Tangible Wealth of the U.S., 1900-1968
(Billions of 1947-49 dollars during 1900-1958: thereafter billions of 1958 dollars)

| Year | Corporate Business | | Noncorporate Business | | Government, Household, and Other Sectors | | All Sectors of the Economy | |
|---|---|---|---|---|---|---|---|---|
| | Amount | Percent | Amount | Percent | Amount | Percent | Amount | Percent |
| 1900 | $75.9 | 24.1 | $23.7 | 7.5 | $215.0 | 68.3 | $314.6 | 100.0 |
| 1912 | 125.1 | 26.9 | 32.1 | 6.9 | 307.5 | 66.2 | 464.7 | 100.0 |
| 1922 | 165.7 | 28.2 | 44.0 | 7.5 | 378.5 | 64.3 | 588.2 | 100.0 |
| 1933 | 196.4 | 26.5 | 54.0 | 7.3 | 491.8 | 66.3 | 742.2 | 100.0 |
| 1945 | 190.4 | 25.4 | 57.5 | 7.7 | 500.5 | 66.9 | 748.4 | 100.0 |
| 1950 | 258.1 | 27.2 | 65.0 | 6.8 | 626.0 | 66.0 | 949.1 | 100.0 |
| 1955 | 315.0 | 27.8 | 71.3 | 6.3 | 745.5 | 65.9 | 1,131.8 | 100.0 |
| 1958 | 348.8 | 28.0 | 75.9 | 6.1 | 819.8 | 65.9 | 1,244.5 | 100.0 |
| (1958 dollars) | | | | | | | | |
| 1958 | 363.0 | 27.1 | 91.0 | 6.8 | 886.0 | 66.2 | 1,340.0 | 100.0 |
| 1960 | 390.0 | 27.2 | 97.0 | 6.7 | 946.0 | 66.0 | 1,433.0 | 100.0 |
| 1965 | 485.0 | 27.4 | 123.0 | 7.0 | 1,154.0 | 65.5 | 1,762.0 | 100.0 |
| 1968 | 577.0 | 28.7 | 147.0 | 7.3 | 1,286.0 | 64.0 | 2,010.0 | 100.0 |

SOURCES: R. Goldsmith, *The National Wealth of the United States in the Postwar Period* (New York: National Bureau of Economic Research, 1962), p. 139, for figures during the years 1900 through 1958. Figures for the recent period 1958-1968 are the author's own estimates.

TABLE 7

*Corporate Profits in Relation to U.S. National Income, 1930-1969*

(Amounts in billions of dollars)

| (1)<br>Year | (2)<br>National<br>Income | (3)<br>Corporate<br>Profits<br>Before Taxes<br>(Including<br>Inventory<br>Valuation) | (4)<br>Percent<br>(3) / (2) | (5)<br>Corporate<br>Profits<br>After Taxes<br>(Excluding<br>Inventory<br>Valuation) | (6)<br>Percent<br>(5) / (2) |
|---|---|---|---|---|---|
| 1930 | $ 75.4 | $ 6.8 | 9.0 | $ 2.9 | 3.8 |
| 1935 | 57.2 | 3.2 | 5.6 | 2.6 | 4.5 |
| 1940 | 81.1 | 9.6 | 11.8 | 7.2 | 8.9 |
| 1945 | 181.5 | 18.9 | 10.4 | 9.0 | 5.0 |
| 1950 | 241.1 | 36.7 | 15.2 | 24.9 | 10.3 |
| 1955 | 331.0 | 45.3 | 13.7 | 27.0 | 8.2 |
| 1960 | 414.5 | 48.0 | 11.6 | 26.7 | 6.4 |
| 1965 | 559.0 | 70.1 | 12.5 | 44.5 | 8.0 |
| 1969 | 769.5 | 85.8 | 11.2 | 38.7 | 5.0 |

SOURCES: U.S. Department of Commerce, *The National Income and Product Accounts of the United States, 1929-1965*, and *Survey of Current Business.*

TABLE 8

*Number of Direct Shareowners in U.S. Public Business Corporations, 1952-1970*

(Figures in millions)

| Year | Number of<br>Shareowners | U.S.<br>Population | Percent<br>Shareowner<br>to Population |
|---|---|---|---|
| 1952 | 6.5 | 156.2 | 4.2 |
| 1956 | 8.6 | 167.4 | 5.2 |
| 1959 | 12.5 | 176.4 | 7.1 |
| 1962 | 17.0 | 185.2 | 9.2 |
| 1965 | 20.1 | 193.5 | 10.4 |
| 1970 | 30.9 | 204.4 | 15.1 |

SOURCE: *Census of Ownership* for respective years, New York Stock Exchange.

## NOTES

1. See Charles Reich, *The Greening of America* (New York: Random House, 1970). Reich built upon many of the central concepts of John Kenneth Galbraith in *The New Industrial State* (Boston: Houghton Mifflin, 1967). Other social scientists who share some visions of the "corporate state" are W. Lloyd Warner, *The Corporation in the Emergent American Society* (New York: Harper, 1962), and Peter F. Drucker, *The Concept of the Corporation* (New York: John Day, 1946).

2. *The Trustees of Dartmouth College v. Woodward*, 4 Wheaton 518 (1819).

3. G. H. Evans, Jr., studied only corporation *entries* in his *Business Incorporations in the United States, 1800–1943* (New York: National Bureau of Economic Research, 1948).

4. See article by Edward S. Mason in *International Encyclopedia of the Social Sciences,* Vol. 3, p. 396.

5. *Statistics of Income, Corporation Returns 1965* (Washington, D.C.: U.S. Government Printing Office, 1965), pp. 4–5. All except a few thousand of the reporting corporations were actively in business. The number of returns filed somewhat understates the total number of active corporations because an affiliated group of corporations (connected through stock ownership with a common parent) may elect to file a single return, and also because of the failure of some companies to file any return. The estimate of 1.6 million in 1968 was made by fitting a linear function to the available data for 1946–1966 by the least squares method and extrapolating.

6. That the growth rate of the corporation population has been much higher than that of the human population for more than 150 years may be inferred from the fact that there were 335 business corporations in the United States in 1800 and about twenty in England and France. See Thomas C. Cochran, *Basic History of American Business* (Princeton: D. Van Nostrand, 1959), p. 40.

7. Although real GNP grew at a compound rate of 3.3 percent a year in the United States and 2.2 percent a year in the United Kingdom between 1929 and 1966, the British corporate population growth rate was higher than the American during that period. U.S. Bureau of the Census, *Statistical Abstract of the United States 1969* (Washington, D.C.: U.S. Government Printing Office, 1969), p. 313. Also, *General Annual Report on Companies* (London: Board of Trade, H.M. Stationery Office, various years).

8. The Office of Business Economics of the U.S. Department of Commerce formerly published annual estimates of the average number of business firms in operation, based upon data from the Bureau of Old Age and Survivors' Insurance; but it discontinued the series after 1963, in which year 4,797,000 firms were listed. The number of firms in 1968 was estimated by fitting a curve to the time series over the period from 1945 to 1963 and extrapolating. Because the coefficient of variation of actual from computed values was only 0.623 percent, a high degree of confidence in the estimate is justified. Dun and Bradstreet, Inc., publish figures showing the annual number of "operating business firms" in the United States, but they include only firms seeking commercial credit—2,418,000 in 1968—which formed about half the total enterprise population.

9. Robert R. Doane, *The Measurement of American Wealth* (New York: National Bureau of Economic Research, 1953), table 18, p. 53.

10. Based on data from *Census of Manufacturers, Census of Business,* and *Census of Mineral Industries* (Washington, D.C.: U.S. Government Printing Office, various years).

11. This estimate excludes those persons whose incomes were too small to have reportable gross income.

12. The 7.4 million individual tax returns showing self-employment income formed 14 percent of civilian employment in 1945, whereas the 11.1 million tax returns reporting self-employment income formed 14.6 percent of civilian employment in 1968.

13. This point is made in Evans, *Business Incorporations in the United States,* Ch. 2.

14. *Ibid.,* p. 9.

15. Source: *Statistical Abstract of the United States 1969, op. cit.,* pp. 53, 49, 55.

16. See Neil H. Jacoby, "Corporate Concentration, Conglomeration and Competition" in *Role of Giant Corporations,* Hearings before the Subcommitte on Monopoly of the Select Committee on Small Business, U.S. Senate, July 1969 (Washington, D.C.: U.S. Government Printing Office), p. 508.

17. For example, in its widely-quoted *Economic Report on Corporate Mergers* of 1969, the staff of the Federal Trade Commission stated that between 1948 and 1968 the hundred largest manufacturing companies had increased their share of total manufacturing *assets* from 40.03 to 49.3 percent, and the two hundred largest manufacturing companies had increased their share from 48.3 to 60.9 percent. This *Report* was published as *Economic Concentration,* Hearings before the Subcommittee on the Judiciary, U.S. Senate, 91st Congress, 1st Session, pursuant to S. Res. 40 (Washington, D.C.: U.S. Government Printing Office, 1969). However, the statistical procedures utilized in this study render the conclusion of rising concentration tenuous. The proportion of value-added—a more significant measure of concentration—was much lower during the past ten years. See Betty Bock, "Statistical Games and the '200 Largest' Industrials: 1954 and 1968," *Studies in Business Economics,* No. 115 (New York: National Industrial Conference Board, 1970).

18. The Gini Coefficient measures the extent to which the Lorenz curve, showing cumulated percentages of the actual numbers (here, of firms), in each of the size-classes, to the total population, deviates from a diagonal of equal distribution of that population among the size-classes.

19. See Betty Bock, *Concentration, Oligopoly and Profit: Concepts and Data* (New York: The Conference Board, 1972).

20. Between 1954 and 1968, "large" acquisitions directly contributed only 15 percent to the combined growth of assets of the "two hundred largest" industrial corporations. For a fuller discussion see Chapter 4.

21. See A. D. H. Kaplan, *Big Enterprise in a Competitive System* (Washington, D.C.: Brookings Institution, 1954), p. 141. Kaplan's study of turnover of the largest corporations through 1948 is extended here through 1968.

22. Technological changes may not affect the mean size of enterprises, but they may increase the standard deviation from the mean. See Neil H. Jacoby, "Impacts of Scientific Change upon Business Management," *California Management Review,* Vol. 4, No. 4 (Summer 1962).

23. This view is documented in Eli Ginsberg, Dale L. Hiestand, and Beatrice G. Reubens, *The Pluralistic Economy* (New York: McGraw-Hill, 1965), Chs. 1 and 2.

24. Based on data of the U.S. Department of Labor.

25. Victor R. Fuchs, *The Service Economy* (New York: National Bureau of Economic Research, 1968), p. 10.

26. See Jeanette Fitzwilliams, "Employment in Corporate and Non-Corporate Production," *Survey of Current Business* (November 1959), p. 19.

27. See R. Goldsmith, *The National Wealth of the United States in the Postwar Period* (New York: National Bureau of Economic Research, 1962), p. 139. "Net tangible wealth" refers to the estimated market value of the physical assets owned by each sector of the economy.

28. For these reasons many proposals have been made for wider distribution of corporate shares among the population. See, for example, Louis O. Kelso and Mortimer J. Adler, *The Capitalist Manifesto* (New York: Random House, 1958).

29. The findings of the New York Stock Exchange *Census* for 1970 are borne out by a 1970 study, *Survey of Consumer Finances,* by the Survey Research Center

of the University of Michigan, which showed that one out of every four American family units owns shares of stock.

30. Adolf A. Berle, Jr., and Gardiner C. Means, *The Modern Corporation and Private Property* (New York: Macmillan, 1932), p. 36.

31. Temporary National Economic Committee, *Distribution of Ownership in the 200 Largest Nonfinancial Corporations* (Washington, D.C.: U.S. Government Printing Office, 1940).

32. Securities and Exchange Commission, *Public Policy Implications of Investment Company Growth* (Washington, D.C.: U.S. Government Printing Office, 1966), pp. 276–277.

33. *Investment Companies 1969* (New York: Arthur Wiesenberger Services, 1970), p. 18.

34. See Roger F. Murray, *Economic Aspects of Pensions: A Summary Report* (New York: National Bureau of Economic Research, 1968), p. 30.

35. Projector, Weiss, and Thorensen, "Composition of Income as Shown by the Survey of Financial Characteristics of Consumers," in *Six Papers on the Size Distribution of Wealth and Income* (New York: National Bureau of Economic Research, 1969), pp. 109–110.

36. Robert J. Lampman, *The Share of Top Wealth-Holders in National Wealth 1922–56* (Princeton: Princeton University Press, 1962), pp. 21, 25.

37. Projector, Weiss, and Thorensen, *op. cit.,* p. 11.

38. Lampman, *op. cit.,* p. 26.

# PART II

POSTWAR
DEVELOPMENTS IN
ORGANIZATION AND
OPERATIONS

# CHAPTER 3

# Corporate Management: Adding Science to Art

S O FAR, we have looked at the corporate institution from the perspective of its critics, and we have delineated its role in the economy of the American nation. The evolution of both corporate criticism and corporate economic performance over the past half-century has been noted. In order to understand this institution fully, however, it is also necessary to examine recent salient developments in its organizational structure and operating processes.

*The evolution of the American business corporation since World War II has been marked by three primary and interrelated developments: a quantum leap in the development of the science and practice of management; a burgeoning of conglomerate enterprise; and a mighty expansion of multinational business.* Of the three, the advance in management science and practice has been the most fundamental; and, in fact, more than any single factor, it has enabled corporations to conglomerate and to multinationalize on an unprecedented scale. Indeed, it is hard to conceive how a large multinational conglomerate, such as International Telephone and Telegraph, could survive without the concepts and practices

This chapter originated as the P. S. Ross Inaugural Lecture, given at McMaster University in Hamilton, Ontario, Canada, on March 15, 1968, under the title, "The Continuing Revolution in Management Education." I am grateful to the then President of McMaster University, Dr. Henry G. Thode, for his kind invitation. I have drawn also upon my article, "Impacts of Scientific Change Upon Business Management," published in the *California Management Review*, Vol. 4, No. 4 (Summer 1962). Professor Harold D. Koontz made valuable comments on this chapter's themes.

of modern management, as well as the computers and information systems, and the elaborate communications facilities, that characterize contemporary management.[1] Modern management science has made it feasible for corporations to expand the scope and variety of their operations. It has created new economies of scale through which larger aggregations of men, materials, and funds can be efficiently deployed and controlled over larger areas. We come now to examine these developments in management practices and the related changes in the education of professional managers.

## POSTWAR INNOVATIONS IN MANAGEMENT PRACTICES

By the "science" of management we will mean that body of concepts, principles, and techniques whose validity has been tested by business executives in real business situations. The operation of a business enterprise is an art as well as a science, in that it calls upon those ineffable factors of human intuition and judgment—and plain luck. Yet, managerial action is increasingly guided by concepts and models that extend the area of rationality and reduce reliance upon hunch and guesswork.

Let us make a quick inventory of the major developments in the management of large American corporations that either originated or have attained widespread usage since World War II. It is convenient to group these managerial innovations under the five major functions into which, according to one of the best statements of modern operational theory, the managerial process may be divided: planning, organizing, staffing, directing, and controlling.[2] Of course, both in theory and in practice, each of these five functions is closely interrelated with the others.

### Planning

As understood in modern operational theory, planning means the selection of objectives for an enterprise from among alternatives and the development of the best methods of reaching them. During recent years the scope of corporate planning has become more systematic and comprehensive as business executives have come to see the complex interconnections between the performance of the enterprise and the multifaceted and changing environment for business. *Environmental forecasting*—the effort to envisage the probable social, political, economic, and technological changes of the future—is used increasingly by large companies as a basis for their plans and strategies. *Long-term, "rolling" plans*, involving the setting of goals and the making of general plans for a five-year period—or longer—and including a detailed, firm plan of operations for the ensuing year, are now common. Each year, such a plan is updated by adding a year. The *Planning-Programming-Budgeting System* (PPBS) is a method of allocating resources (capital or expenditures) so as to maximize their effectiveness through the rational exploration of all alternative courses of action to attain a specified goal. Originated by RAND Corporation for use in the Department of Defense, its use has spread rapidly through government. Basically, PPBS is a technique for formulating governmental budgets more in terms of major goals sought, rather than in the traditional "line item" format, and for using cost/benefit analyses to help determine goals.[3] In a significant sense these innovations were adaptations of the "project" budgeting and "feasibility studies" long employed in private business.

*Time-event network analysis,* also known as "critical path scheduling," exemplified in the Program Evaluation and Review Technique (PERT), was first applied productively to the planning and scheduling of complex engineering programs in the aerospace industry. Basically a refinement of the Gantt Chart—itself a notable innovation of the nineteenth century— critical path scheduling has found wide usage in such complex projects as the construction of office buildings, bridges, and highways. The *capital budgeting* technique has come into general usage by corporate executives in their effort to identify prospectively the highest yielding projects for capital investment. This technique makes use of the discounted cash flow rate of return on each investment, after adjustment, with the use of probability theory, for the degree of risk involved. Production planning and control today commonly makes use of *operations research,* a methodology developed during World War II. Linear and dynamic programming, queuing or waiting-line theory, the building of financial and other models of enterprise operation, the running of simulations of such models to test out the consequences of possible courses of action—all are intellectual tools of the contemporary manager. Needless to say, application of these methods depends upon the availability of the electronic computer.

## Organizing

Possibly the most dramatic postwar change in corporate organization has been the widespread adoption of *divisional, or "profit-center," organization.* This approach, first introduced by du Pont and General Motors in the early 1920's, more than anything else made possible the efficient management of giant enterprises.[4] The central concept of this approach is the organization of the corporation into a cluster of semi-autonomous divisions, each with a wide delegation of authority to operate on its own and each a "profit-center" whose manager is held accountable for overall results. The corporate headquarters group retains broad powers over the budgets, capital expenditures, and operations of each division. In essence, it serves as a capital-allocating and operations-monitoring agency, making decisions on matters affecting the success of the whole company and performing specialized financial and management functions at lesser cost than would be possible if performed separately by each division for itself.

Stemming from research in the behavioral sciences, which revealed the importance of informal groupings of people within formal business organizations, was the postwar development of the *use of informal organization to serve formal organizational objectives.*

*Matrix organization* for "project" or "product" management has been another innovation. It combines functional with project or product modes of departmentalization within the same organizational structure. Thus, the "project manager" of a new weapons system would have overall responsibility for the successful completion of his project within assigned time and cost limitations, and he would be given budget support to use in "buying" the necessary manpower, space, equipment, and other needed resources from the "functional" executives of the enterprise.

Other organizational changes during the past generation include the *enlargement of corporate staff offices* and the *wider use of executive committees.* These functions were needed as decision-making by the chief executive became more complex. Such successful enterprises as Standard Oil (New Jersey) are run by a plural executive, but a single responsible executive carries out the policies decided upon.

## Staffing

There have also been significant developments during the last quarter-century in the methods of manning corporate organizations. Companies have found that thorough, company-wide *executive job design and description* makes for higher morale and greater productivity, by clarifying authority-responsibility relationships. Similarly, a wider use of *incentive compensation,* including profit-sharing, bonuses, stock options, and deferred and retirement benefits, has been used to motivate executives to creative and energetic action; mediocre performance is often due not to ignorance of what should be done, but to an erosion of commitment to action. Along with incentive plans, schemes have been introduced for *regular executive performance evaluation* by a manager's superiors; such evaluations provide an opportunity for counselling, salary adjustments, and the fixing of incentive compensation.

The postwar era has been marked by a burgeoning of *management development programs* intended to expand the capabilities of the company's executives especially in the middle years of their careers. Such programs are conducted by many companies, and they have multiplied in the graduate schools of management. We now know that the most important asset of any enterprise is its people—a principle well-exemplified by the outstanding performance of International Business Machines. Because corporate success ultimately depends upon the degree of dedicated and creative effort made by human beings, shareowners and executives should know how much a company is investing in its people, and how the value of that investment is changing. *Human-asset accounting,* a technique suggested by Likert, is now being actively explored for that purpose.[5]

## *Directing*

The managerial function of communicating with, motivating, and leading the organization has likewise undergone considerable postwar development. As enterprises have grown in size and complexity, *employee communications systems* have become increasingly necessary to keep a company's personnel informed about the aims of their organization and their relationships with fellow employees. Publication of house organs, as well as corporate sponsorship of recreational and social events for employees, are means to this end. Extensive research has been conducted to measure the effectiveness of different *styles of executive leadership*—authoritarian, paternalistic, permissive, and participative, but the results have been inconclusive. Apparently, the optimum style varies with the type of organization, its mission, its personnel, and many other factors. Both research and practice have made it clear, however, that *the most effective managers are supportive* in the sense that they create an environment in which people can and will perform well. They remove obstacles to achievement and utilize methods of leadership that help people reach their highest levels of attainment.

As Americans became more affluent and better educated during the postwar years, styles of corporate management became more democratic and participative in order to motivate less dependent, more sophisticated employees. Contrary to Weber's prediction, corporate business became *less* bureaucratic. Organizations became more flexible, rules and procedures less rigid and detailed, opportunities for the individual wider, personal relationships more significant, job satisfactions more varied. Corporate executives had strong reasons to adopt these more productive techniques of management; they would serve to improve their own performance and the rewards that came with it.

Nevertheless, the problem of routinized jobs and employee boredom, especially among blue-collar production workers, has continued to challenge the ingenuity of American managers. The "flexi-time" concept may be a solution. It offers workers, now all forced into the eight-to-five, five-day-a-week format, a menu of different work-days and work-weeks from which each could choose that one meeting his personal preferences. Designing jobs to fit the physical and psychological requirements of people, rather than asking men and women to perform tasks determined by available technology and equipment, is another approach that is being increasingly adopted. Job rotation and enrichment are other techniques being used.

## Controlling

Much of the day-to-day activity of the corporate manager concerns the measurement of the enterprise's progress toward planned objectives, and the initiation of corrective action when operations go off course. Indeed, the modern concept of corporate control is that of a cybernetic system which feeds back to the executive information on the operation of the system, so that he can take corrective action on any deviation from plans. Related to this is a concept of planning and control that has attained widespread use in the postwar era, namely, *management by objective.* This is simply the principle of identifying the key result sought, setting up verifiable objectives, and judging the responsible manager's effectiveness in achieving them. A related idea is *management by exception,* the notion that the executive is more productive when he focuses his attention sharply on exceptions, or deviations, from the plan and how they may be corrected. Of course, the application of these ideas presumes the existence of well-developed corporate operating plans, as well as an organizational structure that makes clear who is responsible for results.

Among the many techniques for the efficient guidance of business operations that have come into common usage are the following: *statistical analysis,* applied to the control of the quality of products; *variable budgets,* in which estimated sets of costs are arrayed against various volumes of production or sales of products; *direct costing of products,* which more accurately measures the incremental costs of additional output than does traditional "absorption" accounting; *inventory control models,* that reveal the trade-offs between the holding costs of additional stocks and the reduction of waiting time in filling orders; *distribution logistics models,* that show how the company can minimize the costs in its total system of purchasing materials, manufacturing, warehousing, and shipping products, while meeting specified constraints upon inventories and customer service it provides.

A recent, potentially significant tool of corporate control is the *company social audit.* There is now a consensus that business has a social responsibility to aid in the resolution of such problems as poverty, slum housing, minority unemployment, air and water pollution, and other forms of environmental deterioration.[6] Some corporations are exploring the idea of making an annual audit of their operations—quantified to the maximum feasible degree—which would measure their responsiveness to social action. Because the concept is sound, the company social audit will probably come into wide usage.

This summary of major postwar developments in corporate management has emphasized theories, concepts, and ideas. Broadly, these are the "software" of management. One must, however, also recognize the postwar revolution in managerial "hardware" that accompanied the development of these ideas and made their application possible. Indeed, hardware and software developments interacted. Sometimes the availability of hardware (e.g., powerful computers) led to the discovery of a new concept or technique; at other times, the invention of a new concept was the motive for developing hardware to apply it. In any event, business could not manage on the contemporary scale without the computers, peripheral electronic data-processing equipment, electronic calculators, bookkeeping machines, electric typewriters, recording equipment, and copying and other apparatus. Equally vital is the hardware of transportation and communications—the jet airplane, telegraph, telephone, television, facsimile teleprinter, microwave transmitter, and communications satellite.[7]

## MANAGEMENT EDUCATION
## BEFORE WORLD WAR II

Paralleling the postwar evolution of management practices has been a striking change in university education for management. Slowly, during the past quarter-century, it was recognized that a science of management had grown to respectable proportions and that it should be the central discipline of the university school of business. This recognition led to profound alterations in the nature of management education, the caliber of business school students, the status of business school faculties within universities, and the standing of their alumni in the world of affairs.

When the author began teaching in the Graduate School of Business of the University of Chicago in the late 1930's, the curriculum was based upon two main disciplines—economics and accounting. At that time, accounting was held to be *the* preeminent subject of business study. Indeed, the first business school to be founded within an American university was named the Wharton School of Accounts [sic] and Finance, established at the University of Pennsylvania in 1898. Most business students at that time sought to prepare themselves to become practitioners of public accounting. This was a natural ambition because accounting was the first business subject to acquire a theory, an organized body of knowledge, and a professional stature. Emphasis was placed upon drill in bookkeeping, practice in applying the rules of professional accounting bodies, and proper accountability to stockkholders, tax collectors, and regulatory agencies. The profession of accounting was, indeed, thrust into prominence in American society by the enactment of three laws—the Federal Income Tax in 1913, the Securities Act of 1933, and the Securities Exchange Act of 1934—which compelled individuals and enterprises to maintain adequate accounts of their affairs.

Economics was the other foundation discipline of the prewar business school. The faculties of progressive schools saw that economic theory could be applied to the solution of such business problems as planning and forecasting, pricing, cost-analysis, and capital budgeting. Applied economics—or, as it came to be more generally known, "business economics"—was a root discipline in education for management.

A significant prewar development, originating at the University of Chicago, was the so-called "business functions" organization of the curriculum.[8] Sequences of courses were offered in production, finance, marketing, personnel, and risk-bearing. Most of these courses were long on description and short on operationally useful theory. The textbook in corporation finance, for example, devoted hundreds of pages to descriptions of financial markets and institutions, and to case studies. The lecturer in marketing likewise spent most of his time describing marketing institutions and their operating practices. The course in production leaned heavily upon the work of Frederick Taylor on "scientific management"; it was concerned with production line layout, job definition, time and motion studies, and similar techniques. Personnel management was approached by describing current business practices in job classification, manpower procurement, and compensation systems. While the prewar business school student took basic courses in statistics and financial mathematics, his training in quantitative analysis was limited.

In the development of a discipline, the description and classification of phenomena are the earliest stages; empirical generalizations and theoretical constructs come later. Certainly, the reliance of the Harvard Graduate School of Business Administration upon "cases" drawn from real-life situations was a valuable contribution to management education in the early years. And, business cases still have a useful role to play in management education. But theories for the analysis of problems are now of much greater value.

# POSTWAR CHANGES
# IN MANAGEMENT EDUCATION

World War II generated a revolution in management education. It brought full employment and a need to allocate resources efficiently. It required more effective methods for planning, mobilizing, and allocating manpower and matériel on a larger scale. Under the pressure to resolve these problems, new mathematical and statistical controls were devised and applied in government and business. Efforts were begun to synthesize the pioneering work of men like Fayol, Gulick, Urwick, and Barnard into a general theory of management. Mathematicians began to work on the military problems of transportation, convoying, and inventory control, and the new science of "operations research" was born.

Meanwhile, as a result of the pioneering work in national income accounting of Kuznets and others, and of the theoretical framework provided by Keynes in his classic, *The General Theory of Employment, Interest and Money,* published in 1936, macroeconomics emerged as a science. Leontief furnished another powerful intellectual tool with his theory of input-output relationships between industries. Probability theory and statistical inference techniques were applied more widely to business. Mathematical programming was invented. Aiken's crude Mark I electronic computer, developed for wartime research, opened a new chapter in man's history that is still unfolding. These were among the manifold events that reshaped the business curriculum.

A potent factor in raising management education from a technical undergraduate level to professional graduate stature was the work of the Ford Foundation and of the Carnegie Corporation. Both philanthropic bodies commissioned inquiries into the prevailing state of management education; and both inquiries revealed shocking deficiencies that stimulated reforms.[9] The Ford Foundation followed up its study with a substantial program of financial grants during the period from 1955 to 1965. This helped considerably to upgrade the intellectual quality of many university schools of business and narrowed the gap that separated them from the leading graduate schools of management.

After World War II, the curricula of progressive American business schools began to change rapidly. The following changes are particularly notable:

> • The development of economics, which more and more qualified it as a science useful to business.
> • The development of accounting as a *managerial* tool and, more recently, its treatment as a business information system.

- The emergence of behavioral science as an integral part of the curriculum.
- The extension of quantitative methods to a wide variety of business problems—a development given a powerful thrust by the electronic computer.
- Possibly most significant of all, the evolution of an integrated theory of operational management.

Economics in the modern business school is a highly quantified course of study, which makes use of simulation techniques and mathematical models of the economy and of the enterprise. Enterprises can now have much more information available for the formulation of their operating plans, information which can be utilized in ways that enable management to approach ideal conditions for decision-making. Economists can now predict the future course of the national economy and of regional economies with much greater accuracy and confidence than before. Businessmen can use models of an enterprise to develop forecasts of sales, profits, expenses, cash flow, and financial requirements within much finer limits than before.

The postwar years also witnessed a new emphasis upon "managerial" accounting in contrast to the earlier emphasis upon public accounting. Courses dealing with systems of internal control, costing, budgeting, and recording needed to generate the data for management decisions were introduced into curricula. It was recognized that the accountant should be educated to help the manager optimize the outcome of corporate operations, not merely to report them to the public. Later, another step was taken by business schools—to consider accounting as basically a management information system and to train accountants in the design and operation of computerized information systems. This new concept widened the scope of accounting education and elevated the role of accountants in enterprise management.

Courses in behavioral science form another pillar of the new business school curriculum. Knowledge of man's behavior, as an individual and in social groups, is now recognized to be an integral part of the intellectual equipment of the manager. As business organizations have grown in size and complexity and as people become more affluent, the manager has found it necessary to devote more attention to problems of human motivation, organizational behavior, and morale. It avails him little to know the right solution to a problem, if he is unable to lead the people in his organization to carry it out. Drawing upon individual and social psychology, sociology, and political theory, behavioral science has developed principles and concepts that are of considerable value to operating managers.

Still another new pillar in the curriculum of the progressive business school is the study of quantitative methods, including mathematical programming, stochastic processes, optimization techniques, simulation, statistical decision theory, game theory, systems analysis, and operations analysis. Quantitative methods are being increasingly applied to problems in the traditional "business functions" courses. As a result, these subjects—particularly production and finance—have become more analytic in character. Problems such as optimizing the location of factories or warehouses, controlling inventories, production line balancing, production scheduling, and capital budgeting can now be dealt with precisely. Resources can be more effectively conserved and allocated.

*A signal postwar innovation was the development of general operational management as a field of study.* In the prewar era, courses had been offered in "production management," focusing upon work layout, job definition, production scheduling, and motion and time study. During the same period practicing executives like Chester Barnard and Henri Fayol, and political theorists like Luther Gulick, had written about the wide-ranging functions of executives. Accounting theorists had begun to develop theories and practices of corporate control. From these several strands of thought there was woven an integrated body of concepts and principles, a theory, very useful in general management, which was refined and expanded through research. A leader in this task, beginning in the late 1940's, with many other schools subsequently participating, was the Graduate School of Business Administration at UCLA.[10]

# THE RISING STATUS OF SCHOOLS OF MANAGEMENT

Management education has become more rigorous than it was in the past. It now calls for considerable mathematical and statistical sophistication, a knowledge of computers, and a grasp of applied social science. With a more challenging curriculum, the modern management school is now attracting a larger proportion of the brightest graduate students in the university than it did previously. Many able young people who used to enter graduate work in other fields are coming into the graduate schools of management.

At the same time, the quality and versatility of the faculty required by the school of management has risen. A faculty drawn from many disciplines, in addition to accounting and economics, is needed, including mathematics, history, psychology, sociology, and jurisprudence. The developing science of management draws upon more of the traditional scholarly disciplines than do any of the other professional schools. Indeed, many contributions to the basic disciplines now originate in the schools of management.

At the same time, the central task of a school of management is to educate managers; and the criticism has justly been made that the faculties of such schools contain too few members who have had first-hand executive experience, and some who are not even acquainted with the theory of operational management. Appointment of business executives for temporary service as "adjunct" professors or lecturers can help to cure this fault. *More than any other professional school, the graduate school of management walks a tightrope that divides the world of affairs from the world of scholarship. Maintaining a balance of critical independence and close association with business is a challenging task.*

The management schools have achieved academic respectability by developing theoretical capabilities; but one of the costs has been a neglect of factual observation and the testing of theories for their ability to explain and predict events in the real world. In the 1950's, the Ford and Carnegie studies helped to elevate the intellectual stature of the schools. Now, in the 1970's, the primary need is to develop useful theories and strategies of business management that are based upon close observation of real managerial problems and processes. The current state of management science resembles that of economic science, which has been pithily described by Professor Mishan:

> It is only during the last few years that it has begun to occur to some of us that so-called theoretical economics touches the real world at very few points. To glance through the journals of the last ten to twenty years is to lose oneself in a carnival of possibility theorems. With so few empirical checks to speculative fervour, the opportunities for economic science-fiction are practically boundless. . . . The apparent vitality of theoretical economics today must be attributed to the keen interest in abstract models for their own sake, rather than for the light they shed on real problems.[11]

Management schools, like economics departments, need a new thrust toward the integration of theory and practice.

The management school has now taken its place in the university alongside the older professional schools of medicine, law, and engineering. Increasingly, it is being seen as an integrating faculty of the university, one able to design optimal organizational systems for projects requiring manpower, matériel, machines, and funds. It has the capability to marshal the intellectual resources of the university in attacks upon many of the great problems that confront our industrialized and urbanized society. Nearly all human organizations are obliged to economize in their use of scarce resources. Most of what the management school teaches is as applicable to the administration of governmental departments, hospitals, or educational systems, as it is to profit-seeking private enterprises.

In both the more and the less developed economies of the world, well-trained managers are, relatively, the scarcest resource. The proof of this statement lies in the high incomes that able managers command. Any society that puts social progress high on its list of priorities must necessarily exert strong efforts to expand its supply of trained managers. For example, the Soviet Union and other socialist countries are now engaged in a determined effort to provide a broader education for the managers of their state enterprises—managers who have heretofore had only engineering training. It is as muddle-headed to believe that industrial leaders are best educated by studying the classics as it is to think that scientific leaders can be produced by the study of theology or left to the chance emergence of inventive geniuses like Henry Ford or Thomas Edison! Management today is a distinctive subject with *its own* body of operationally useful theory. Those who aspire to careers in management should make the mastery of this new science their first objective.

## THE FUTURE OF MANAGEMENT EDUCATION

The revolution in management education will continue, and one may forecast the following strong future trends:

### Further Development of the "Management Sciences"

The sciences of management will surely continue to develop. This will occur particularly in marketing, which is still mainly descriptive in character. As we learn more about human behavior, we will be able to measure reactions to advertising and sales stimuli more accurately. Product planning, sales forecasting, and marketing policies will become more scientific and less intuitive. Other areas of management, such as finance, will also become more widely subject to scientifically based decisions. Knowledge of decision-making, under conditions of uncertainty, will grow.

### Convergence of Management and Engineering Curricula

A second probable development is the convergence of the curricula of business and engineering schools. The new emphasis on quantitative methods has brought the management school curriculum closer to the engineering curriculum, and management students are acquiring more of the same intellectual equipment that engineering students possess. But the engineering curriculum also seems to be moving toward the management curriculum. Because a large proportion of engineers enter managerial positions at some stage in their careers, progressive engineering schools are introducing more economic analysis and behavioral science into their programs, along with general operational management. Convergence will not, however, lead to coincidence.

## Programs for Practicing Executives

A third probable evolution is the burgeoning of management development programs for *practicing executives*. As the science of management has advanced, the ideas and practices of existing managers have been subject to a rising rate of obsolescence. To overcome this handicap, practicing managers must return to the university every five or six years for "intellectual re-tooling." To date, few university schools of business have developed complete programs for this need. Some schools have Executive or Management Development courses designed to bring either middle managers or senior executives *au courant* with contemporary concepts and practices. However, no management school has squarely faced the task of serving its profession with a *sequence* of extension programs, at intervals of five or six years, throughout the executive's career. The productivity of the executive can be enhanced by periodical "sabbatical leaves" to participate in such programs of continuing education, and more business corporations will undoubtedly grant such leaves in the future.

## Convergence of Business and Public Administration

The management school has come to embrace public administration. Allied to this tendency will be closer cooperative relationships between the schools of management and other professional schools, such as medicine, public health, law, and education. All of these schools educate members of professions that encompass large managerial tasks. The *management of hospitals, public health facilities, educational and cultural institutions, and the judicial establishment, all pose enormous problems in contemporary society*. It is not enough to equip those who will bear these responsibilities with the traditional education. They need managerial education as well. Specialized programs in *public* administration have not, in general, thrived on the campuses of American universities because their intellectual bases have been too narrow. The more broadly based school of management is better equipped for the task of educating men and women for the leadership of public organizations.

## *Emphasis upon Social Responsibilities*

Still another trend supports greater emphasis upon the social responsibilities of business firms and greater interest in the interactions between business and public policies. The great problems of contemporary society, such as environmental pollution, waste disposal, unemployment, poverty, urban renewal, and mass transit, are most likely to be solved by combining the organizational discipline of the action-oriented business corporation with the legal and taxing powers of government. Private corporations will more frequently be used to attain public purposes. At the same time, the public has made it clear that it will no longer tolerate the thrusting of private costs upon itself. American automobile makers have recently found, for example, that they are expected to build safe vehicles which produce a minimum of air pollution; and the petroleum industry is being forced to reduce the lead and sulfur content of its products. Schools of management confront the task of developing the new concepts that will relate business and public policy.

## *Evolution of Comparative Management Studies*

Much progress will be made during the next decade in adapting management processes to the manifold cultural and political settings found throughout the world. Management practice cannot be the same in Brazil as in the United States, or in Indonesia as in Canada; it must be adapted to the particular cultural milieu of each country. Studies of comparative management will be of immense value in revealing the nature of these adaptations. So far, the surface has only been scratched.

## THE GLOBAL TASKS OF MANAGERS

Within the last generation, the science of management has come to play a vital role in the society. Its role will continue to expand. Despite growing affluence, the economic tasks faced by the industrialized nations, and the demands of their people, expand faster than their incomes. The pressures to economize in the use of resources, to manage public and private undertakings more efficiently, are mounting steadily. The order of President Johnson in 1965 to introduce Planning-Programming-Budgeting Systems (PPBS) into all agencies of the federal government is symptomatic of the trend.

State and municipal governments are also making broader use of advanced management techniques. Our competitive market economy continually forces private enterprises to rationalize and improve performance. The demand for sophisticated managers, for experts in solving policy-oriented business problems, will continue to mount.

In the less developed countries, it has been increasingly clear that a real bottleneck to development is a shortage of entrepreneurial and managerial talent. This resource, more than land, labor, or capital, is the constraint upon economic progress. As this fact becomes more widely recognized, we may expect that larger numbers of the youth of the less developed countries will receive managerial education.

The manager is skilled in allocating scarce resources to the most urgent uses. He knows how to discover new markets and to correlate production with market demand. He is ingenious in financing the enterprise. He designs human organizations. Through his knowledge of people, he selects and welds them into efficient working teams. He plans for the future. He establishes standards of performance. He designs and operates controls of the organization. To do all these things well requires a mastery of the science of management, along with an artistry in its practice that comes with experience. The development of the science of management and the education of managers in this discipline are indispensable conditions of progress in our times.

## NOTES

1. For a description of the organization and management methods of ITT, see *Investigation of Conglomerate Corporations,* Hearings before the Antitrust Subcommittee of the Committee on the Judiciary, H.R., 91st Congress. November 20, 21, 26, and December 3, 1969. Serial No. 91–93 Part 3. (Washington, D.C.: U.S. Government Printing Office, 1970). See especially pp. 245–257.

2. See Harold D. Koontz and Cyril O'Donnell, *Principles of Management: An Analysis of Managerial Functions,* 5th ed. (New York: McGraw-Hill, 1972). Also Harold D. Koontz, *Toward a Unified Theory of Management* (New York: McGraw-Hill, 1964).

3. See David A. Novick, ed., *Program Budgeting,* 2nd ed. (New York: Holt, Rinehart and Winston, 1969).

4. See Alfred P. Sloan, *My Years with General Motors* (Garden City, N.Y.: Doubleday, 1962), Ch. 3. Oliver E. Williamson has described the economies of multidivisional corporate organization in his *Corporate Control and Business Behavior* (Englewood Cliffs, N.J.: Prentice-Hall, 1970).

5. See Rensis Likert, *The Human Organization* (New York: McGraw-Hill, 1967).

6. See Chapter 10, *infra.*

7. There has been an immense amount of research into various aspects of management, and a ferment of interesting ideas. Here, we focus only on concepts that have proven their value in practice.

8. Leon C. Marshall has described this development in *The Collegiate School of Business* (Chicago: University of Chicago Press, 1930).

9. See R. A. Gordon and James E. Howell, *Higher Education for Business* (New York: Columbia University Press, 1959) and F. C. Pierson, *The Education of the American Businessman* (New York: McGraw-Hill, 1959).

10. Daniel A. Wren has given an account of this process in "Principles and Process: The Search for Unity," Chapter 19 of his *The Evolution of Management Thought* (New York: Ronald Press, 1972).

11. E. J. Mishan, "Britain, the Economist and the Six," *The Bankers Magazine,* No. 1421 (August, 1962). Based on a lecture delivered at the University of Buenos Aires, July, 1962.

# CHAPTER 4

# The Conglomerate Corporation: Monstrosity or Model?

THE DEVELOPING science of management, along with astonishing advances in the equipment for data recording and processing, communicating and traveling, has made possible important changes in the structure of business corporations. One of the most pervasive of these structural changes since World War II has been that kind of diversification of corporate operations generally known as "conglomeration." In the 1960's, it was the dominant feature of the third great wave of corporate mergers in the American economy during the past eighty years. During 1968, more than forty-four hundred companies disappeared by mergers involving an estimated $43 billion in securities—an all-time record.[1] In this tidal wave of mergers, which subsequently crested and receded, conglomerate firms accounted for either a substantial or a preponderant fraction, depending upon the definition of "conglomerate" adopted.

Why did this merger wave emphasize conglomeration? Is the conglomerate a stable and efficient form of business, the heir apparent to American corporate power? Or, is it a financial fad, a source of monopoly, a threat to small business? Does it pose new problems of public regulation? Is it an ego-gratifier for ambitious entrepreneurs? Is it a monstrosity, or is it a model of the future?

The initial version of this chapter was written in 1969 at the Center for the Study of Democratic Institutions and was published in *The Center Magazine*, Vol. 2, No. 4 (July 1969), under the title, "The Conglomerate Corporation." The criticisms of Professor J. Fred Weston were especially helpful in refining this paper.

# THE CONGLOMERATE
# CORPORATION DEFINED

"Conglomerate corporation" will be used here to mean *a business corporation producing goods or services that are unrelated with respect to raw material sources, product development, production technology, or marketing channels.* A "conglomerate merger" brings together two or more enterprises engaged in unrelated lines of business; it is a particular mode of enterprise growth in which a firm penetrates industries and markets outside its current operations.

Many managers of diversified firms avoid the use of "conglomerate," believing that it denotes a lack of any inner logic and has a pejorative ring. They prefer to describe their companies as "multi-market" or "multi-industry" firms. But a "conglomerate corporation" is a special kind of multi-industry firm, and the term has simply gained too wide a currency to be discarded.

The modes of enterprise expansion may be classified as follows:

1. Vertical
   (a) Backward (toward raw material sources)
   (b) Forward (toward consumers of the final products)
2. Horizontal (market extension within the same industry)
3. Product extension (into additional industries)
   (a) Producing related products (concentric)
   (b) Producing unrelated products (conglomerate)

*Merger has been a minor method of growth for American business corporations, the predominant method having been through the investment of internally generated funds.* Until recent years, most mergers have been of the vertical or horizontal types, in which firms acquired other firms within the same industries or industrial groups. During the 1960's, however, most large mergers involved firms operating in different industries. Some brought together firms producing goods that were *related* with respect to sources of raw materials, production technology, or marketing channels; these have been aptly termed "concentric" companies.[2] Others joined *unrelated* enterprises—these are the true conglomerates.

The degree of product relatedness within a diversified company is, of course, a matter of opinion or judgment. Spokesmen for multi-industry firms often offer tenuous theories of centrality to avoid the brand of "conglomerate." Are such traditional giants as General Motors (diesel locomotives, refrigerators, as well as motor vehicles) and General Electric (jet engines, radars, and metallurgical chemicals, as well as hundreds of electrical products) conglomerates or concentrics? And, if conglomerates, were they not such before World War II? Should Transamerica be classed as a concentric because its avowed field is "services"? Norton Simon because it "serves the needs of the individual as a consumer, homemaker, and person"? Bendix because it is committed to "growth through technology"? Or Occidental Petroleum because it describes itself as a "producer and processor of natural resources"? The latter company, for example, rejects the conglomerate label because common technologies are used in exploring for and producing oil, natural gas, coal, sulfur, and phosphates, and all of these raw materials enter into fuels, fertilizers, industrial chemicals, and plastics, its major products.

On the other hand, there are many huge corporations whose activities are so disparate that their managements do not even attempt to formulate a theory of centrality. Among them are Litton Industries, which, among many other activities, makes office equipment, builds ships, operates restaurants, sells packaged foods, and operates national development plans. Textron, Avco, International Telephone and Telegraph, Gulf and Western Industries, and Tenneco are other conglomerates whose manifold products clearly lack common raw materials, production technology, or marketing channels. Even the names of some conglomerates imply an all-encompassing generality, such as National General.

Although concentric companies are sometimes grouped with conglomerates, it is preferable to adopt a strict definition which focuses attention upon the managerial and financial economies that distinguish the true conglomerate corporation. *The conglomerate corporation has managerial and financial control over products so diverse that negligible economies of scale can be realized in performing the functions of product-development, purchasing, production, or marketing.* Thus it differs from multi-plant, multi-product, or multi-industry firms that do achieve these economies. The conglomerate corporation differs, on the other hand, from the investment company, which does acquire ownership interests in firms producing unrelated products, but does *not* have management and financial responsibility for them.

## LESSONS FROM THREE MERGER WAVES

We may more confidently assess the meaning of the recent wave of conglomerate mergers, and forecast the economic effects and public regulations it may produce, by examining the course of past merger activity in the United States. *Economic historians generally agree that the American economy has experienced three major business merger episodes since the 1890's.*

The first wave, in which activity rose markedly above its long-term trend, occurred between 1897 and 1902, reaching a peak in 1899.[3] In the peak year, approximately twelve hundred mining and manufacturing corporations with total capitalizations of $2.3 billion (about $10 billion in 1968 dollars) were involved. The major thrust of this wave was the joining of local and regional railroads into national systems, and of one-plant manufacturing companies into national multi-plant entities. U.S. Steel, U.S. Rubber, and American Can were born in this manner.

The second episode, marked by a high level of merger activity, came between 1924 and 1930, reaching its peak in 1929. In that year, some 1,250 mergers were reported, probably involving securities of much larger total value than in 1899. Vertical and horizontal combinations of manufacturing, public utilities, and merchandising companies were prominent in this wave.

The third period of hyperactivity began about 1965, when the graph of annual mergers broke sharply upward from its long-term trend line. Mergers continued to rise through 1968, when some twenty-five hundred mining and manufacturing companies, involving around $20 billion of securities, were acquired. The most prominent actors in this wave were the conglomerates.

The long-term curve of merger activity displays much peakedness. A four- or five-year buildup to a peak year of activity has been followed by a year or two of swift decline. The high point of the recent wave was reached in 1968, thereafter subsiding. Thirty years, therefore, separated the first and second peaks, while thirty-nine years separated the second and third. Over the past seventy-five years, merger activity has risen at an *average* rate of somewhat under 4 percent a year. Because this has been little more than the rate of growth of real GNP, merger activity does not appear to have become relatively more important over the long term.

Although the statistics of merger activity are incomplete and the two or three known waves of mergers are an inadequate basis for generalization, the evidence certainly supports the conjecture that *the hectic merger activity of 1968 will not be matched again for a number of years.* The economy is probably not moving up an accelerating long-term trend of business concentration through merger, and conglomeration should not be viewed in apocalyptic terms. The 4,400 business corporations that disappeared by merger during 1968 were a small number compared with the 2,000 that disappeared by failure, or the 207,000 new corporations that were formed.[4] Even the $43 billion in securities exchanged in mergers that year were only 3.3 percent of the market value of corporate securities.[5]

# A MERGER WAVE HYPOTHESIS

Why has corporate merger activity, historically, taken the form of a strong wave at long intervals? We know that merger peaks have not corresponded closely with peaks in production, commodity prices, or overall business activity. Of all economic indicators, merger activity has been most closely related to movements in industrial stock prices.[6] A booming stock market has been present at the crest of all merger waves. Yet a high level of mergers has not accompanied *all* stock market peaks.

In the extensive literature on mergers, three theories have been advanced to explain their motivation and economic effects. Many observers have seen in business combinations only the elimination of competitors so that surviving firms can reap monopoly profits. Others have stressed the dominance of promoters and bankers, who engineered mergers in order to sell securities to the public at inflated prices. Still others have viewed mergers as a natural response of businessmen to new opportunities to reduce costs and expand sales in a competitive environment.

No single theory provides a satisfactory explanation of the long periods that have separated peaks of merger activity. None explains why the quest of businessmen for monopoly power should mount to a climax after thirty or forty years. Stock market cycles have been much shorter than a decade in their duration. Population growth and technological changes, which father business opportunities, take place more or less continuously.

How are these periods of intense merger activity to be explained? We propose that long-term merger waves in the United States are explained by the infrequent conjuncture of two preconditions: (1) *an accumulation of perceived, but unexploited, profit-making opportunities for enlarging the scale of enterprises, which have arisen from basic technological and social changes; and* (2) *a buoyant capital market with a strong demand for new securities.*

This Merger Wave Hypothesis, which is put forth here simply as conjecture, asserts that, before merger hyperactivity can occur, there must be both an unusually large number of opportunities for enlarging profit by combining independent firms *and* strong public demand for the new securities created in the merger process. Because these two preconditions have not often coincided, merger hyperactivity has been much less frequent than stock market peaks.

It is assumed that the *predominant* motives for mergers have been the drive of businessmen to realize profits by taking over poorly managed firms or by capitalizing upon newly perceived economies of scale, and the desire of bankers and brokers to earn fees selling new securities to the public or profitable terms. It rejects the notion that monopoly power has been an important motive for corporate mergers during the past half-century. The quest for monopoly power apparently reached its high point in 1899, at which time antimonopoly laws were not vigorously enforced. Since World War I, however, the Sherman Act, the Federal Trade Commission Act, and state antimonopoly laws have generally forbidden combinations that threaten to create undue market power. The Merger Wave Hypothesis does not, of course, imply that substantial advantages of more efficient management or of larger enterprise scale are in fact present in all mergers. In the hyperenthusiasm of a stock market boom, many mergers are launched that later founder.

Why does the conjunction of a large number of perceived opportunities for profits from enlarging firms and of buoyant capital markets occur infrequently? The idea that change is the only constant in modern society is by now a cliché. Less well understood is the distinction between tactical (small, superficial) and strategic (salient, structural) changes. Most tactical changes cancel or offset each other through time; a few cumulate into strategic shifts in the structure of technology and society. Not only do strategic changes take many years to accomplish, but there is a time-lag between their occurrence and their general perception. Many strategic changes create opportunities for profit which can be achieved by enlarging enterprises. In the pervasive optimism of a stock market boom, once-overlooked opportunities, or known opportunities which were not financeable previously, are acted upon. Given the rapidity of communication in financial markets, such perceptions multiply and build to a climax. Wall Street goes through a phase of "merger madness."

Later, the pool of profit-making opportunities for business combinations is drained, and financial expectations deteriorate. Merger activity falls off as quickly as it previously mounted. Many years pass before structural changes in both technology and society create a new pool of perceived changes for gains from enlarging the scale of corporate operations. When a new reservoir of opportunities develops, and when knowledge of it permeates the business and financial communities, its conjuncture with a boom in equity security prices will trigger another merger wave.

## FOUNDATIONS OF
## THE EARLY MERGER WAVES

Let us test this hypothesis by considering the merger waves of the past. Certain structural changes in the economy had set the stage for the first merger peak which occurred in 1899. One was the creation of a national railway network during the 1880's, by the connection of hundreds of local and regional lines and the building of new lines. The same era witnessed the completion of national telegraphic and telephonic communications. These facilities greatly reduced the cost and increased the speed of transportation and communication. National markets became a reality. By 1895, opportunities for profit by combining firms into larger units and reaping the benefits of lower costs through economies of scale in production had grown enormously. Meanwhile, the nation had developed a national securities market, and by 1895, rising security prices joined with the new opportunities for profit, and the first merger wave occurred. That stock promotion gains played a significant role in this merger wave is suggested by the fact that a large number of the combinations made in that era subsequently failed.[7]

The structural changes that led to the second merger peak in the 1920's also took place in transportation and communication. With the development of reliable mass-produced motor vehicles and the completion of a national network of all-weather roads, the economy of the United States was motorized after World War I. Automobiles and trucks gave people and goods unparalleled mobility, thus enlarging markets, destroying local monopolies, and creating new economies of scale. Concurrently, the home radio made national advertising cheap and effective, built the value of national brand names, and enhanced the advantages of national marketing. Single-store distribution was doomed. By the mid-1920's, businessmen generally perceived the astonishing opportunities for chain stores that had been opened up by these changes. The booming stock market from 1921 to 1929 satisfied the other precondition, and the second great merger episode was under way. Its economic rationale focused upon economies of scale in marketing.

## FOUNDATIONS OF THE
## CONGLOMERATE MERGER WAVE

*The Merger Wave Hypothesis is also consistent with the main facts about the great merger wave of the 1960's.* Structural changes in the United States after World War II had, by the early 1960's, created a pool of perceived opportunities for profits which could be achieved by diversifying and enlarging the scale of corporate operations. The buoyant capital market in the last half of the decade triggered the merger boom that began about 1965, by making it easy to sell new securities to the public. The most fundamental and powerful of the underlying structural changes was a revolution in management science. Other contributing factors were the postwar research and development explosion, the rise of the service economy, a quantum increase in taxation, a doubling of the price of capital, and enforcement of antitrust laws. Let us look at the role of each of these.

## Management Science and Computers

Radical changes occurred in the science of enterprise management after World War II, as we have seen.[8] Intuitive judgment was progressively superseded by rational decision-making processes. The concurrent phenomenal development of electronic computers facilitated the expansion of management science. In 1950, only a few computers were operating in businesses; at the end of 1971, there were over fifty thousand.

These fundamental developments created opportunities for profits through mergers that removed assets from the inefficient control of old-fashioned managers and placed them under men schooled in the new management science. The modern managers were able to control effectively a larger set of activities. Management science made possible the reductions in financial and managerial costs and risks that are associated with the acquisition of firms in *diverse* industries. These gains differed from the familiar economies of scale in production, purchasing, or marketing that normally accrue from vertical or horizontal mergers. Thus, the new management science was a primary force behind conglomeration.[9]

## The Research and Development Explosion

In the postwar era, outlays for scientific research and development grew nearly 14 percent a year, from $1.5 billion in 1946, to nearly $24 billion in 1968. This dramatic increase in the national commitment to applied science and technology was a seminal factor in the evolution of the American economy. By the 1960's, it had created whole new industries: in lasers, cryogenics, oceanography, electron optics, xerography, and so on. It had generated thousands of new products in established industries; plastics, synthetic fibers, color television, electronic equipment, among others. Most important, it had evolved a proven method for deliberately creating commercially needed products through research.

Research and development is now an established function of corporate business. Its economics calls for organizations of considerable scale and specialization, which, in turn, require large sales volumes to keep down costs per unit. Also, research produces unexpected findings and leads enterprises into diverse industries and product-lines. These, too, are powerful drives toward conglomeration.

## The Rise of the Service Economy

During the past quarter of a century, the United States has been transformed from a "commodity" to a "service" economy. As real incomes have risen and leisure time has expanded, a larger part of income has been spent on personal and professional services, transportation, education, and recreation, and a smaller part on food, clothing, and shelter. Most working Americans now provide services rather than produce commodities. White-collar jobs outnumber blue-collar jobs. Established service industries like insurance, banking, consumer finance, medical care, air transportation, television, motion pictures, and education have expanded greatly. Whole new service industries have come into being, such as computer leasing, automobile rental, credit card services, and travel agencies. Data generation and processing in service industries—which, by definition, serve large masses of people—have grown enormously. Service industries have generally been in the forefront in computerizing their operations and using advanced management controls. It is no accident, therefore, that some of the largest conglomerates, including Transamerica and International Telephone and Telegraph, specialize in services.

## Higher Income Taxation

A fourth factor underlying the merger wave of the 1960's was the steep rise in the load of corporate income taxation since World War II. In 1940, the effective federal corporate income-tax rate was 27 percent; in 1968, it was 50 percent. Rates of state and local taxes on business incomes have risen commensurately.

The manifold impacts of heavy income taxation on corporate policies can scarcely be exaggerated. They are a prime mover behind conglomerate mergers. International oil and minerals companies with unused foreign tax credits acquire companies whose incomes can be "sheltered" by those credits. American petroleum producers with large drilling expenses acquire firms for the same reason. Companies having profits merge with those which have losses that can be used to offset the profits. Many railroads found that diversification enabled them to use their past losses to reduce the tax liabilities of the companies they acquired. A central motive behind Container Corporation's union with Montgomery Ward to form Marcor was to defer several years the payment of Federal income taxes by taking fuller advantage of Ward's ability to defer taxes on profits arising from its installment credit sales. Thus, tax avoidance has been a powerful motive for conglomerate mergers.

## A Doubled Price of Capital

Since World War II, the price of capital—the going rate of return to investors—has doubled. Medium-grade industrial bonds that yielded 4 percent in 1945 returned 8 percent in the late 1960's. Home mortgage loan rates went from 4 percent to 8 percent in the same span of time. The dominant cause of the doubled price of capital was a vast expansion of demand for investment funds in relation to the available supply. Also, high interest rates reflected the widespread inflationary expectations of investors.

The higher price of capital had many consequences. Corporations have tried to use their capital more efficiently. Cash management programs have proliferated. Investment projects have been screened more rigorously. More to the point, aggressive managers have looked for merger partners laden with cash or liquifiable assets. Banking, insurance, and finance companies have been especially sought after by industrial companies because of their steady inflows of deposits, premiums, or loan repayments. Thus, the pervasive quest for financial resources has been the motive behind many a conglomerate merger.

## Antitrust Enforcement

A final factor behind conglomerate mergers was, paradoxically, more vigorous action by the Federal Courts, the Antitrust Division, and the Federal Trade Commission to inhibit vertical and horizontal mergers. Frustrated in their efforts to expand their enterprises along the traditional merger routes, growth-oriented businessmen turned to conglomerate acquisitions as a substitute.

# PRIVATE GAINS FROM CONGLOMERATION

But what, we might ask, are the private and social gains to be anticipated from business mergers? We will suggest that *public policies should encourage those mergers that have the potentiality of yielding net gains to society; they should not actively encourage those that result only in transfers of wealth or income among individuals.*

The two principal kinds of private gain from mergers are promotional profits and reductions in tax liability. While they may or may not be accompanied by social benefits, both are present in most conglomerate mergers.

Consider the extreme case of a merger whose *sole* purpose and effect is to generate profits for promoters and bankers, who take advantage of the optimism of the public during a stock market boom. The standard gambit is to have a "growth" company, whose stock is selling at a high multiple of its annual earnings, acquire another company, whose stock is evaluated at a low multiple of earnings, in the expectation that, after a pooling of interests, the market will value the equity of the expanded survivor at the higher multiple. In the atmosphere of a boom this expectation is often realized. Earnings per share of the acquiring firm will increase as a result of the merger. The market will apply the high multiplier and bid up the price of the stock. This makes further acquisitions through exchange of stock attractive. They are the basis of a further expansion in reported earnings per share and further inflation of the market price of the stock.

This game can continue until the public recognizes that there has been no growth in the *operating* earnings of the acquired companies. The price of the conglomerate's stock then plummets to a point where the price-earnings ratio is normal. At this much lower price, further acquisitions are unattractive and cease.[10] Meanwhile, promoters will probably have unloaded their shares on less sophisticated investors, and bankers will have pocketed their commissions. What will have occurred is a transfer of capital values from one to another set of individuals.

Government should do nothing to prevent such mergers, beyond enforcing Securities and Exchange Commission regulations requiring full disclosure of all material facts. If speculators ignore the *caveat emptor* rule, they suffer the consequences. Given the dynamism and complexity of business life, predictions are inevitably hazardous, and there is no feasible means of distinguishing with certainty, in advance, viable mergers from other mergers. The public is best protected by education and full disclosure.

The second type of private gain from mergers is a reduction of tax liability. If a company with carried-over losses is merged into a profitable company, reducing the taxes of the survivor, government may be obliged to impose heavier taxes upon other firms in order to restore the preexisting level of revenues. There is a shift of tax burden from stockholders of the merged companies to those of the other firms. Society will be unaffected, except for a possible deterioration in the equity of the tax system. Public policy can inhibit mergers arranged solely to cut taxes only by radical simplification of the structure of federal taxation of corporate income. This structure is now highly differentiated and shot through with special treatment of particular industries.

# SOCIAL GAINS FROM CONGLOMERATION

Several types of potential gains from conglomerate mergers may be of value to society by leading to better or lower priced products. They deserve emphasis because the dominant public attitude toward conglomerate companies after the stock market recession of 1969–1970 was one of hostility rather than objectivity.

## *Increase of the Reward/Risk Ratio*

By definition, the conglomerate firm combines operations that are unrelated with respect to raw materials, technologies, or markets. The annual profits of its different divisions will be negatively correlated; that is, at any given time some will be comparatively high and others comparatively low. In the aggregate, they will be more stable through time than the sales or profits of a specialized firm. For any given rate of return on investment, risk will be less; for any given risk, expected reward will be higher. The standard gains from portfolio diversification will be realized. This benefits society as well as the conglomerate's stockholders because the reduction in the premium for risk is equivalent to a cut in the company's costs and, *via* market competition, in the prices of its products.

## *Financial Economies of Scale*

Closely related to the gains of diversification are the advantages reaped by the conglomerate of lower capital costs and avoidance of "Gambler's Ruin." The conglomerate can often raise funds at lower cost than could its smaller constituents. In addition, having a "long purse," it is in a position to finance temporary operating losses of a subsidiary that would bankrupt the latter if it were an independent firm. The conglomerate is in a position to "out-spend, out-dare, and out-wait" smaller and financially less secure firms in its effort to win a market. This is socially beneficial, provided that the conglomerate continues to face adequate competition in its several markets—a subject to which we shall return.

## *Economies of Scale in Management*

Acquisitions can enable the conglomerate firm to apply over a wider sales base the talents of a skilled general management team. The central corporate management of the conglomerate commonly delegates wide authority to each divisional management and holds it accountable for a "target" rate of return on the investment in its division. The central corporate officers enforce a planning and controlling discipline upon all divisional managers. They make the major decisions on capital allocation. Characteristically, they provide management consulting services to the entire organization. The conglomerate, with its larger and more diverse activities, can utilize efficiently specialized experts in operations analysis, computer science, behavioral science, incentive systems, taxation, industrial relations, and other subjects.

## Transfers of Assets to More Efficient Management

A real social gain occurs when the assets of an enterprise are transferred, *via* merger, to the control of a superior management. Striking advances in management science, combined with great inequalities among firms in its application, have opened up extensive opportunities for gains from such transfers. Through more informed decisions and better information systems, a modern management can deploy resources with greater efficiency, resulting in lower costs and product prices. While this kind of social gain can flow from any kind of merger, it is most likely in conglomerates. The reason for this is that market competition generally compresses differences in the quality of management of firms in the same industry to a smaller dimension than is present among firms in different industries.

Any company with a "sleepy" management, under-used assets, or stock selling at a low multiple of earnings is a logical candidate for a merger. Sharp-eyed promoters will probably buy up its shares with the aim of gaining control and then merging it into an aggressively managed firm. Merger-makers are often denounced as "corporate raiders," and their takeover of a company is regarded as an unethical act. But there is another side to the coin. They perform a socially useful function by keeping the managers of all companies on their competitive toes and by helping to redeploy business assets into more competent hands. Surely, no one would seriously contend that the public interest would be served by *protecting* all corporate managements in their control of companies.

In what proportion of conglomerate mergers are social gains realized, and how large are those gains? Regrettably, these questions cannot be answered, given the present state of knowledge. Answers would require intensive, elongated case studies of the costs, prices, and profits of conglomerates and their constituents, both before and after merger. Most conglomerate corporations have had too short a life history to permit the confident drawing of conclusions.

## CONGLOMERATION AND COMPETITION

What has been the effect of conglomeration upon the vigor of competition? Traditionally, mergers have been identified with tendencies toward monopoly because, historically, most mergers have been of the horizontal or vertical types.[11] Many have increased industrial concentration—the percentage of the total sales or output of an industry accounted for by its leading four to eight firms. It is generally believed—although proof is lacking—that there is a positive correlation between the level of concentration of an industry and the probability of noncompetitive behavior by its leading firms. When the preponderance of the output of an industry is produced by three or four leading corporations, collusion among them is thought to be easier; or there may be a tacit mutual recognition that all can profit from higher-than-competitive prices. As the level of industrial concentration drops, the chances of noncompetitive behavior diminish; and when the number of competitive firms becomes very numerous they become negligible. Proposed mergers of important members of the same industry are, therefore, generally frowned upon by the antitrust authorities. Nevertheless, there is vigorous competition in many highly concentrated industries (e.g., automobiles); and mergers of several weak firms in such industries have sometimes created a strong enterprise capable of offering sharper competition to its rivals than did its components.

A conglomerate merger, however, involves a joining of firms in *different* industries. It thus leaves the ratios of concentration in those industries unchanged. Conglomeration does replace two or more smaller firms with one larger enterprise and thus may increase macroeconomic concentration, i.e., the percentage of total industrial activity in the economy accounted for by the leading hundred or two hundred nonfinancial corporations. Indeed, *conglomeration by large firms appears to have held industrial concentration in the economy about constant, in the face of increasing macroeconomic concentration.*[12]

Manifestly, it is *industrial* concentration that is directly related to the vigor of competition. Macroeconomic concentration need not be of concern, as long as the number of giant diversified corporations is large enough to preclude overt or tacit collusion among them. Since it requires more than one hundred corporate giants to account for even half of all manufacturing assets in the nation, the American economy is far from the possibility of noncompetitive behavior because of an inadequate number of corporate participants.

Conglomerate mergers can invigorate industrial competition. By strengthening the managerial and financial support available to each of its constituents, the conglomerate is able to make each a more energetic competitor in the industry in which it operates. Each entity can draw upon the conglomerate's pool of specialized managerial talent, utilize its management science, obtain financial assistance, and assume a more innovative and risk-taking posture than it could as an independent firm.

*The conglomerate corporation also expands potential competition.* It is more likely to possess the financial and other resources—and the motive—needed to enter additional industries heretofore closed to its smaller constituents. Established firms in those industries will, as a result, tend to behave more competitively than before in pricing their products, in the hope of deterring the entry of the conglomerate. It has been aptly said that the conglomerate "sits on the edge of any and all markets," ready to enter, and thus keeps the established firms on their toes. Indeed, a German economist has interpreted the conglomerate merger as a self-correcting force in American capitalism, making it more competitive and, in effect, denying the Marxist prophecy of increasing monopoly.[13]

While conceding the probability that conglomeration energizes competition, many observers contend that large diversified corporations may engage in predatory pricing, cross-subsidization, reciprocity, or other anticompetitive actions. Thus, it is said that the large conglomerate can engage in predatory pricing in one of its lines of business, covering its losses with profits earned in other lines, until its smaller competitors are driven from the field. In practice, instances of cross-subsidization are rare. Not only does it violate antimonopoly laws, but it flies in the face of accepted principles of management. In a multi-industry company, it is not feasible to force the manager of one subsidiary to operate unprofitably, i.e., to require abandonment of established profit targets and management incentive plans. Also, unless barriers to the entry of new firms are very high, the subsidized division cannot reap monopoly profits once its competition has been eliminated because its efforts to raise prices will attract new competitors and deny it an opportunity to recoup its losses.

Somewhat related to the cross-subsidization argument is the idea that the large financial resources of the conglomerate (its so-called "deep pocket") enable it to engage in temporarily losing activities, such as expensive product development or large-scale advertising that smaller companies are unable to finance, which ultimately give it the competitive edge in the market. While there may be some truth in this contention, the advantage of the larger firm arises from superior resources and not from conglomeration. Unless one believes that public policy should protect smaller firms at any cost, one cannot object to product and market development activities which are in the consumers' interest, even though they are open only to enterprises with ample financial means.

Yet another standard objection to large firms, whether conglomerate or not, is that they achieve such important advantages of scale that they raise the barriers to entry into an industry. Here again there is some truth in the argument. Conglomeration, as well as other modes of business diversification, can enable the surviving firm to benefit from reductions in risks or costs through the enlargement of operations. By increasing the stakes in the industrial game, they make it harder for poor players to survive. If these economies are real, society benefits—provided, of course, that competition remains effective and obliges the conglomerate to pass the economies along to the public through lower prices or product improvements. Few will defend the perpetuation of inefficient small-scale firms at heavy cost to the public. What is important is that a sufficient number of firms remains in each industry to discipline each other.

The possibility that the conglomerate firm will cause its constituents to practice commercial reciprocity to the disadvantage of its small competitors is usually mentioned in assessing the effects of mergers upon competition. If intradivisional sales are made on competitive terms, there can be no complaint. Is it realistic, however, to expect the manager of one division of a conglomerate to do business with another division on unfavorable terms, counting upon recouping the loss by selling the other division some of his own product at higher than competitive prices? The answer is negative because, as previously noted, it violates basic principles of "profit-center" management.

Business reciprocity can also be practiced in purchases and sales among different corporations in such subtle ways as to escape detection by antitrust authorities. However, there is no clear evidence that conglomerates are more culpable than other large firms. Corporate organizations normally delegate to divisional managers the authority to buy and sell in the cheapest market, and corporate incentive programs strongly motivate them to do so.

Finally, there is concern that conglomeration may be a new route to dangerous aggregations of economic and political power. (This was the central concern that led to the massive hearings on conglomerate business in 1970 by the Antitrust Subcommittee of the Committee on the Judiciary of the House of Representatives.) Nevertheless, macroeconomic concentration is not at a dangerous level. The number of large manufacturing corporations remains so large as to preclude the possibility of oligopolistic behavior. Levels of industrial concentration have not risen, and they are the relevant criteria for judging competition, as the 1964 guidelines published by the Attorney General recognized.

American courts have consistently held that large size is not, *per se,* an offense against the antitrust laws. If corporate giantism had been adjudged antisocial, the government should long ago have proceeded to break up the larger nonconglomerate giants. In a ranking of 130 members of the "billion dollar club," in descending order of their 1968 sales revenues, the five largest conglomerates were International Telephone and Telegraph, fourteenth; Ling-Temco-Vought, thirtieth; Tenneco, forty-fifth; Litton, forty-eighth; and Textron, fifty-ninth. If public policy required a dismantling of these largest conglomerates, some fifty-four other giants should first be broken up. And only eight conglomerates were found among the two hundred largest manufacturing corporations.

To sum up: *corporate conglomeration can have mixed effects, but it is far more likely to enliven than to dampen competition. Public policy therefore should not penalize conglomerate mergers.* These conclusions, reached by the author in 1969, have subsequently found increasing support. Public animosity toward conglomerates has abated. The vigorous legal campaign launched against conglomerates during 1969 by the antitrust authorities has long since been moderated. The highly publicized hearings during 1970 by the House Antitrust Subcommittee led to mild and neutral findings.[14] A preponderance of economists who contributed to the massive symposium on conglomerate mergers, published in 1970 by the *St. John's Law Review,* agreed that conglomerates could yield social benefits as well as costs; and many called for further study.[15]

## POTENTIAL FINANCIAL EFFECTS

Conglomeration can have potentially important effects upon the place given to the internal financing of business, upon investment policies, and upon the relationship of banking to industry. It tends to increase internal financing of business enterprises by reducing a firm's use of external sources for funds. In a diversified firm, some divisions may be expected to have expanding needs for cash, while others may be throwing off cash. The aggregate demand for external funds by the conglomerate, therefore, will fluctuate less through time than will the demands of a set of specialized firms of equal overall size. Other things being equal, conglomerates will have less recourse to the commercial banking system for short-term financing.

Another potential consequence of conglomeration is a restructuring of investment portfolios. If a rising proportion of publicly owned corporations conglomerate, each following the principle of portfolio diversification, managers of mutual funds, trust officers, and individual investors will find it less necessary to diversify their portfolios. Thus, an investor might achieve the same protection against extreme fluctuations in the value of, and income from, his holdings by buying a million dollars of stock in "International Everything," as by buying fifty thousand dollars of stock in firms in each of twenty industries. Of course, the possibility of mismanagement at the top of the conglomerate, which might endanger all of its constituents simultaneously, must be kept in mind.

One possibility that was implicit in the process of conglomeration was the joining of commercial banks and industrial corporations in a common ownership. The Banking Act of 1935 had required commercial banks to maintain an arm's length relationship with nonfinancial institutions. One purpose was to prevent banks from underwriting corporate securities, a practice that had contributed to the wave of bank failures after the stock market crash of 1929. A more important purpose was to maintain banking impartiality in supplying credit to businesses. For a period in the 1950's, however, conglomeration brought some commercial banks and industrial corporations under common control. Since the passage of the Bank Holding Company Act in 1956, however, conglomerates have been able to remain in banking only through use of the "one-bank holding company." For example, the Chase Manhattan Corporation owns the Chase Manhattan Bank and other financial subsidiaries; and BankAmerica Corporation owns the Bank of America and other companies rendering a variety of financial services. A one-bank holding company is usually created when a sponsoring commercial bank issues the stock of a new holding company to its shareholders in exchange for their present shares. Thus it acquires a corporate vehicle, capable of diversifying into fields not open to commercial banks, such as computer leasing, credit cards, mortgage banking, or the sale of mutual investment company shares. Up to the end of 1969, some forty-three of the nation's one hundred largest banks had formed such holding companies.

But commercial banks are instrumentalities for the execution of national monetary policies. A bank controlled by an industrial conglomerate could discriminate in favor of its parent's industrial subsidiaries in times of tight money. In order to stop the incipient merging of banking and industry, federal legislation was enacted in 1970 to block the acquisition of commercial banks by industrial conglomerates and to prohibit one-bank holding companies from engaging in activities not closely related to banking. The historic separation of American commercial banking from industry is thus being preserved.

# PUBLIC POLICY FOR CONGLOMERATES

What new public regulation is needed to assure that conglomerate mergers and the diversified corporations they create serve the public interest?

Because some conglomerate, and other, mergers have proved to be unsound and failed, it has been proposed that government should prohibit such mergers. But *there is no feasible way to identify bad mergers in advance; only time and the test of market competition reveal them.* A foundational concept of the American economic system is that business enterprises should be free to try out new organizational patterns, management concepts, and financial structures as well as new products. To require advance decisions would be to deprive society of possible gains from innovation and to substitute a political judgment for a decision by the market. Prevailing law properly protects the right of each individual to deploy his funds as he wishes, provided there is full disclosure of all material facts necessary for an informed decision. While this policy costs society something in misallocated capital, the benefits are certainly worth the price.

Conglomeration has thrust into public consciousness knotty problems of the transference of corporate ownership and control. For example, are special restraints needed on conglomerate acquisition of communications media such as radio and television broadcasting stations or publishing companies? Are restraints upon ownership required for such important agencies of American foreign relations as international airlines? How can and should society guard against the use of multi-industry corporations by criminal elements to expand their economic influence? There are no easy answers to such questions, which require further study.

## *Accounting and Reporting Needs*

*The conglomerate merger movement threw into bold relief faults in the current system of financial reporting, and it created new problems. One longstanding fault is the lack of standard accounting rules and procedures.* This permits opportunistic businessmen to vary reported profits within wide limits. A corporate manager, interested in playing a numbers game with stock price-earnings ratios for quick profits, is able to inflate current reported profits at the expense of future profits. The methods are legion: shift from accelerated to straight-line depreciation; defer or stretch out maintenance expense; deplete inventories held at low cost; sell assets for "one-shot" income. Excessive flexibility in permissible accounting methods creates opportunities for misleading reports of profits.

The American accounting profession is the custodian of the information system upon which investors rely in allocating society's scarce capital. *Standardized* accounting methods are essential to enable bankers and investors truly to compare the performances of firms within each industry, and in different industries. Standardized methods can inhibit corporate managers from creating illusory profits—or losses. If the profession fails to meet the legitimate public demand for financial reports that are more revealing, more meaningful, and more comparable, the Securities and Exchange Commission will surely impose standards upon it, as SEC Chairman William J. Casey warned.[16] Hopefully, the newly formed Financial Accounting Standards Board of the American Institute of Accountants will press forward vigorously on this difficult, but vital, mission.

The other problem is the information gap created by the pooling of the accounts of acquired companies in the published financial statements of diversified companies. All publicly held business corporations should be required—by appropriate regulations of the Securities and Exchange Commission, state security commissioners, and the stock exchanges—to report sales and either net income or operating earnings *for each industry* in which they are operating. Diversified companies need this information for efficient management; similarly, investors need it for intelligent investment.

## PERSPECTIVE

The conglomerate corporation is neither a "monstrosity" lacking in economic and social justification, nor is it a "model" of the future to which the enterprises of the United States will increasingly conform. Its true role in the American economy cannot be known for at least another decade. If time and trial prove that its theoretical potential for lowering risk and raising returns on corporate capital are realized, the conglomerate form will spread further. But should these benefits elude capture or be offset by faults yet unseen, many of these firms will disappear. Market competition will dictate their future role in the U.S. economy. Viewed in a broad perspective, however, conglomeration attests to the flexibility of the corporate institution in responding to pervasive social and technological changes.

## NOTES

1. Press Release, Federal Trade Commission (Washington, D.C., February 1969).

2. See J. Fred Weston, "The Nature and Significance of the Conglomerate

Firm," in *Conglomerate Mergers and Acquisitions: Opinion and Analysis,* Vol. 44, *St. John's Law Review*—Special Ed. (1970), pp. 66–80.

3. Merger activity may be measured by the annual number of reported mergers, by the annual number of firms disappearing through merger, or by the value of securities issued in mergers. The only continuous reporting since the 1890's has been of the annual number of mergers. See S. R. Reid, *Mergers, Managers and the Economy* (New York: McGraw-Hill, 1968), p. 15. Reid's series is derived from data collected by Ralph A. Nelson and published in *Merger Movements in American Industry 1895–1956* (Princeton: Princeton University Press, 1959), and by the Federal Trade Commission in *Report on Corporate Mergers and Acquisitions* (Washington, D.C., 1955) and in subsequent press releases.

4. See *Economic Report of the President of January 1969* (Washington, D.C.: U.S. Government Printing Office, 1969), p. 316.

5. The market value of corporate securities was estimated roughly by multiplying the $25 billion of dividends paid on equity securities by a factor of thirty-three, which assumes an average yield of 3.0 percent, to attain a market value of business equity of $825 billion. To this was added an estimated $375 billion of debt securities to attain the total of $1.2 trillion.

6. See Ralph A. Nelson, *op. cit.,* p. 7. See also J. Fred Weston, *The Role of Mergers in the Growth of Large Firms* (Berkeley and Los Angeles: University of California Press, 1953).

7. See Shaw Livermore, "The Success of Industrial Mergers," *Quarterly Journal of Economics,* Vol. 69, No. 4 (November 1935). In a study of the results of 328 mergers at the turn of this century, only 146 succeeded. Of these, 139 owed their success to technological and managerial improvements, promotion of quality brand names, development of new products, entry into new lines, commercial exploitation of research, or other real economies of scale. Only sixteen survived because of monopolistic power. The results suggest that stock promotion gains were an important motive behind the first merger wave.

8. See Chapter 3.

9. See David N. Judelson, "A Philosophy for a Conglomerate Company," *Business Horizons* (June 1968). See also his testimony as President of Gulf and Western Industries to the Antitrust Subcommittee of the Judiciary Committee, U.S. House of Representatives, July 30, 1969.

10. See Marvin M. May, "The Chain Letter Revisited," *Financial Analysts Journal* (May–June 1968), pp. 1–5.

11. Jesse W. Markham, "Survey of the Evidence and Findings on Mergers," in *Business Concentration and Price Policy* (Princeton: Princeton University Press, 1955), p. 143.

12. William G. Shephard, "Trends of Concentration in American Manufacturing Industries, 1947–1958," *Review of Economics and Statistics,* Vol. 45, No. 2 (May 1964), pp. 200–212.

13. M. Neumann, "Conglomerate Mergers and the Degree of Monopoly," *Zeitschrift für die Ges. Staats* (October 1967).

14. See "Celler's Slingshot Misses the Giants," *Business Week* (September 11, 1971). The Department of Justice brought five major cases against conglomerate firms during 1969, three against ITT, one against LTV, and one against Northwest Industries. Only the LTV case had been won by early-1973. However, ITT agreed to divest itself of Hartford Fire Insurance Company.

15. See *Conglomerate Mergers and Acquisitions, op. cit.* Thus, Weston concludes, ". . . there are substantial potential economic benefits from . . . the recent conglomerate merger movement. However, it is clear that undesirable effects may also result. . . . More study and analysis is required. . . ." (p. 80) Jules Backman concluded, "Many such mergers involve the acquisition of companies which may be laggard in their competitive activity. . . . By 'shaking things up' the conglomerate can add a new dimension to competition in many markets." (p. 132) David R. Kamershen concluded, "I find myself in more agreement with the moderate group that argues that each conglomerate case must be judged on its own merits. . . ." (p. 146) E. S. Birdzell said, ". . . there are a number of recognizable and potentially valuable functions for the headquarters level of management in conglomerate firms. Whether they will realize their potential cannot be known without some years of experiment. . . . The case for cutting off the experiment is particularly weak if one views a free economy as, among other things, a laboratory for the development and testing of new forms of organization." (p. 315) Jesse W. Markham expressed agreement with Professor Turner that ". . . the presumptions on anticompetitive effects of conglomerate mergers are not as strong as those of other mergers. . . ." (p. 290) And John C. Narver concluded that "conglomerate mergers are not inherently procompetitive or anticompetitive. Under some conditions they very probably can promote competition and under other conditions they can very probably decrease competition." See Narver, *Conglomerate Mergers and Market Competition* (Berkeley and Los Angeles: University of California Press, 1967), p. 138.

16. See *Wall Street Journal,* October 3, 1972. The potential legal liabilities of accountants as a result of stockholders' suits provide an additional incentive to improve accounting standards.

# CHAPTER 5

# The Multinational Corporation: Imperialist or Pacifist?

M ULTINATIONALIZATION has been a structural change in corporate enterprise that has had far more important effects upon American and world society than conglomeration. The emergence of the multi-national private corporation as a powerful agent of world social and economic change has been a signal development of the postwar era. Its evolution has been regarded with mixed feelings by public officials both of the investing and the host countries, as well as by observers of corporate and international affairs.

The multinational corporation is, among other things, a private "government," often richer in assets and more populous in stockholders and employees than some of the nation-states in which it carries on business. It is simultaneously a "citizen" of several nation-states, owing obedience to their laws and paying taxes to their treasuries, yet having its own objectives and being responsive to a top management that may be located in another nation. Small wonder that some critics see in the multinational corporation an instrument of irresponsible private economic power, or even an agent of economic "imperialism" by its home country. Others view it as an international carrier of advanced management science and technology, an agent for the global transmission of cultural values, bringing closer the day when a common set of ideals will unite mankind.

What forces and motives have thrust the corporate institution into

This chapter was developed in a manner similar to Chapter 4; an original version was published in *The Center Magazine,* Vol. 3, No. 3 (May 1970), as "The Multi-national Corporation." Professor Barry Richman's comments were helpful.

the world arena? How is it characteristically managed? What effects does it produce on investing and host nations, and on international relationships and institutions? Above all, how can the policies of multinational companies and of the nations in which they operate minimize international conflicts and advance the cause of world order?

## THE MULTINATIONAL CORPORATION DEFINED

*A multinational corporation owns and manages businesses in two or more countries. It is an agency of direct, as opposed to portfolio, investment in foreign countries,* holding and managing the underlying physical assets rather than securities based upon those assets.

Almost every large enterprise has foreign involvements of some kind. Whatever its home, it will probably send agents to other nations, establish representative offices abroad, import foreign materials, export some products, license foreign firms to use its patents or know-how, employ foreign nationals, have foreign stockholders, borrow money from foreign bankers, and may even have foreign nationals on its board of directors. None of these, however, would make an enterprise "multinational" because none would require a substantial *direct investment* in foreign assets nor entail a responsibility for *managing* organizations of people in alien societies. Only when an enterprise confronts the problems of designing, producing, marketing, and financing its products within foreign nations does it become truly multinational.

Although we define the multinational corporation by the ownership *and* management of businesses in several nations, in reality this is generally only one stage in the process of multinationalization. Characteristically, the expanding corporation traverses the following stages:

1. Exports its products to foreign countries.
2. Establishes sales organizations abroad.
3. Licenses use of its patents and know-how to foreign firms that make and sell its products.
4. Establishes foreign manufacturing facilities.
5. Multinationalizes management from top to bottom.
6. Multinationalizes ownership of corporate stock.

Upward of 100,000 American business enterprises are stage one exporters; many fewer have reached the second and third stages; only about 4,500 firms are fourth stage multinationals; a mere handful of giant firms are approaching stages five and six.

A domestic corporation may become multinational by establishing foreign branches, by operating wholly or partially owned subsidiaries in other countries, or by entering into joint ventures with enterprisers in other countries. Whatever the form, it becomes a working corporate citizen within many nations. Although the business transactions of the multinational corporation typically cross many national boundaries, no company is strictly "international" or "transnational." All the subsidiaries of the multinational corporation are chartered by national governments.

# THE RISE OF
# CORPORATE MULTINATIONALISM

Multinational operations by private business corporations are comparatively recent in man's history. The companies of merchant traders in medieval Venice and the great English, Dutch, and French trading companies of the seventeenth and eighteenth centuries were forerunners, but not true prototypes, of today's multinational corporation. They were essentially trading rather than manufacturing organizations, with comparatively little fixed investment. And they operated mainly within the colonial territories or spheres of influence of their own nations rather than under the jurisdiction of foreign sovereign states.

During the nineteenth century, foreign investment flowed extensively from Western Europe to the undeveloped areas of Asia, Africa, and the Americas, including the United States. In this age of empire building, Victorian Britain was the great capital exporter, followed by France, the Netherlands, and Germany. Little of this capital flow was direct investment outside imperial boundaries. Although British firms made large investments in India, Canada, Australia, and South Africa; French companies deployed capital in Indochina, Algeria, and French Africa; and Dutch firms helped to industrialize the East Indies; corporate investment was conducted mainly within the boundaries of empire. When British and European capitalists helped to finance the railroads and canals of the United States, Argentina, and other countries outside of their imperial jurisdictions, they did it by purchasing the securities of American governments or corporations. They engaged in portfolio investment. Rare was the profit-seeking business corporation that ventured outside the imperial realm to make commitments directly in brick and mortar under an alien regime. Nevertheless, by the turn of this century, American firms were producing, in Britain, such products as farm equipment, sewing machines, printing presses, and revolvers, and a book entitled *The American Invasion* was published in London in 1902.[1]

The first *substantial multinational corporate investment came in the mining and petroleum industries during the initial years of the twentieth century*. A wide geographical separation existed between the great mineral deposits of the world and the consuming markets in the United States and Western Europe. Hence, large oil companies like British Petroleum and Standard Oil (New Jersey) and hard-mineral corporations, such as International Nickel, Anaconda Copper, and Kennecott Copper, were among the first true multinationals. Singer, Coca-Cola, and Woolworth were early American manufacturing and merchandising multinationals; Unilever, Phillips, and Imperial Chemical Industries entered the foreign arena from Britain and the Netherlands. Bayer and Thyssen went abroad from Germany. The Suez Company and the Wagons Lits Company were early entrants from France.

Multinational corporate investment spread further in the years after World War I, spurred by rising barriers to international trade and led by the burgeoning automobile and associated industries. General Motors and Ford acquired ownership of automobile companies in Britain, France, and Germany. American companies making tires, plate glass, and automobile accessories followed. By 1940, some six hundred American firms had invested more than half a billion dollars in factories in Britain.[2] But the worldwide economic depression of the 1930's ended this incipient movement, and foreign corporate investment languished until after World War II.

After the war, the multinational corporation flowered, as American firms invested heavily abroad in a wide variety of manufacturing and merchandising operations. At the end of 1950, direct foreign investment by American corporations was $11.8 billion, mostly committed to the petroleum and minerals industries of Canada, Latin America, and the Middle East. By the end of 1969, the figure had more than sextupled to $71 billion.[3] Paralleling this explosive growth were shifts in the type of industry and in the location of the investment. Two-thirds of the total was invested in manufacturing, mercantile, and other *non*-extractive industries. Almost two-thirds was invested in Western Europe, even though commitments in other parts of the world had also expanded greatly.

Increasingly, foreign corporations have become multinational also. Direct foreign corporate investment in the United States stood at nearly $12 billion at the end of 1969, having risen by 25 percent during the preceding three years, as more foreign businesses gained the financial means and the managerial confidence to enter the huge American market. Most of this investment was made by enterprises from Britain ($3.4 billion), Canada ($2.6 billion), the Netherlands ($1.7 billion), and Switzerland ($1.2 billion), with smaller sums from France, Germany, and Japan.[4] Long used to the presence of such firms as Shell, Lever, and Rolls-Royce,

Americans became conscious of new corporate immigrants like British Petroleum, Courtaulds, Pechiney, Aluminium, Massey-Ferguson, Sony, and Toyota.

This increasing European and Japanese business intrusion into the American continent, as well as the increasing American business involvement throughout the world, demonstrates that *corporate business is outgrowing national boundaries.* Increasingly we find that nineteenth-century political organization provides an archaic framework for a twentieth-century economy.

American corporations led the world trend toward business multinationalism. The great size and wealth of the economy of the United States generated capital for investment. Companies were attracted by the relatively higher foreign rates of return on investment. There is a strong growth dynamic in American business thinking. American capital outflow took the form of corporate *direct* investment because of the superior organization of American capital markets and the larger capabilities of American managers. With its multitude of stockholders, ready access to equity capital and credit, experience in coordinating business operations over a continental area, growth-and-profit orientation, and its use of advanced techniques of management, the large American corporation was far better prepared for foreign investment than the typical European enterprise, with its smaller size, narrower market, emphasis upon security and stability, and traditional mode of management. Also, European capital markets were small and public ownership of corporate securities was limited. These factors made it difficult for a European company to acquire external funds.

American corporate investment abroad is, as would be expected, concentrated in the hands of the largest firms. Of a total investment of $65 billion at the end of 1968, the five hundred largest American industrial corporations had invested more than $50 billion. A score of these firms had a third or more of their total assets in other countries; an even larger number derived more than one-third of their income from foreign operations. For the great majority, however, foreign operations constituted a minor segment of their business.

## THE EXTENT OF FOREIGN
## ECONOMIC PENETRATION

American corporate investment has penetrated deeply into the economies of a few advanced nations, such as Canada and Britain. It stands out in certain raw material producing countries in Central and South America and in the Middle East. Foreign firms—primarily American—

owned 63 percent of Canada's petroleum and mining industries and 35 percent of all its mining, manufacturing, transportation, and merchandising business in 1962.[5] In Australia, foreign firms owned about one-quarter of all business corporation assets in 1965.[6] They controlled about one-fourth of Brazil's rail and electrical industries and about 18 percent of its manufacturing in the early 1960's.[7] British subsidiaries and joint ventures of American corporations accounted for 10 percent of the industrial output of the United Kingdom and for 17 percent of that country's exports in 1965, according to a recent study.[8] This investment was concentrated in high-technology industries (pharmaceuticals, computers) and in industries for whose products people spend a rising fraction of their incomes as their standard of living increases (automobiles, cosmetics, packaged foods). American companies also owned considerable parts of the industrial apparatus of Honduras, Chile, Panama, and many oil exporting countries.

*In the European countries, American corporate investment forms less than 5 percent of total business investment.* What concerns Europeans, however, is the deep penetration by American companies of high-technology sectors of their economies. In France, American firms controlled two-thirds of the photographic film, paper, farm machinery, and telecommunications industries. In Europe as a whole, they produced 80 percent of the computers, 95 percent of the integrated circuits, 50 percent of the semiconductors, and 15 percent of consumer electronic products.[9] Thoughtful Europeans have been haunted by the spectre of domination of their most advanced industries by American firms, relegating native enterprises to conventional tasks.

Taken globally, it has been estimated that the value of the output of all foreign affiliates of American corporations was a staggering $200 billion during 1970.[10] This was nearly five times American exports of $40 billion in that year. Evidentally, the preponderant linkage of the United States to other markets is foreign production rather than foreign trade. Thus *United States industry abroad had become the third largest "economy" in the world,* outranked only by those of the domestic United States and the Soviet Union. Moreover, foreign production of American firms during the 1960's has grown about 10 percent a year, twice as fast as domestic economies. Multinational corporations are rapidly increasing their shares of the world's business.

## MOTIVES TO MULTINATIONALIZE

Direct investment in foreign manufacturing facilities is usually an alternative to exporting homemade products. Why have manufacturers endured the harder tasks and larger risks of foreign operations instead of shipping their products abroad? Evidently, direct investment appeared to be a relatively profitable use of corporate funds.

The most frequent reason for direct foreign investment is that entrepreneurs confront foreign barriers to their exports. Nationalistic sentiment leads most nations to try to build their own industrial capabilities. By raising barriers against imports of manufactured products, they induce foreign as well as local firms to establish domestic industries. Large numbers of American corporations became multinationals simply to maintain or expand markets in Canada or in the European Economic Community that could not be as profitably served by exports.

Business firms also multinationalize because their presence as a producer in a foreign nation enables them to adapt their products to local demands more effectively. For example, during the 1920's General Motors acquired Vauxhall in Britain and Opel in Germany and opened assembly plants in fifteen foreign countries. It sought thereby to meet consumer demand that had expanded to a point where local manufacturing was more profitable than exporting from the United States.[11]

The relative attractiveness of direct investment in foreign nations had many other causes. The creation of larger free-trading regions, such as the European Economic Community, opened up opportunities to capitalize upon economies of scale that American firms were prepared to seize more quickly than their European counterparts. The rapid postwar expansion of European markets, with a spreading wave of mass consumption, opened doors to profits from the introduction of mass manufacturing and marketing methods. The EEC also created competition among its members to attract American firms. A foreign corporation, denied entry to one country, could build a plant in another from which it could ship products into the recalcitrant nation. The Common Market thus served to frustrate myopic nationalism. Entry by American firms into Europe was also facilitated by the typically large amounts of credit supplied by European bankers on a limited equity base.[12]

Another reason for direct foreign investment was that antitrust laws and keen competition at home tended to restrict the expansion dynamic of American business, channeling corporate attention to opportunities abroad.[13] An important factor, already noted in Chapter 3, was the development of management science. Growing confidence in the political stability and economic strength of the advanced nations appeared to reduce the risk of foreign commitments. Also, geographical diversification of a corporation's operations into many national markets offered a means of stabilizing the growth of its total earnings.

By multinationalizing, a company also acquires certain competitive advantages. It can monitor technological developments in many countries. It can borrow at low interest rates in one country to finance working capital shortages in a high-interest country. It can move surplus funds between its multiple bases, to minimize the cost of borrowed funds or to take advantage of expected changes in exchange rates.

Clearly, there are many cogent reasons for corporate multinationalism; and there is little doubt that it will continue to expand long into the future, so long as nations permit it.

## MANAGEMENT PATTERNS AND PROCESSES

A multinational business corporation may adopt one of two basic organizational forms: a *world corporation* form, in which the basic business functions of finance, marketing, manufacturing, and research and development are the primary pillars of the organization, and domestic and foreign operations are merged; or an *international division* form, in which foreign business is done in separate national divisions, apart from the domestic operations.[14] There are strengths and weaknesses in each form, and both have been used by successful firms. As firms gain experience, a wider use of the world corporation plan is likely because it achieves more complete integration of foreign and domestic management.

In both types of multinational organization, the head office normally makes policy decisions, such as those concerning expansion of product lines, marketing territories, and capital budgets. It delegates to the managers of its foreign affiliates broad authority to operate under those policies within their respective countries. Policy control of foreign affiliates is exercised, first, through the use of annual budgets that specify goals to be attained and, secondly, through periodic reports by the affiliates' managers on progress toward the specified goals.[15] Coordinated control of policy through central staff functions, and decentralized operating responsibility with a clearly defined line authority—the management technique developed within General Motors—has been the key to successful multinational management.[16] To manage a many-based enterprise with a tight rein is simply not feasible.

What is the desirable extent of ownership of a foreign affiliate? Up to the present time, the predominant vehicle of direct corporate investment abroad has been the wholly owned subsidiary. Thus, 72 percent of the net assets of American firms in the United Kingdom in 1965 were held by wholly owned subsidiaries, 14 percent by subsidiaries more than 50 percent American-owned, and only 9 percent by entities financed mainly by British firms.[17] Many American and European managers believe that sole ownership is necessary to enable them to base their operations upon objective economic factors, free from the influence of foreign partners.[18]

Although complete ownership may facilitate the enforcement of corporate discipline, it goes against the prevailing opinion in most host countries. Host countries strongly and increasingly prefer an equity interest by local businessmen because it reduces the danger of foreign control of their economies. In addition, local partners can help to improve the affiliate's relations with the foreign government and its people. The examples of Japan and Mexico, which have admitted foreign companies mainly as minority owners of joint ventures, demonstrate that successful foreign investment does not require 100 percent or even majority ownership. *Although joint ventures are not free of difficulties, it is desirable— and probable—that more multinational business will assume this form in the future.* Another route to joint ownership, of course, is multinational ownership of stock in the parent company. This is desirable for the additional reason that it can help to minimize international frictions.

Comparative studies of management in different countries indicate that the similarities are far greater than the differences. With appropriate adaptations to local conditions, American management techniques have proved to be a hardy transplant in foreign soils. As Lilienthal has perceptively observed, the most important managerial problems of multinational corporations are their relations with governments. The legal systems of host countries often conflict with those of the home country. Interminable negotiations with government officials is the lot of the foreign manager.[19]

Managers of the foreign affiliates of multinational companies once had the reputation of being "second-stringers," sidetracked from the main line of advancement to top management. This has changed as companies have learned the folly of entrusting markets with high profit potentials to men of less than topflight abilities. A foreign assignment now is part of the grooming process for leadership in the multinational company.[20] Overseas placement is typically not a preconceived career goal for the young executive, but a step in broadening his experience.[21]

# EFFECTS ON LESS DEVELOPED HOST COUNTRIES

*The economic, political, technological, and cultural effects of multinational corporate investment are most striking in the less developed countries.* There, corporate investment has made a strong impact on development. This conclusion emerges clearly from twelve case studies made over a fifteen-year period by the National Planning Association, whose credentials as an objective observer are unquestioned.[22] In each of these cases the American corporation played an innovating and catalytic role, founding new industries, transmitting technological and managerial skills as well as capital, and in many cases creating entire social infrastructures, including schools, housing, health facilities, and transportation, in order to conduct its business.

Sears, Roebuck, for example, pioneered the modern general supermarkets of Mexico, initiated a credit system for consumers with lower incomes, and established a large coterie of native manufacturing industries to stock its stores.[23] United Fruit, one of the earliest American multinationals, was the major force in developing the international trade in bananas, pioneering in every aspect of the industry from plantation production through disease control techniques, land and ocean transport, and sales promotion.[24] It enormously expanded the real incomes and welfare of the peoples of the six Central American republics in which it operated, while earning a profit on its investment that averaged *less* than that realized by corporate business in the United States.

International Basic Economy Corporation, organized for profit by the Rockefeller family for the purpose of introducing new industries and business methods into less developed countries, had established 119 subsidiaries and affiliates in thirty-three countries by the end of 1968. Its efforts were focused upon agribusiness. Its subsidiaries made many innovations in the production of food and low-cost housing and in the economical distribution of food through supermarkets. Because of its heavy developmental and innovational costs, which broke the ground for later entry by local entrepreneurs, IBEC's return on investment was subnormal.[25]

The conduct of American business abroad has not always been impeccable. Foreign complaints that American firms have failed to transfer technology or to train local personnel, or that they have corrupted local officials or intervened in national politics, doubtless have some foundation. Yet these forms of conduct are rare today. The overall record strongly encourages an extension of this mode of "foreign aid." Indeed, the constructive developmental results of private business investment led the U.S. Agency for International Development (AID) to launch private enterprise support programs in 1958 and, thereafter, to rely increasingly upon private enterprise in carrying out developmental tasks.

In the face of a generally constructive record, how can one explain the widespread denunciation of American corporations abroad by foreign politicians, as well as by American critics? Charges of "exploitation," "plundering," and "greed for profits" are often made, especially in the Latin-American countries. As the authors of the United Fruit Company study have pointed out, there has been a "striking disparity between the reputation and the performance" of the company.[26] Foreign ignorance of the realities of private enterprise, of the hard tasks to be performed, and of the high risks to be run, is surely one part of the answer. For those ventures that succeed, profits may appear to be inordinately high. Yet, as Vernon has remarked, "the history of such investment is littered with the bleached bones of many enterprises; and taking the failures with the successes, it is not clear that the investment has been handsomely rewarded." [27] Many companies have been obliged to deal with a range of problems vastly wider than those confronted at home. They have had to create whole communities out of wilderness environments, usually in countries with unstable governments. It is in the light of this imperative that their occasional interference with local governments should be interpreted. The foreign company is always a convenient whipping boy for local politicians.

American corporate investment abroad has been gradually shifting from an earlier emphasis upon the mining, extractive, and raw-material industries toward diversified manufacturing and merchandising operations. One important consequence has been a great increase in American exports of technological and managerial skills and knowledge, important values to the recipient country. This shift should serve to reduce the frequency of charges of "foreign exploitation."

The potential contribution of private corporations to the development of poor countries is large. Its realization depends mainly on the development of stable governments in those countries and their actions to encourage private investment. Any less developed country that offers political stability, respect for contracts, financial responsibility, and equitable taxation will attract investment, foreign and domestic. The remarkable evolution of such lands as Hong Kong, Malaysia, and Taiwan testify to this truth. If more low-income countries adhere to codes of foreign investment that reduce political risks, private firms will quickly expand their developmental roles.

The political risks of expropriation, civil war, and the inconvertibility of currencies have risen in less developed lands. The reasons have been rising nationalism and changed world attitudes toward intervention by one nation into the domestic affairs of another. *When an American corporation goes abroad today, it cannot expect the United States government to protect its foreign properties.* Since the expropriation of American business properties by the Soviet government in 1917, there have been major expropriations by the governments of Mexico, Cuba, Argentina, Peru, Indonesia, and Eastern European countries involving estimated losses of some $2.5 billion.[28] "Prompt, adequate, and effective compensation," required by international law, has rarely been paid. The American company loses; but so does the expropriating country and the region in which it is located.

Thus the fears aroused by Cuba's expropriation in 1960 probably cost Latin America some $500 million of business investment from the United States in the following two years.[29]

The AID offers insurance to American corporations against major political risks of investment in those less developed countries that receive American economic assistance. If the flow of private investment is to be expanded, this insurance should be extended to cover more risks and more countries. At the same time, low-income countries should adopt and respect codes of foreign investment and assure fair adjudication of disputes. The establishment in 1966 of the International Centre for the Settlement of Investment Disputes was a desirable move in this direction. By mid-1972, some sixty-seven nations had ratified the convention establishing the Centre, thereby agreeing to submit to its panels of experts any disputes arising between their governments and foreign private investors.[30]

*Private business investment is inherently superior to governmental aid as an instrument of development because it combines transfers of managerial and technical assistance with that of capital.* General dissatisfaction with bilateral governmental aid makes it important to expand the flow of business investment.[31] While measures to limit or to insure against risks will help to enlarge this flow, they will not remove the root causes of international tensions. The foreign subsidiary of the American corporation will still be charged with "exploitation" of local resources and with taking out too much profit. When it pays higher than prevailing wages and benefits to its employees, their higher living standards will provoke envy and resentment among other local citizens. Ways must be found to ameliorate this problem.

*A promising approach is for the American company to agree with the foreign government on a reciprocal reinvestment program.* The company would agree to reinvest a specified percentage of its profits, in return for which the host government would agree to spend (invest) specified amounts of its revenues from corporate operations on schools, health, housing, and other forms of welfare for people in the communities in which the company is operating. Disparities in living conditions would be lessened and a source of social unrest would be removed. Because the agreement would be of mutual benefit, the American company could not be accused of "interference" with local affairs.

The political and social effects of American corporate investment in poor countries are not as clear as the economic effects. The process of development is inherently unsettling to a society. By producing shifts in the distribution of income and wealth, and by redistributing economic power among social classes, development creates political stresses. Often these tensions can be relieved by peaceful political reforms; not infrequently they are followed by more or less violent upheavals. Indeed, being an agent of change, the foreign corporation is seen in the developing country as a threat to privileged positions in the traditional society. And it is often attacked by the Right as well as by the Left. Local criticism of the foreign company may indicate only that it is operating as an effective agent of change. Curiously, some prominent development economists have counseled Latin-American countries that their best interests would be served by compelling foreign firms to sell affiliates to local owners or to the government. They argue that the foreign affiliates stunt the growth of local enterprise. While nationalistic pride may be bolstered by such a policy, its cost in slower development appears to be high.[32]

The cultural consequences of American corporate penetration of the poor countries can be plainly seen in the ready acceptance by native peoples of soft drinks, packaged foods, electrical appliances, automobiles, brand names and advertising, and much of the paraphernalia of American life. At a more fundamental level, it is likely that the status and value systems, the social attitudes and behavioral patterns, the arts and the essential cultural foundations of many of these countries will also undergo profound changes. Such changes ultimately should reduce barriers to communication between peoples and lay a common basis for a stable world order. Yet the transition from poverty to self-sustaining development inevitably will be marked by much international friction.

## EFFECTS ON DEVELOPED HOST COUNTRIES

In Europe, the impact of American multinational business was on politically mature societies, technologically advanced economies, and socially integrated peoples proud of their nations' long histories of achievement. Nevertheless, the physical presence in Europe of more than three thousand American corporations with forty thousand American employees could not help but be significant.[33]

A major economic result of the American "invasion" was the stimulation of the growth of production, incomes, and living standards of Europeans. American corporate investment improved the efficiency of resource allocation. It also improved the balance of international payments of host countries, which benefitted both from capital inflows and also from the exports generated by the foreign-owned affiliates.[34] More subtle and profound economic effects flowed from the new competition introduced by the Americans: hard-sell advertising, mass-marketing techniques, price competition, packaging, branding, and continental marketing strategies—t name a few. Mass production of a host of new consumer products, such as fresh-frozen foods, electric home appliances, and plastic containers, was both a response and a stimulus to the rising levels of European family income. *The primary thrust of the American "assault" on the Continent was to accelerate the pace of a peaceful consumer revolution.*

The newcomers were, of course, criticized for their "disruption of orderly marketing," "extravagant wages and salaries," "reckless financial practices," primarily by those in the old business establishments whose comfortable oligopolies were threatened by the new competition. And American corporate managers did, on occasion, display insensitivity to local customs in their drive for lower costs and greater efficiency. General Electric was condemned for closing a computer plant and dismissing French engineers when it consolidated its foreign computer operations to improve efficiency. Goodyear and Goodrich provoked loud cries of protest from French tire-makers when they doubled the traditional discounts to dealers in order to make initial penetration of the French tire market. Effective competition inevitably disturbs the status quo. As Schumpeter said long ago, it is a "process of creative destruction." However, available evidence indicates that affiliates of American corporations have generally earned higher rates of return on investment in both Britain and on the Continent than have local enterprises in the same industries.[35]

Although the American "invasion" was received calmly in most European countries, de Gaulle's France reacted sensitively. The French government changed its policy toward American direct investment three times. After 1959, it encouraged the entry of American corporations. As a result of popular disapproval of the actions of General Motors in laying off workers, of Chrysler's purchase of Simca, and of the sale to General Electric of the controlling interest in Machines Bull, American investment was severely restricted in 1963. When American firms reacted by switching their investments to other Common Market countries from which they could still penetrate France, Premier Pompidou once again relaxed the restrictions beginning in 1971. In this, as in several other instances, we see that any Common Market country that restricts American investment only helps its rivals.[36]

The technological consequences of the American corporate invasion received much attention from European observers. American investment was concentrated in the high-technology industries of computers, electronics, aerospace, and petrochemicals, and in such fast-growing industries as automobile manufacturing. American firms led or dominated those industries in many European countries. They excelled in the innovation of products and processes. They spent twice as much of their sales dollar on research and development as their European competitors. They were fast-footed in converting laboratory findings into commercial products. To many Europeans, there appeared to be an insurmountable "technological gap" between Europe and the United States.

Europeans responded vigorously to the American challenge. Their governments fostered business mergers designed to create companies able to compete with the American giants. They expanded their research and development activities supporting industry. Basic European science has always been at least equal to American science. Given adequate governmental and industrial support and an efficient scale of business operations, there is no reason why European industrial technology should fall behind, and when taken overall, it is not clear that it is lagging. *There is now general recognition that the key "gap" between European and American business is managerial rather than technological.*[37] Europeans are now taking vigorous steps to close this gap by establishing graduate schools of management and by replacing nepotism with meritocracy in choosing industrial leadership.

What will be the ultimate social and cultural consequences of American corporate multinationalism in Europe? Mass consumption of durable goods, supermarkets, the vanishing personal servant, the ubiquitous automobile—all are indices of the rising social and geographical mobility of Europeans, of the reduction of class barriers, of the equalization of personal opportunities. The multinational corporation is leading Europe toward a more egalitarian, homogeneous, and democratic society. While traditionalists will deplore the gradual blurring of class and national distinctions, such segmentations cannot in the end withstand the onslaught of technological and economic changes. These changes create new political attitudes, just as multinational business has generated new economic pressures. Ultimately, they may facilitate the joining of all Europe in an enduring political and economic union. Should this come to pass, the American multinational corporation, as a primary carrier of social change, will share in the credit for an achievement that eluded Caesar, Charlemagne, and Napoleon.

## EFFECTS ON THE SOCIALIST COUNTRIES

Multinational corporate business has begun, in novel ways, to penetrate the socialist nations of Eastern Europe, and with effects that may ultimately be even more momentous for the world than their operations within Western economies. The novelty lies in the cooperation between private firms and public corporations. These arrangements are called "industrial cooperation" in socialist countries, probably because "joint venture" has a capitalist ring. Typically, a Western private company agrees with an Eastern European public corporation to sell specialized machinery and equipment on installment credit terms, and to provide technical and managerial services necessary to produce certain products. The Eastern European country, in turn, agrees to provide the land, buildings, and labor necessary to produce those products and, often, to pay for imported equipment with exports of its products. The joint venture may market its output in the host country or in third countries. The Western company profits from the sale of equipment and products and is paid a fee for its technical and managerial services. The Eastern European enterprise gains technological and managerial know-how and title to specialized industrial equipment that it will operate by itself later on. While differing in legal form, the essential elements of multinational corporate investment are present: international transfers of capital, management, and technology.[38]

Such East-West "industrial cooperation" appears to have emerged initially in Yugoslavia during the 1950's. Now, all socialist countries have industrial cooperation agreements with Western firms. Rumania had no fewer than nineteen in effect during 1969. For example, Renault of France had agreed with a Rumanian enterprise to build automobile transmissions, partly for domestic use and partly for export. Fiat of Italy, during 1968, agreed with the government of the Soviet Union to supply machinery, management, and technology to create a Russian industrial community capable of making 600,000 automobiles a year. Sharply rising East-West trade in capital equipment shows that the magnitude of such industrial cooperation increased during the 1960's. Mainland China has also purchased industrial plants and equipment from Western countries on long-term credit.

East-West industrial cooperation had involved only European and Japanese enterprises up to 1972 because American firms were barred from exporting most high-technology products to communist countries. The result was that communist countries imported both American and foreign products from companies in third countries rather than from American companies. President Nixon's journey to Moscow in 1972 marked a fundamental change in American policy, by opening up trade relations between the United States and the Soviet Union. Occidental Petroleum quickly signed an agreement with the Soviet government for "scientific and technical cooperation" in five industrial fields. Other American companies followed suit. *Because the Soviet Union is eager to have access to advanced managerial and technological knowledge, trade between the superpowers is bound to expand.* The ultimate involvement of the People's Republic of China in commercial intercourse with the United States also holds great promise for lowering barriers to international understanding.

Socialist ideology, which precludes private ownership of fixed capital, has caused East-West industrial cooperation to take place on a basis of loans rather than equity capital. Yet cracks have appeared in this ideological barrier. The Foreign Investment Law of Yugoslavia was amended during 1967 to permit joint ventures of Yugoslavian and foreign companies to acquire ownership of domestic fixed assets.[39]

Expanding East-West industrial cooperation could help to relax international tensions and create an environment favorable to peace. It promotes travel and communication. It emphasizes the *common* economic goal of more efficient production and a better life for all peoples. Technological and managerial knowledge is diffused, accelerating gains in productivity and standards of living. Because the peoples of *both* cooperating countries manifestly gain from such arrangements, there is no basis for feelings of "exploitation."

## EFFECTS ON INVESTING COUNTRIES

Multinational corporate investment has had an important economic, political, and cultural impact upon investing countries. Thus, the United States balance of payments was in substantial deficit during most of the 1960's, and foreign long-term investment is believed to have contributed to it. An Interest Equalization Tax was imposed in 1963 to deter Americans from making foreign loans or portfolio investments. Later, voluntary and then mandatory direct controls were imposed upon foreign direct investment by American corporations in an effort to reduce capital outflow and to strengthen the dollar in the world's money markets.

*Whether foreign investment controls are achieving their aims and serving American interests is doubtful.* Large American multinational firms are able to raise needed capital from foreign bankers or in the Eurodollar market. The heaviest impact of American controls is felt by smaller enterprises which are unable to tap these financial sources. More fundamental is the argument that any improvement in the United States balance of payments resulting from controls can be temporary at best. In the long run, controls have the perverse effect of enlarging the deficit of the United States by reducing the inflow of interest and dividends from foreign affiliates of American companies.[40]

A basic objection to foreign investment controls is that the deficit in the United States balance of payments they are designed to curtail vanishes when international transactions are measured *on an assets basis* rather than on a liquidity basis. At present, when an American company invests in a foreign country, it acquires a long-term asset in return for which it pays dollars—a short-term liability of the United States. Although the transaction enlarges the United States deficit on the liquidity basis, it does not change the value of assets owned in the two countries. As a result of the creation by the International Monetary Fund of the Special Drawing Rights (SDR's) as a new form of international currency reserve, dollar liquidity has become less important. A deficit in the United States balance of payments on the liquidity basis should no longer be a compelling reason for restricting United States capital outflow, especially when, on the basis of the value of assets held, the financial position of the United States is strong.

Virulent criticisms are directed at multinational corporations by labor unions. Multinationals are viewed by unions as "runaway" firms that produce cheap products abroad by paying "substandard" wages, thereby taking jobs away from Americans. Unions sponsored the Burke-Hartke bill in the United States Congress during 1971; it would have imposed quotas on most imports, raised taxes on foreign earnings, and tightened governmental regulations. *Yet U.S. government studies have shown that foreign investment by American companies has expanded American employment.* The import restrictions and penalties on foreign earnings sought by the unions would actually have *curtailed* the real incomes and job opportunities of American workers.

# EFFECTS ON INTERNATIONAL RELATIONS

The foreign operations of American—and European—enterprises have generated many misunderstandings and tensions with the governments and peoples of host countries as well as with their home governments.

As corporate citizens of many nations, multinational corporations daily confront conflicts between divergent national policies, economic and social systems, and values. As agents of technological and cultural change, they naturally provoke critical reactions from foreign businessmen and governments.

Foreign criticism of American corporate operations abroad has focused on: the "exploitation" of local manpower or natural resources; the conflict between the national policies of the United States and the national interests of the foreign country; the overcentralization of managerial decision-making in American headquarters; the locating of advanced research in the United States; the insensitivity of American managers to local laws and customs; investment behavior that destabilizes foreign economies; and political support by the U.S. government. Let us examine each of these charges.

## "Exploitation"

The charge of "exploitation" is often made against American firms in the less developed countries where the firms extract minerals or produce other materials. It is based upon the naive idea that the company "takes away" irreplaceable natural resources without providing a *quid pro quo*. What critics commonly overlook are the heavy risks assumed by the American company in searching for and developing local resources, its large investment of capital, the huge losses incurred in unsuccessful ventures, and the large contribution made to their own country's material welfare by the foreign company that succeeds. After the fact, it is easy to point to "extravagant" profits being realized from a successful foreign operation, and to forget the many unsuccessful ventures, uncertainties, and delays experienced in creating a profitable enterprise.

"Exploitation" of a country's natural resources, in the economic sense, is possible only when monopsony (a single buyer) prevails. As long as world markets for natural resources are effectively competitive, the terms on which a foreign company enters a country to explore for and produce its natural resources reflect a careful balancing of estimated risks and rewards. Today, any country possessing natural resources finds that exploration and development rights are eagerly sought by a multitude of firms from many foreign nations. It can charge substantial bonuses for limited agreements and impose heavy taxes and royalties on the production from successful concessions. Dozens of oil companies from many nations compete intensely in bidding for petroleum agreements with such countries as Libya, Nigeria, and Venezuela. The terms of entry into the foreign oil business have become so onerous that the oil-producing country typically makes over six times as much per barrel of oil produced (from *successful* concessions) as the oil company, although it invests no capital, incurs no expense, and takes no risk. Natural-resource agreements today are rarely exploitative, whatever may have been true in the past. The host country profits from the public income generated by royalties and taxes, from the private income derived from wage payments and other expenses in the local economy, and, above all, from the acquisition of modern technology and management skills. The overall return on American foreign oil investments has not been excessive.

## Disparities Among National Policies

More serious is the allegation that the foreign affiliates of American companies, being under the policy control of their home offices, are obliged to pursue policies that serve American interests rather than those of the host country. For example, it has been charged that American companies limit the exports of Canadian subsidiaries to third countries, or force them to purchase raw materials or components from their American plants instead of from Canadian suppliers.[41] More generally, it is said that the efforts of a multinational firm to maximize its *aggregate* profits do not necessarily require it to do so in a particular country.

There is no basic conflict between the multinational company's goal of maximizing profits in each country and overall profit maximization. The multinational company will serve its own interests best by investing in its affiliates in each country up to the point where the marginal return on capital, after adjusting for risks, is the same in all countries, and by allowing each of its affiliates the freedom to enter the parent company's home market as well as the markets of third countries.

Comparative costs will dictate the amount of exports of a foreign affiliate, just as they do in a locally owned company. Indeed, A. E. Safarian found that the foreign trade of Canadian subsidiaries of American companies was actually greater, relative to their total sales, than that of independent Canadian firms in the same industries.[42]

Conflicts between the national policies of investing and host countries can put the multinational corporation in a quandary. For example, the policy of the United States has barred certain exports to the People's Republic of China, whereas Canadian policy permits such trade. A Canadian subsidiary of an American corporation, under instruction from its home office to obey United States law, clearly cannot serve Canadian interests in expanding exports.

Frictions also arise between American multinational companies and governments over antimonopoly laws. The government of the United States seeks to prevent foreign affiliates of American companies from engaging in such anticompetitive practices as price fixing or market sharing.[43] Host governments, on the other hand, resent the application of American commercial policies to firms operating within their own boundaries. European policies have been much more permissive in regard to trade practices and business combinations.

Fortunately, antimonopoly law enforcement has not been a serious problem in international relations. Foreign affiliates of American companies have generally conducted their affairs in conformity with the more rigorous standards of the United States. Also, foreign countries have moved rapidly toward antimonopoly policies that resemble those of the United States, so that potential conflicts are being reduced.[44] The 1958 Treaty of Rome barred monopoly for members of the EEC, and set up machinery to prevent restrictive practices.

*Nearly all differences between multinational corporations and host governments can be resolved by harmonizing national policies.* In a rational world, the United States and Canada would pursue the same trade policy toward the People's Republic of China. The tax systems of different countries would be reconciled. Tax treaties would assure equitable allocations of tax liabilities arising from multinational business. Multinational business did not create disparities between national policies; it merely threw old disparities into bolder relief and made urgent the task of removing them.

## Overcentralized Management

A third genre of complaints against the multinational corporation is that it overcentralizes management decisions in its head office. A related indictment is that it uses little foreign managerial talent, even in foreign operations. In a study of this matter, conducted among the French affiliates of American firms in 1965, Allan Johnstone concluded that the American multinational firms in France did indeed drive with a tight rein; in fact, home offices often made policy decisions with little consideration of the local consequences in France.[45] On the other hand, Safarian's conclusion with respect to the Canadian subsidiaries of American firms was different: wide delegations of authority were made to the managers of Canadian subsidiaries by their American parent companies. The parents interfered *less* in their Canadian operations than in their American subsidiaries.[46] The stronger cultural similarities of Canada and the United States and the comparative recency of American direct investment in France may have accounted for the difference. Delegated authority to the management of a foreign subsidiary usually widens through time as confidence is gained from successful experience.

The record of American companies in developing foreign management personnel is good. A study in 1957 revealed that only one thousand of the thirty-five thousand supervisory, technical, and professional personnel of American companies in Canada had been sent from the United States. The situation is probably much the same in Europe, although figures are lacking. American multinational businesses have a strong economic reason for employing local personnel to the maximum extent: the salaries are much less than those of Americans would be.

## Overcentralized Research

A fourth criticism is that American multinational companies centralize scientific research and engineering in the United States, while relegating foreign personnel to routine operations. This stricture is clearly refuted by the evidence. Safarian found that most of the spending on industrial research and development was concentrated in the *foreign-owned* sector of Canadian industry. Half of the Canadian subsidiaries performed industrial research in Canada; most of the remainder did not because they had access to the technical knowledge of their parent companies.[47] Dunning found that British subsidiaries of American firms spent larger parts of their sales dollar on research than did British firms in the same industries. As in the case of management skills, international transfer of technology is an important gain from foreign investment for a host country. A multinational corporation entering a foreign nation is likely in the first stage to import its technical knowledge from its home country. Later, as local personnel are trained, it usually establishes local research facilities. It has a strong incentive to do so because foreign research costs normally are much lower.

## Insensitivity to Local Business Practices

American managers of foreign subsidiaries are said to be insensitive to local business customs. Often cited are the laying off of factory workers from a Parisian refrigerator plant by General Motors in 1963, Remington Rand's similar action with a Lyons typewriter plant in the same year, and the previously mentioned closing of a computer plant by General Electric.[48] These episodes provoked angry comment by the French press, even though the American corporations amply justified their actions as a quest for efficiency in the face of shifts in market demand. French consternation was due to the French tradition that the employer, rather than the employee, bears the manpower adjustment costs of such shifts; in the United States, of course, these costs are mainly borne by the employees. The multinational company often plays the role of an outsider testing the viability of local business practices.

## Destabilization of the Economy

It is charged that foreign affiliates of American corporations frustrate the stabilization policies of the host country. Canadians complain that fluctuations in inflows of American capital complicate their problems of attaining stable economic growth without inflation. They also feel vulnerable to shifts in American policies that reduce investment outflows, such as the Interest Equalization Tax and foreign investment controls. French government officials have objected to the ability of American corporate subsidiaries to escape the constraints of French national economic planning.

The French government possesses formidable powers to control investment by its own enterprises through its control of many credit facilities. Having foreign funds available, the French affiliate of an American firm can elude this control.

The Canadian complaint about uneven investment inflows is simply the other side of the American problem of uneven foreign investment outflows. The efforts of private investors to profit from changing opportunities and international inequalities in investment returns thus poses a problem for both countries. When recognized as a *mutual* problem arising from natural economic forces and not as an extraterritorial imposition of American laws, this problem can be resolved by consultation and harmonizing actions by the two governments. Although the multinational corporation magnified these problems, it did not create them.

## An Instrument of National Power

Critics charge that the multinational corporation is an instrument of "imperialism," collaborating with its home government to enhance its national power in the world. They contend that multinational companies use the economic, diplomatic, and military power of their home government to gain profits. American foreign policy is determined, they say, by American business interests abroad.

Clearly, the government of the United States—as does every other national government—acts in many ways to support American private enterprise abroad. The Departments of Commerce and State negotiate treaties of commerce and friendship with foreign countries, maintain consular services, promote American exports, insure against some risks of investment in less developed countries, and support international trade fairs. Historically, this support once went beyond economic and displomatic measures into the realm of military action. "Trade followed the flag" and *vice versa,* as the naval attack on the Barbary pirates in 1801, Admiral Perry's expedition to Japan in 1850, the American intervention in the Boxer Rebellion in 1900, and the Marine forays into Latin-American republics demonstrate.

*Since World War II, however, there has been a radical "de-politicization" of private foreign investment. The era of "gunboat diplomacy" is past.* When an American corporation invests abroad today, it carries its own risks. If it loses property by civil war or expropriation, without fair compensation, it cannot expect economic or military sanctions to be applied against the offending country by the government of the United States. The recent expropriations of American corporate property in Bolivia, Peru, Chile, and Algeria stand witness to this statement; in no case did the government of the United States intervene. It did not even apply the

Hickenlooper Amendment (shutting off economic aid) to Peru when that country seized International Petroleum's property in 1970.

Even more telling evidence that business today has little influence on the foreign policy of the United States is found in American actions in the Middle East. One of the largest concentrations of American corporate investment is in the petroleum industry of Arab countries around the Persian Gulf and in North Africa. Yet the government of the United States has given economic and military support to Israel, whose economic significance to the United States is not great, thereby arousing the bitter hostility of the Arab states and provoking threats of expropriation of the property of American oil companies.

This de-politicization of American business investment abroad is desirable because it reduces the risk of military conflict growing out of economic intercourse between nations. Private economic interests in profit are separated from national political interests in power and security. Although the risks and costs of foreign investment are higher for private entrepreneurs, the more important risks and costs of war are lower for all of us as citizens. Moreover, the knowledge that private foreign investment stands on its own feet is likely to make the behavior of both the investing and host countries more responsible in the future.

## EFFECTS ON INTERNATIONAL AND TRANSNATIONAL INSTITUTIONS

Multinational corporations have helped to create transnational financial institutions because the large scale of their operations generated financial needs beyond the capabilities of national institutions. Notable examples are the Eurodollar market, the Eurobond market, and the multinational banking syndicate. The many billions of American dollars held in Europe are actively traded, borrowed, and lent by banks and businesses in the Eurodollar market for both short- and long-term purposes. Multinational businesses frequently borrow funds by selling Eurobonds—debt securities denominated in one European currency, but sold and held by investors in many countries. Transnational finance has become commonplace, as syndicates composed of European and American investment bankers underwrite large corporate issues and distribute them throughout the world. The multinationalization of manufacturing and trading enterprises has been followed by the multinationalization of commercial banking. Bankers of many nations have established overseas branches and affiliates. All these developments again show that the world's business has long since outgrown national boundaries. The concepts of national currencies and exchange rates have become anachronistic in the age of multinational business.

Multinational business is likely also to bring the multinational labor union in its wake. Many companies in high-wage countries like the United States have built plants in low-wage nations in order to reduce costs and stay competitive in world markets. Their success in avoiding the cost-raising effects of the economic power of the national union is motivating labor unions to multinationalize. More unions are beginning to organize, to bargain, to boycott products,˙and to strike *across national boundary lines.* While yet incipient, labor union multinationalism may be expected to gain force in the future. If it does, it could slow the pace of multinational corporate investment.

The rise of multinational business has not yet brought much change in *international* institutions. The United Nations and its affiliated bodies so far have not been intimately involved in multinational enterprise. Nevertheless, a new era of such involvement may be dawning. Resolutions have been introduced into the General Assembly of the United Nations for the establishment of an international government of the oceans and seabeds of the world which are beyond national jurisdiction. Should such an Ocean Regime be established, one sphere of its action could be the formation and monitoring of agreements with business enterprises for the exploration and exploitation of the oceans and seabeds.[49]

This opens up a startling prospect. For the first time in history, a major part of the world's surface would become the common property of all nations, ruled by a supranational government.[50] For the first time, a supranational government would be dealing extensively with multinational corporations—*a double bypassing of national boundaries.*


## A WORLD CORPORATION AUTHORITY

So far, multinational companies have been chartered and regulated by the respective countries in which their affiliates do business. Is such national regulation enough, or should regulation by a *supranational* authority supplement or supplant it?

This issue is analogous to the long-discussed question of federal chartering of business corporations in the United States. A strong case can be made for a federal monopoly of chartering of corporations engaged in interstate commerce. Nearly all large American corporations would be required to obtain federal charters under such a regulation. Corporate powers would become less diverse and more easily understood by stockholders and directors. Corporations could no longer shop around among the states to obtain the best combination of broad powers and low taxes. By analogy, *there is a strong case for supranational chartering of multinational companies.*

Ideally, one may visualize a World Corporation Authority, established under the aegis of the United Nations, to charter and regulate multinational enterprises, as George W. Ball has suggested.[51] Corporation laws are very general, specifying broad methods of governance and finance, so that a single law could be compatible with diverse business cultures. The European Economic Community has drafted such a law for presentation to the legislatures of its member countries.

During 1972 the Economic and Social Council recommended that the Secretary General of the United Nations initiate a broad study of multinational corporations by a group of independent experts. The study is to examine their impact upon the evolution of the less developed nations and upon international relations, and to propose effective regulatory machinery. If it is thorough and objective, and not a mere "witch hunt" intended to produce ammunition for political attacks upon multinational business, this study could well be the vehicle for formulating a world corporation law.

## POLICIES TO EXPAND MULTINATIONAL BUSINESS

Because multinational business is demonstrably beneficial to both investing and host countries, and tends to strengthen the forces of world order, its expansion should be encouraged. We recommend the following policies:

### Corporate Policies

The multinational company can alleviate criticism and improve international relations by adopting the following policies:

• Publicize in the host country the costs and risks the company has assumed and the economic benefits it brings the people.
• Identify the interests of the company with those of the host country in every possible way. (For example, American petroleum companies have developed water resources and built modern farming communities to reduce the food deficits of North African and Middle Eastern countries.)
• Conform to local business practices, except when efficiency clearly demands a change; and then make changes only after consultation with local authorities.

• Decentralize authority to the managers of foreign affiliates to the maximum feasible extent.

• Perform a maximum of research and product-development activities in the host country.

• Adopt a specific program for progressively nationalizing the personnel of foreign affiliates while reducing the number of Americans.

• Establish stock-ownership loans for foreign employees and list the company's securities for trading on the exchanges of host countries.

• Be receptive to joint ventures and to part ownership of a foreign affiliate. They are the wave of the future.

## National Policies

Nations should refrain from actions that would retard the international flow of capital and should act to expand that flow. In the case of the United States, we propose that it should:

• End domestic price inflation; this would materially strengthen the economy of the Unitde States and contribute to a stable world environment for foreign investment.

• Harmonize United States policies on taxation, competition, and international trade with those of other nations; this would remove a fertile source of friction and misunderstanding.

• Remove the Interest Equalization Tax and restrictions upon direct corporate investment abroad. The general rise in domestic interest rates and investment returns during recent years has brought them up to European levels, so that American capital is no longer tempted abroad by generally high rates of return.

• Extend the foreign investment guaranty program of the Agency for International Development to cover more risks and more countries.

• Encourage investment agreements between American corporations and the governments of less developed countries; this would help to diminish the disparities between living conditions of local citizens and those of employees of foreign companies.

Host countries should remove barriers to capital flows and create favorable climates for investment. There are other constructive measures they should take:

• Enact and adhere to fair codes of foreign investment that would enable the foreign company to know its legal status.

• Liberalize foreign exchange regulations to the maximum degree feasible in order to facilitate movements of capital and income.

• Become associated with the Centre for the Settlement of Investment Disputes, so that foreign investors could be assured of an impartial forum to hear any grievances.

• Use their comparative advantages in international trade rather than seek economic independence.

# THE FUTURE OF THE MULTINATIONAL COMPANY

*The multinational corporation stands at the beginning of its development.* Today, few corporations are multinational in *all* dimensions. Most are national corporations that have gone abroad to do business, but retain the ownership, management, and world-view of their country of origin. Professor Perlmutter has drawn a perceptive distinction between "ethnocentric" companies, run from their home countries and sending management abroad; "polycentric" companies, having strong subsidiaries operated by local management, but subject to firm central control; and "geocentric" companies that have stockholders throughout the world, find management anywhere, and have a global flexibility.[52] Currently, the great preponderance of multinational firms are ethnocentric, a small minority are polycentric, and a mere handful, such as Shell and Unilever, are geocentric.

Through time, native officers of the subsidiaries of large multinational companies may be expected to rise to the top of the corporate hierarchy. Shares of stock in more multinationals will be traded on the security exchanges of more nations. Equity ownership will spread through many lands. Geocentric companies will become numerous, polycentric companies typical, and ethnocentric companies will be exceptional.

While one may foresee more American direct corporate investment abroad, it is likely that the reverse flow of foreign corporate investment into the United States will expand even faster. Rates of return for investment in the United State have risen and converged with those available abroad. The growing managerial and technical competence of European and Japanese enterprisers will lead more of them to enter the American market. Such a development would enhance domestic competition, reduce the outflow of capital, and improve the American balance of payments. *In the long run, multinational business may prove far more effective than international trade in equalizing interest rates, real wages, and living standards throughout the world.*

The multinational corporation, able to assemble resources and to organize production on a worldwide scale, has evolved in response to human needs for a global instrument of economic activity. As it evolves further in this direction, it will find itself increasingly frustrated and constrained by national governments. The outcome of this conflict will depend upon the nature of the future world order. Will it continue to be a system of ·nation-states, weakly joined in the United Nations? Or will it become a true world government, as men come to recognize that the present order is too unstable to survive the population explosion and the technological revolution? In the confrontation between the multinational company and the nation-state, it is the former that is at bay. The rising tide of nationalism in the less developed world poses a serious threat both to their own material progress and to multinational business. While much has been said about the great power of the multinational company, the simple truth is that no company can enter and do business in any nation except by the sufferance of its government and upon the terms it dictates.

The multinational corporation is, beyond doubt, the most powerful agency for global economic unity that our century has produced. It is fundamentally an instrument of peace. Its interest is to emphasize the common goals of peoples, to reconcile or remove differences between them. It cannot thrive in a regime of international tension and conflict. The instrumentality of multinational business is man's best hope for achieving political unity on this shrinking planet.

## NOTES

1. F. A. McKenzie, *The American Invasion* (London: Grant Richards, 1902).

2. John H. Dunning, *American Investment in British Manufacturing Industry* (London: Allen and Unwin, 1958).

3. U.S. Department of Commerce, *Survey of Current Business* (October 1969), p. 35.

4. *Ibid.*

5. A. E. Safarian, *Foreign Ownership of Canadian Industry* (Toronto: McGraw-Hill of Canada, 1966).

6. D. J. Brash, *American Investment in Australian Industry* (Canberra: Australian National University Press, 1966).

7. Claude McMillan, Jr., and Richard F. Gonzalez, with Leo G. Erickson, *International Enterprise in a Developing Economy* (East Lansing: Michigan State University Press, 1964).

8. John H. Dunning, *The Role of American Investment in the British Economy,* Political and Economic Planning Broadsheet 507 (London, February 1969), p. 119.

9. Jean-Jacques Servan-Schreiber, *The American Challenge* (New York: Atheneum, 1968).

10. Judd Polk, *The Internationalization of Production* (New York: U.S. Council of the International Chamber of Commerce, May 7, 1969).

11. See Frederick G. Donner, *The Worldwide Industrial Enterprise* (New York: McGraw-Hill, 1967).

12. See Sanford Rose, "The Rewarding Strategies of Multinationalism," *Fortune* (September 15, 1968).

13. Jack N. Behrman, *Some Patterns in the Rise of the Multinational Enterprise,* Graduate School of Business Research Paper 18 (Chapel Hill, N.C.: University of North Carolina, 1967), pp. 6–8.

14. *Organizing for Worldwide Operations* (New York: Business International Corp., 1965).

15. See George A. Steiner and Warren M. Cannon, *Multinational Corporate Planning* (New York: Macmillan, 1966).

16. See Alfred P. Sloan, Jr., *My Years With General Motors* (New York: Duell, Sloan & Pearce, 1963), Ch. 4.

17. Dunning, *The Role of American Investment in the British Economy,* p. 126. See also Behrman, *Some Patterns in the Rise of the Multinational Enterprise,* pp. 58–60.

18. Donner, *The Worldwide Industrial Enterprise,* Ch. 4.

19. David Lilienthal, "The Multinational Corporation," in Melvin Anshen and Leland Bach, eds., *Management and Corporations 1985* (New York: McGraw-Hill, 1960), Ch. 5.

20. Richard F. Gonzalez and Anant R. Neghandi, *The U.S. Overseas Executive: His Orientation and Career Patterns* (East Lansing: Michigan State University Press, 1967).

21. See E. Paul Imhof, "Foreign Service—Multinational Corporation Techniques," *Intereconomics,* No. 10 (1970).

22. Publications in the program of studies, United States Business Performance Abroad, since 1953 have analyzed the cases of Sears in Mexico, Grace in Peru, Creole Petroleum in Venezuela, Firestone in Liberia, Stancvac in Indonesia, United Fruit in Latin America, TWA in Ethiopia, General Electric in Brazil, IBM in France, Aluminium of India, U.S. Plywood in the Congo, and International Basic Economy Corporation worldwide.

23. *Sears, Roebuck de Mexico, S.A.* (Washington, D.C.: National Planning Association, 1953).

24. Stacy May and Galo Plaza, *The United Fruit Company in Latin America* (Washington, D.C.: National Planning Association, 1958).

25. Wayne G. Broehl, Jr., *The International Basic Economy Corporation* (Washington, D.C.: National Planning Association, 1968).

26. May and Plaza, *op. cit.,* p. 239.

27. Raymond Vernon, "The Role of U.S. Enterprise Abroad," *Daedalus* (Winter 1969), p. 1130.

28. Franklin Root, "The Expropriation Experience of American Companies," *Business Horizons* (April 1968).

29. *Ibid.,* p. 69.

30. See International Centre for Settlement of Investment Disputes, Washington, D.C., *Convention on the Settlement of Investment Dispute, in force October, 1966, 1966–67 Annual Report,* and *1971–72 Annual Report.*

31. See Jack N. Behrman, "International Divestment: Panacea or Pitfall?" *Looking Ahead,* Vol. 18, No. 9 (Washington, D.C.: National Planning Association, Nov.–Dec. 1970). Behrman criticizes Hirschmann's, "How to Divest in Latin America and Why," *Essays in International Economics,* Princeton University, International Section (November 1969), and Raul Prebisch's "La Marcha de la Integracion," *Boletin de la Integracion,* INTAL, No. 51 (March 1970).

32. Reasons for "de-politicizing" foreign aid, by replacing bilateral with multi-

lateral assistance and private investment, are set forth by the author in *The Progress of Peoples,* Occasional Paper, Vol. II, No. 4 (June 1969), of the Center for the Study of Democratic Institutions, Santa Barbara, California.

33. Estimates are from Edward A. McCreary, *The Americanization of Europe* (Garden City, N.Y.: Doubleday, 1964).

34. Evidence for Britain is given by Dunning, *The Role of American Investment in the British Economy,* pp. 142–45.

35. *Ibid.,* p. 130.

36. Servan-Schreiber, *The American Challenge,* Ch. 2. Also Raoul Aglion, "French Policy and American Investments in France," *California Management Review,* Vol. 14, No. 4 (Summer 1972).

37. Servan-Schreiber, *The American Challenge,* Ch. 7. See also *Gaps in Technology,* A General Report of the Organization for Economic Cooperation and Development (Paris, 1968).

38. See "Note on Industrial Cooperation," in *Economic Survey of Europe in 1967* (New York: United Nations, 1968), pp. 79–86.

39. See *Joint Business Ventures of Jugoslav Enterprises and Foreign Firms* (New York: Columbia University Press; and Belgrade: Institute of International Politics and Economy, 1968).

40. See *U.S. Business Abroad,* an Economic Report of the Manufacturer's Hanover Trust Company (New York: March 1969). The short-run effect of investment controls on the U.S. balance of international payments depends on the length of the recoupment period. See F. Michael Adler and G. C. Budbauer, "Foreign Investment Controls: Object—Removal," *Columbia Journal of World Business,* Vol. III, No. 3 (May–June 1969).

41. See Safarian, *Foreign Ownership of Canadian Industry.*

42. *Ibid.*

43. As long ago as 1911 the U.S. Supreme Court held that the Sherman Act applied to the foreign activities of American corporations. *U.S.* v. *American Tobacco Company,* 221 U.S. 106.

44. See Sidney E. Rolfe, *The International Corporation* (Paris: International Chamber of Commerce, May 1969), pp. 82–88.

45. Allan Johnstone, *United States Direct Investment in France* (Cambridge: Massachusetts Institute of Technology Press, 1965), Ch. 7.

46. Safarian, *Foreign Ownership of Canadian Industry,* Ch. 3.

47. *Ibid.,* Ch. 6; and Dunning, *The Role of American Investment in the British Economy,* p. 157.

48. Johnstone, *op. cit.,* Ch. 7.

49. See Elizabeth M. Borgese, *The Ocean Regime,* Occasional Paper, Vol. I, No. 5 (October 1968), of the Center for the Study of Democratic Institutions, Santa Barbara, California.

50. Problems of enterprises in an ocean regime were explored at three *Pacem in Maribus* international convocations to explore peaceful uses of the oceans and ocean floor, conducted on the island of Malta in 1970, 1971, and 1972 under the sponsorship of the Center for the Study of Democratic Institutions, Santa Barbara, California.

51. George W. Ball, *The Discipline of Power* (Boston: Little, Brown, 1968).

52. H. V. Perlmutter, Lausanne School of Management Studies.

## Selected Bibliography

Eells, Richard. *Global Corporations: The Emerging System of World Economic Power.* New York: Interbook, 1972.

Eells' work constitutes a definitive exploration of the relationships between multinational companies and national governments.

Vernon, Raymond. Publications of the Multinational Enterprise Project directed by Professor Vernon of the Graduate School of Business Administration of Harvard University are valuable sources of data and analysis, especially on multinational corporate management.

Brown, Courtney C., ed. *World Business.* New York: Macmillan, 1970.

Contains a useful symposium of articles by specialists on different aspects of multinational business.

Hellmann, Rainer. *The Challenge to U.S. Dominance of the International Corporation.* New York: Dunnellen, 1971.

Presents a European view of multinational corporate investment and forecasts a surge of European investment abroad.

Kindleberger, Charles, ed. *The International Corporation: A Symposium.* Cambridge: Massachusetts Institute of Technology Press, 1970.

Economists and lawyers discuss a variety of multinational business topics; includes several industry and country case studies.

Mikesell, Raymond F., *et al. Foreign Investment in Petroleum and Mineral Industries.* Baltimore: Johns Hopkins Press, 1971.

Case studies of investor-host country relations; emphasizes the increasing economic and political control exercised by host countries.

Penrose, Edith T. *The Large International Firm in Developing Countries: The International Petroleum Industry.* Cambridge: Massachusetts Institute of Technology Press, 1968.

Useful analysis of trends in the relationships of oil companies to host governments, emphasizing the increasing control exercised by the latter.

Wilkins, Myra. *The Emergence of Multinational Enterprise.* Cambridge: Harvard University Press, 1970.

An account of the evolution of American multinational business from the Colonial era to 1914.

# PART III

## LEADING ECONOMIC AND POLITICAL ISSUES

CHAPTER **6**

---

# Corporate Economic Power: Concentration or Fragmentation?

O UR INQUIRY thus far has focused on the many criticisms that have been made of the corporation, on its role in the economy, and the adaptations it has recently made to basic social and technological changes. In Part III, we will consider three critical problems resulting from the interaction of this institution with society: the problems of corporate economic power, corporate political power, and corporate government.

Perhaps the oldest of these problems has to do with whether corporate concentration produces undue economic power. Does the great size of some corporations and the concentration of the production of certain goods in the hands of a few companies make competition ineffective as a regulator of business behavior, as many critics maintain? Is monopoly rising and competition declining in the American economy? Is it necessary to curb corporate growth by law to protect the public interest in good products at reasonably low prices? Should large corporate mergers be forbidden? Should government fragment giant enterprises like General Motors and International Business Machines? Should big businesses be regulated

The basic thoughts of this chapter were originally presented in testimony before the Subcommittee on Monopoly of the Select Committee on Small Business of the United States Senate under the chairmanship of Senator Gaylord Nelson of Wisconsin, July 11, 1969, in Washington, D.C. Subsequently, this and other testimony was published by the Subcommittee under the title, *The Role of Giant Corporations in the American and World Economies: Automobile Industry 1969* (Washington, D.C.: U.S. Government Printing Office, 1969). Professor J. Fred Weston made useful comments on this chapter.

further by public commissions, or even owned and operated by government? If market competition can be effective in protecting the public interest, what should be done to enhance its vigor?

# TWO PERSPECTIVES ON CONCENTRATION AND COMPETITION

The belief that big corporations have excessive power over markets, owing to the reduction of competition through concentration, has been expressed in a number of ways by critics. They assert that:

- Aggregate concentration in the economy has been rising.
- Concentration in many individual markets is high.
- Economies of scale do not require giant firms and existing high levels of concentration for maximum efficiency.
- Excessive market concentration has given corporate managers discretionary market power to fix prices, products, and outputs.
- Monopoly power has produced inefficiencies, high prices, inflated profits, and a loss in public welfare.

The critics conclude that to improve these conditions requires breaking up giant companies into smaller units and setting severe limits on business mergers. This perspective on American corporate structure and behavior has been repeated so often and is so widely held in academic and political circles that it should be called the *conventional criticism*.[1] Its central theme is that the classical model of "atomistic" competition is still the proper norm for the organization of the business system.

The conventional criticism has been set forth comprehensively in Blair's *Economic Concentration*.[2] This monumental work was based upon hearings and reports, produced between 1957 and 1971, by the Subcommittee on Antitrust and Monopoly of the United States Senate, while the author was its chief economist. Because the mission of the Subcommittee was to detect monopoly in the American economy, the evidence it examined, naturally, was selective and not representative. Blair's treatment of the issues was also—perhaps subconsciously—*ex parte* rather than judicial in nature. Thus, he blamed price inflation during the period 1966 to 1970 upon the monopoly power of big corporations and held that direct controls of pay and prices would not have been necessary in an economy of medium and small firms. He overlooked the inconvenient fact that price increases during this period were inversely—not directly—related to concentration! And he was strangely silent about the monopoly power of labor unions, which figured heavily in wage inflation and the imposition of direct controls. Blair's book missed an opportunity to advance our understanding of the real causes and effects of industrial concentration. For too long, economists have been repeating each other's speculations about big business behavior. What is urgently needed is more attention to the facts of actual corporate performance.

Opposed to the conventional criticism is another perspective on the problem of corporate economic power, which an increasing number of economists appear to be embracing. We shall call it the *dynamic perspective*. This perspective starts from the premise that changes in business structure are the result of business population dynamics, i.e., changes in business entry, exit, and growth rates, in which mergers play but a minor explanatory role. It sees the contemporary business structure as pluralistic in nature. Present concentration ratios are generally appropriate to their respective industries and not excessive, when viewed against the expanding size of markets and the dynamic nature of competition. Basing its assessment upon a multi-vectored, dynamic model of competition, it argues that markets are, on the whole, effectively competitive, and that competition is in fact rising rather than declining. Hence, it concludes that the market system on the whole is producing an effective allocation of resources, is resulting in normal profits over time, and is stimulating innovations and improvements of products at a satisfactory rate. Accordingly, merger bans and corporate breakups are not in the public interest. Instead, *public policy should focus on preventing specific acts of anticompetitive behavior by businesses, and on opening up of all kinds of markets to new competition.* We propose now to examine both the conventional criticism and the dynamic perspective in the light of the available evidence. (See Figure 1.)

## CORPORATE GROWTH: ATTITUDES AND ACTUALITIES

Americans have always mistrusted large size and concentrated power in their social institutions, whether public or private, political or economic. We have a nostalgia for the modest farming, mercantile and manufacturing enterprises, and the limited governments of the nineteenth century. Our political faith is in democracy and a government of separated parts, each checking and balancing the other. Our society is one of institutional pluralism. We believe that no organization should be able to dominate others. Hence the growth of large institutions has always been viewed with apprehension, if not hostility.

Big business, in particular, has been castigated by generations of critics

FIGURE 1

*Two Perspectives on Corporate Concentration and Competition*

| Perspective | Accepted Theoretical Criterion | Central Instruments of Structural Change | Prevailing Industrial Structure | Prevailing Business Behavior | Effects on Public Welfare | Required Public Policies |
|---|---|---|---|---|---|---|
| I. The Conventional Criticism | Classical Model of Atomistic Competition | Mergers | High Concentration<br>Rising Concentration | Monopolistic:<br>High Prices<br>High Profits<br>Stagnant Technology<br>Inefficiencies<br>Low Adaptability | Adverse:<br>Reduction of Real GNP<br>Worsening Enviroment<br>Poor Products | Break up Big Companies<br>Ban Mergers |
| II. The Dynamic Perspective | Multi-vectored Dynamic Model of Competition | Entry Rates<br>Exit Rates<br>Growth Rates<br>Mergers | Rational Concentration<br>Stable Concentration | Effectively Competitive:<br>Efficient Resource Allocation<br>Normal Profits<br>Innovation<br>Normal Adaptability | Beneficial:<br>Gains in Real GNP<br>Improving Environment | Prohibit Anti-Competitive Behavior<br>Lower Entry Barriers<br>Expand Markets |

as an organ of monopoly, a barrier to the entry of new firms, and even as a menace to democratic government. From the Populist movement that led to the passage of the Sherman and Interstate Commerce acts in the 1880's, to the "trustbusting" program of President Theodore Roosevelt before World War I, to the intensive inquiries into monopoly by the Temporary National Economic Committee in the 1930's, up to the federal attack on conglomerate mergers during the 1960's—recurrent campaigns by government to curb big businesses have marked American history.

Despite the anti-bigness syndrome in the American mind, the enormous enlargement of the nation's population, income, wealth, and markets, as well as the continuing advance of technology, have called forth organizations of increasing size to perform society's tasks. Large business corporations have continued to grow along with the economy. So have labor unions, cooperatives, universities and—*most of all*—governments. Giant corporations as a group have grown faster than the economy as a whole during the past generation, but these relative gains have been modest. Total sales of the five hundred largest industrial corporations tabulated by *Fortune* grew 7.4 percent a year from 1955 to 1971, while the GNP rose 6.2 percent a year. Aggregate sales of the top five hundred firms formed 39 percent of the GNP in 1955 and 48 percent in 1971.[3] The long-term growth of General Motors—leader in the world's corporate establishment—was typical. GM's North American sales of $24 billion formed 2.3 percent of a GNP of $1,047 billion in 1971. Yet forty-two years earlier, in 1929, these sales had been $1.5 billion or 1.5 percent of a $103 billion GNP.[4] Over the same period, the size of government in American society, measured by government purchases, rose from 8.2 percent of the GNP in 1929 to 22.6 percent in 1970!

*It is highly improbable that the long-term tendency of large corporations to grow faster than the economy as a whole—a trend confirmed by the analysis in Chapter 2—will persist indefinitely.* The growth rate of large corporations will diminish if their relative profitability is low or declines. It is ominous that the profitability of the top five hundred industrial companies, which was greater than that of other industrial corporations up to 1965 (measured in rate of return on equity investment), fell below the return on investment of the smaller companies in the period from 1965 to 1971. Whether this turn of events was because of higher labor costs incurred by the heavily unionized large corporations, of lower earnings on their foreign assets, of more rigorous competition from foreign business, or of growing diseconomies of large scale, has not been determined.

Our native predilection for a Jeffersonian society provided the animus for the emotional attack on conglomerate mergers in the late 1960's. The old idea was revived that corporate bigness was, *per se,* bad. Ill-considered proposals were made by Congressmen to enact an absolute dollar limit upon corporate size and to impose a moratorium on all large corporate mergers. Such measures would, of course, have inhibited the changes in industrial structure that could produce economies, enhance competition, expand markets, and benefit consumers. Indeed, they would have vitiated the competition they were intended to invigorate! Fortunately, such extremist proposals were defeated, and a more enlightened and objective assessment of the conglomerate movement subsequently was made.

American society requires an adequate dispersion of economic and political power to buttress individual freedoms and to foster social progress. Vigilance in maintaining competition is in the public interest. There is an important role for antimonopoly actions and for Congressional study and surveillance of the industrial structure and behavior. But, apocalyptic interpretations of economic changes have been quite misleading historically and should be avoided. Corporate growth should be assessed in the light of the expanding world economy, and of the new technologies that create financial and managerial economies of scale. Structural changes, such as conglomeration and multinationalism, should be examined as normal entrepreneurial responses to new opportunities for achieving such economies. Let us reject the conspiratorial theory of corporate growth—that it is motivated simply by a quest for monopoly power over markets.

Two ideas that command wide public belief are that big corporations emerge and grow primarily by acquiring other companies, and that merger activities will radically restructure American industry unless restrained by government. We have seen that both propositions are false.[5] A study by the Federal Trade Commission—surely no biased witness on this subject—showed that less than one-fifth of the growth in dollar assets of the two hundred largest manufacturing companies during the period from 1948 to 1967 was attributable to acquisitions.[6] Internal investment has been the predominant source of growth of big firms. We have also seen that merger waves recede after a few years of hyperactivity and do not persist.

## POSTWAR CHANGES IN CONCENTRATION

Has American business activity become so concentrated in the hands of giant corporations that a few companies control the supply of each type of product and, formally or informally, coordinate their pricing and marketing policies so as to reap monopoly profits? In considering this issue the reader should recall the distinction, made in Chapter 4, between *aggregate* concentration (the size of the firm in relation to the size of the economy) and *industry* concentration (the size of the firm in relation to its industry)

In measuring aggregate concentration, the Federal Trade Commission found that, over the period from 1948 to 1967, the two hundred largest American *manufacturing* companies raised their collective share of total manufacturing assets from 48 to 59 percent, and that the hundred largest firms increased their share from 40 to 48 percent.[7] These findings are consistent with those of Chapter 2, which show that the aggregate concentration of *all* corporate business increased at a moderate rate throughout the postwar period. The salient question is whether this increase threatens to damage the public interest.

We should observe, first of all, that the FTC figures exaggerate the trend toward aggregate concentration because they are based upon the *assets* held by the largest companies. A more significant measure is the *value-added* by these companies, which gives a closer approximation to their true relative importance in the economy. Measured by value-added, the share of the two hundred largest industrial companies rose from 30 percent in 1947, to 42 percent in 1967, reflecting a much lower degree of concentration.[8] Moreover, as Weston has shown, most of the high concentration in 1968 was confined to the six industries of petroleum refining, motor vehicles, steel, industrial chemicals, nonferrous metals, and aircraft. Indeed, these industries contained half of the hundred largest firms in the manufacturing sector. Thus, high concentration was located in a limited sector of the U.S. economy.[9]

The postwar increase in aggregate concentration is, moreover, irrelevant to the vigor of competition. The total number of giant competitors is still far beyond the minimum number needed for effective competition, and—as we have seen in Chapter 2—important changes have occurred in the individual firms composing the "largest one hundred."

To the degree that concentration ratios do measure the vigor of competition—and the correlation between the performance and the structure of industries is not high—it is *industry* concentration that counts.[10] Studies show that *industry concentration in manufacturing industries in the United States, taken as a group, did not change significantly during the period from 1947 to 1968.*[11] One may reconcile this with a moderate rise in macroeconomic concentration by recalling that the postwar period was marked by a strong tendency for giant firms to diversify, either by internal investments or by conglomerate acquisitions. Because big corporations tended to compete in a growing number of industrial markets, industry concentration ratios did not rise. Evidently, postwar structural changes in markets for American manufacturing products have not been of a kind to weaken competitive forces.

A more striking conclusion can be reached if concentration is measured in the global market rather than in the American national market, as it should be in the case of such internationally traded products as automobiles, steel, aluminum, and electronic equipment. General Motors may produce 45 percent of the motor vehicles made in the United States, but it produces less than 25 percent of the automobiles manufactured worldwide. The concentration ratio for American-made automobiles in the global market is radically less than it is in the U.S. market. As global markets have emerged since World War II for a rising number of products, the true concentration of supply to American consumers undoubtedly has diminished on the average. Competition has been greatly enlivened by this development, both in the United States and in other industrial countries.

Finally, we may ask whether high concentration is associated with high profits. The orthodox view is that firms in highly concentrated industries enjoy higher profit rates than other firms because they more often practice collusion in pricing their products. In a recent study, Ornstein refuted this notion. After revealing errors in previous work on this subject, he concluded that "the evidence provides scant support for the traditional hypothesis." [12]

## BARRIERS TO ENTRY INTO BUSINESS

Many who mistrust the economic power of the giant corporation will agree that postwar *structural* changes in American business need not cause concern: but they contend that there are other aspects of big business behavior that weaken competition as a protector of the consumer. It is said that big corporations "overawe" small businesses by their vast size and resources, and thereby deter entry into many lines of business and tend to eradicate small firms.

If this were generally true, one should expect to find a decline in the number of business formations and a rise in business failures. Yet the Department of Commerce index of new business formations stood at its all-time high in 1968, the very year in which corporate mergers reached their peak number. A record 240,000 corporations were formed in that year. We have seen that the ratio of the enterprise population to the human population has remained stable for half a century, and that as large a fraction of American income taxpayers work for themselves as ever. [13] Business failures during the 1960's were relatively fewer than during earlier times.

A promising road to fortune for the young entrepreneur of today is to establish a successful small business, sell it to a large corporation for a capital gain, and then repeat the process. This has been done extensively in retailing, service industries, commercial banking, construction and othe fields. Far from "overawing" the would-be entrant, the big corporations *induce* entry by offering buoyant markets for capital assets. That is why a ban on mergers and acquisitions would depress new and small firms more than large ones.

It is true that the barriers to entry of a new business are formidably high in those industries in which economies of production or marketing are very large, as in the automobile and cigarette industries. Yet the big corporation should be seen as the result of the high entry barriers that are indigenous to such industries, not as the cause of those barriers. General Motors grew in an effort to realize the potential economies that were inherent in advancing technologies and changing markets.

# ECONOMIES OF SCALE

It is often said that big business is too big—that all of the economies of scale could be realized by firms of smaller size. The principal evidence cited in support of this proposition is a study by Bain, in the early 1950's, of plant sizes and the associated production costs in twenty industries.[14] Bain concluded that firms in most industries could realize most potential economies of *plant* scale if their productive capacities were about 5 percent of an industry's total capacity. Because 5 percent is well below the market shares of leading firms in most concentrated industries, the implication was that such firms were too large. Society would benefit, it would seem to follow, from lower costs and prices, if these firms were broken into smaller units.

The flaw in Bain's study is that it overlooks the fact that consumers' interests are best served by *enterprises* of the most efficient size in each industry, and not merely by optimum-scale *plants*. The major thrust of postwar changes in management practices—a subject frequently neglected by economists—has been to enlarge the potential economies of scale of enterprises. Increasingly, enterprises have become multi-plant, multi-product, multi-divisional, and multinational. Williamson well analyzed the character of these economies,[15] which he divided into two categories: economies arising from the horizontal (i.e., multi-divisional) expansion of the corporation, and economies arising from the vertical (i.e., multi-stage) expansion of operations.

What gains are possible from these two forms of expansion? Among the potential economies of *horizontal* integration are these: reduction in the amount of information needed and the costs of transmitting it within the organization; better coordination and control of different plants and divisions because the organization can afford specialists in the assessment of performance; fewer errors and inefficiencies in operations because central managers have available comparative data by which to judge the performance of each plant or division; faster reaction to social and environmental changes because the top managers can be free from routine operations; more rapid seizure of investment opportunities because the corporate staff can include specialists in the identification and evaluation of such opportunities. Not all of these potential gains are necessarily realized by the multi-plant or multi-divisional firm; but if they are persistently lost, the firm will lose its position in the market to more aggressive rivals. To the degree that these economies are realized, society benefits from lower prices of products resulting from lower costs.

Potential gains from the *vertical* integration of enterprises can also be impressive; the technical complementarity of successive industrial processes can be better assured; planning of operations can be done with greater certainty because all stages are under the firm's control; savings of time and transportation costs are possible because the firm can coordinate successive operations; the management has more complete data by which to evaluate performance and make improvements; the cost of information needed for planning is less than if data had to be collected from external sources; cost of bargaining and contracting with independent firms for purchases and sales of materials and products are eliminated.

To these potential economies should be added those accruing from purchasing, marketing, and financing on a larger scale. That enterprise economies of scale are significant, where the market is large, is shown by the wave of European business mergers that took place after the Common Market came into existence. It is also noteworthy that *centrally planned* industrial concentration in the Soviet Union is greater than in the United States.[16]

It is logical to conclude, therefore, that *the primary motive behind the growth of giant corporations has been the effort to realize economies of enterprise scale.* Certainly, there is no convincing evidence to the contrary. Under effective competition, such potential economies will be realized in lower costs, and they will be passed on to the public in the form of better products at lower prices. But *is* competition an effective regulator of large firms?

# A MULTI-VECTORED DYNAMIC
# MODEL OF COMPETITION

The argument is commonly made that, when a major part of the output of an industry is concentrated in the hands of a few big corporations there can be no effective competition. All firms will be aware of the inter-dependence of their pricing and production policies, and this will lead to a tacit collusion among them. According to most economic textbooks, "oligopoly" rules in all concentrated markets, with adverse effects upon consumers; it is said that big companies have "discretionary power" to "administer" their prices.

The idea that competition can be effective only when the number of competitors is very large arises from a narrow and outmoded conception of the nature of competition, inherited from classical economics. Classical theory posited a large number of firms in each industry, all producing and selling a homogeneous product to numerous buyers. In the static frame-work of the classical theory, competition was seen to be a simple process of price adjustment by each firm to a position of equilibrium. At that point the rate of supply equalled the rate of sale, and the price equalled the average cost per unit including normal profits. Price and rate of output were the firm's only decision variables. A large number of competitors was essential to assure that none controlled enough of the supply to be able to keep up the price.

Although the classical model of competition was an economic abstrac-tion, it did bear some resemblance to the economic realities of the nineteenth century. In that age, products were fewer and simpler, firms were smaller, markets were predominantly local, supernumerary income (the surplus of disposable income over that required to buy conventional "necessities") was small, product substitution by buyers was a minor factor, and a slowly developing technology offered few new products. Under such circum-stances, it was sensible to conclude that the number of firms and the con-centration ratio of an industry were good indices of the vigor of competition.

The contemporary American economy is radically different from the one from which classical economic theory emerged. It is marked by rapid technological change, large supernumerary income, great uncertainties, continental and worldwide markets for most products, instantaneous com-munication, well-informed buyers, a high mobility of persons and com-modities, and complex terms of sale. A new theory of competition is needed that takes into account the multitude of decision variables that are involved, and which views competition dynamically as a process occurring over time.

Following the seminal ideas of Joseph Schumpeter and J. M. Clark,[17] we propose that *contemporary competition should be described as a multi-vectored dynamic process.* The vectors of the process include the following:

1. *Intra-product competition:*
    (a) Among existing products of firms in an industry.
        (i) price
        (ii) product design and quality

    (iii)  selling costs
    (iv)  services
    (v)  warranties
    (vi)  credit terms and financing
    (vii)  trade-in allowances
  (b)  Between new and secondhand products of the same industry.

2. *Inter-product competition* (from the products of other industries).
  (a)  among existing products (new or secondhand)
  (b)  among newly developed products

3. *International competition* (from foreign-based firms)
  (a)  among existing products (new or secondhand)
  (b)  among newly developed products

4. *Potential competition* (from entering firms)
  (a)  among existing products (new or secondhand)
  (b)  among newly developed products

At any point in time, the large corporation confronts many types of competition from many directions. Through time, the number and strength of these vectors change, often rapidly and unpredictably. Rivals take advantage of new technology, introduce new products, design new sales or financing techniques. Consumers use their supernumerary incomes to buy the products of other industries. Foreign-based companies offer existing or new products. Large conglomerate enterprises stand ready to enter the market *de novo*. Each competitor must quickly react to the moves of his rivals, with his own changed price, product improvement, new sales terms or new product, if he is not to lose his market position and profitability.

*Under contemporary, multi-vectored, dynamic competition, the probability of tacit collusion among a few producers is negligible because the decision variables are so numerous that no producer is able to anticipate the precise actions of his competitors.* Under these conditions competition is usually effective among a few firms in a concentrated market. Concentration ratios are of relatively minor significance. Clearly, measurement of the effectiveness of competition in a market requires an assessment of all vectors, and a summation of their competitive effects. The strength of competition cannot be assessed by confining attention to *prices*.

# CORPORATE DISCRETIONARY POWER UNDER THE MODEL

In the perspective of a modern theory of competition, the market power of the large corporation is normally constrained by many forces whose influence mounts through time. Consider the following:

1. *Intra-product* competition continues, with no significant change in industry concentration during the past quarter-century. Rivalry in the introduction of new and improved products is intensifying as the pace of technological change accelerates. In addition, mounting stocks of used products compete with new products for the buyer's favor.

2. *Inter-product* competition for consumers' supernumerary income is undoubtedly becoming more intense, as the amount of such income rises. Thus, the critical decision for a consumer often is not which brand of automobile to purchase, but whether to buy an automobile, a vacation, a boat, a summer cottage, or a high-fidelity music system. Such inter-product competition puts pressure upon firms in all industries to keep prices down and to offer new or improved products, in order to gain the favor of fickle and fancy-free consumers. As Weston has noted, in an affluent society "product substitution may be the most severe and devastating form of competition." [18]

3. *International* competition obviously has become more vigorous since World War II as hundreds of foreign corporations have penetrated American markets. Twenty years ago, American auto, steel, electrical, and electronic manufacturers had the domestic market to themselves. Today, the behavior of General Motors is disciplined by Volkswagen, Toyota, Datsun, Mercedes-Benz, and Fiat, as well as by Ford and Chrysler. The prices of U.S. Steel are influenced by Mitsubishi and Thyssen as well as by Bethlehem and Youngstown. The bids of General Electric on turbines are tempered by those of English Electric and Brown-Boveri, as well as by Westinghouse.

4. *Potential* competition has also been a vector of increasing force as the postwar corporate conglomeration and diversification movement gained momentum. The strategy of business diversification has meant that many large firms, having both the motive and the resources, are ready to enter any market where profit opportunities appear bright. Established firms in any industry cannot prudently ignore the probability that conglomerates will enter their industry if they maintain high prices and profits.

The thesis that giant companies hold such great economic power that they are able to shape their own environments, and that their planning of products, prices, and production schedules has "replaced the market," was advanced by Galbraith.[19] However, it has been decisively refuted by all we know about the rationale and processes of corporate management. Corporate planning is an attempt by managers to anticipate market signals, and it is based upon market-determined prices. Far from "replacing" the market, it is a technique for utilizing market guidance more effectively.[20] Corporate plans are frequently revised as fresh information is received from the market. Market disfavor caused General Motors to discontinue producing the Corvair, as, at an earlier time, it caused Ford to withdraw the Edsel,

Chrysler the De Soto, and Lockheed the Electra. Inability to compete successfully with IBM in the full-line computer business caused such corporate giants as General Electric and RCA to discontinue their efforts, despite meticulous planning. If the large firm really has the power to make consumers buy what it decides to make, why does it spend millions in market research intended to find out what consumers want? Indeed, the powerful thrust of the recent consumerism movement is, by itself, a refutation of the notion that corporate planning has "replaced the market."

We concur in the conclusion reached by Kaplan: The weight of evidence indicates that contemporary competition is generally effective and that it exerts a strong discipline upon the behavior of large corporations.[21] While this discipline differs from the simple price-changing routine of classical atomistic competition, it is nonetheless effective. As Kaplan observed, "When compared with the improvement in performance that a consumer's dollar has been able to buy in drugs and gasoline, in sound reproducing machines, or in miracle drugs, the downward price pressure of atomistic competition appears relatively feeble."

The keystone of a public policy for effective competition should be to strengthen *all* vectors of the competitive process. A powerful instrument for enlivening *international* competition would be to remove remaining tariffs and import quotas and to convert national into world markets. *When a company bulks large in the American market, public policy should enlarge the market rather than diminish the enterprise.* European governments have organized a continental market, able to absorb the output of firms large enough to achieve economies of scale and numerous enough to assure effective competition. Paradoxically, while Europeans have been enlarging markets and promoting business mergers for competitive efficiency, American critics have been calling for the disintegration of our giant corporations for the same purpose!

Public policy can also increase *potential* competition by lowering the barriers to the entry of new firms into concentrated industries. The important barriers to entry, as Brozen has pointed out, are not national advertising, product differentiation, or economies of scale.[22] They are: the licenses, permits, and certificates required by governmental authorities to enter industries; the tariffs and import quotas on foreign products; and the blockages, imposed by the antitrust authorities, to entrance into industries. The licensing and certifying requirements of federal, state, and local governments should be reviewed, and purged of anticompetitive elements. Barriers to imports of the products of concentrated industries should be leveled. The Antitrust Division of the Department of Justice should recognize that mergers can enhance, and need not necessarily diminish, competition.

When viewed in the light of dynamic multi-vectored competition, the merger "guidelines" published by the Department of Justice in 1968 are sorely wanting. They are based upon the dubious theory that "the conduct of the individual firms in a market tends to be controlled by the structure of that market," that is, by the number of sellers, their market shares, and the height of barriers to entry. In practical effect, they challenge any substantial business acquisition by a company that serves 10 percent or more of its "market." They dogmatically assert that economies and improvements in efficiency *cannot* be used to justify a merger—except in unusual cases. Above all, they neglect market-expanding changes in the nation and in the world, growing inter-product competition, and rising potential competition of large conglomerate corporations. We should compliment the Department of Justice for its effort to provide a map intended to guide businessmen through the antitrust wilderness. Yet, unless the merger "guidelines" are modified to recognize all of the vectors of competition, and are administered with wisdom, they could inhibit rational changes in American industrial organization that would be of great benefit to consumers.

It would be folly to dismember a corporation whose large size has been gained by competitive superiority and maintained without predatory or exclusionary behavior, such as cutthroat pricing. This would be to follow a policy of turning on a company when it succeeds in the competitive game. Rather, public policy toward big businesses should involve, among other things, vigilant observation. The author wrote in 1951:

> In the face of inadequacies of knowledge—which may be inherent in a dynamic economy—may it not be preferable to leave the number and size-distribution of firms to the working out of market forces, in each line of trade where competition appears to be reasonably effective, and there are no real evidences of monopolistic behavior? If the giant firm is really less efficient than its smaller rivals, does not time bring the remedy in a slackened rate of growth for it relative to its competitors? Should not the same uncertainties that preclude a general public policy of enforced merger to achieve efficiency make us pause before adopting a public policy of enforced disintegration for the same purpose? [23]

This observation has as much validity today as when it was written.

Those who view big business and industrial concentration in the dynamic perspective will reject—as unnecessary and unwise—such proposals as those made by Senator Philip A. Hart, during July of 1972, to establish an Industrial Reorganization Commission with power to break up leading firms in concentrated industries.[24] The Hart bill would establish a *presumption* that a company possessed unlawful monopoly power if (1) its average after-tax return on net worth exceeded 15 percent a year for five consecutive years out of the most recent seven years; or if (2) there had been no substantial price competition among two or more companies in any line of commerce in any section of the country for three consecutive years out of the most recent five years; or if (3) any four or fewer corporations accounted for 50 percent or more of the sales in any line of commerce in any section of the country in any one of the most recent three years. Without regard to the above criteria, the Commission would be *required* to develop reorganization plans for seven of the most concentrated industries.

The Hart bill embodies many of the fallacies regarding industrial concentration that have been exposed in this chapter: that a few large firms in an industry behave collusively; that markets are regional or national rather than multinational; that only price competition counts; etc. Its administration would be a nightmare. The Industrial Reorganization Commissioner would be a *de facto* "industrial czar," with power to restructure a large part of the American economy. Although his decisions would be subject to review by an Industrial Reorganization Court, judicial battles over divestment orders would create intolerable uncertainty and would hold up business investment plans for years. The Hart bill fails to go beyond old textbook models of competition and to understand the many dimensions of competitive processes in concentrated industries. It reflects a naive faith in the omniscience of bureaucratic judgments that is quite unjustified by historical experience. Finally this bill wrongly places the burden of proof for justifying their size on the large corporations, whereas it should be the government that is required to prove that large size is contrary to the public interest.

## THE ECONOMIC BALANCE SHEET OF LARGE-SCALE ENTERPRISE

If big businesses in concentrated industries truly behaved as oligopolists, one would find higher prices, persistently higher profits, more extensive advertising, and less product innovation among such industries than among unconcentrated industries. However, the facts show either the contrary or insignificant differences. During the period of price inflation from 1965 to 1970, prices rose most in the *unconcentrated* industries. Over time, the profit rates of businesses move toward an average, whether or not such businesses have above- or below-average profits, and whether or not they are characterized by concentration in large firms.[25] Similarly, Scherer found that differences among industries in the productivity of research and development activities depend mainly on technological opportunities and not upon concentration or profitability.[26] All these findings are, of course, consistent with the modern dynamic theory of competition and imply an absence of great economic power among large firms in concentrated industries.

Finally, what may be said about the overall effects of large-scale concentrated enterprise upon the productivity of the American economy and the welfare of its people? Here, again, there are two quite different perspectives. Scherer estimated the "costs of monopoly power," in 1966, at around 6.2 percent of the GNP.[27] His estimated costs included alleged misallocations of resources, regulated price distortions, poor cost control in the aerospace and other "sheltered" industries, wasteful promotion, below-capacity operations, cross-hauling of freight, and excess capacity in the business system. Clearly, these figures are based upon an idealistic view of how a fragmented business structure might perform under static conditions.

Proceeding from a different—and in the author's opinion a more valid —analysis of the effects of large-scale, concentrated enterprise in a progressive economy, Weston estimated the *net gains* in real output of the present business structure, *vis-à-vis* a fragmented, static structure, at between 2.1 and 7.4 percent of the GNP.[28] In his view, economies of plant scale, of vertical and horizontal integration of firms, of management and cost control, of marketing and financing, and of the avoidance of subsidies to small enterprise (such as the $5 billion a year now paid to farmers) help to lower the costs and the prices of products. Weston's emphasis on benefits from large-scale enterprise are supported by Denison's assignment of nearly 10 percent of the long-term growth of the GNP of the United States to the growth of the national market, which led to large corporations and industrial concentration.[29] The Weston estimate has greater credibility because it does not measure gains and losses from large scale against an unrealistic standard, set by a static theory of competition, as does Scherer's estimate.

We conclude that *the current degree of concentration of business in large corporations is consistent with effective competition. It adds significantly to the welfare of the American people.* To maintain effective competition in the future calls for a positive antimonopoly policy—one that lowers barriers to entry and enlarges markets. Those who would disintegrate large corporations have not sustained the burden of proof that this would serve the public interest.

## NOTES

1. See John Kenneth Galbraith, *The New Industrial State* (Boston: Houghton Mifflin, 1967), for the best of the conventional criticism.

2. See John M. Blair, *Economic Concentration: Structure, Behavior and Public Policy* (New York: Harcourt Brace Jovanovich, 1973).

3. *Fortune* (May 1972), pp. 184–186. Because corporate sales usually involve double counting while GNP represents only sales to final users, corporate growth may be exaggerated.

4. Alfred P. Sloan, Jr., *My Years with General Motors* (Garden City, N.Y.: Doubleday, 1964), p. 199, and *Annual Report of General Motors Corporation 1971.*

5. See Chapters 2 and 4.

6. See *Studies by the Staff, Cabinet Committee on Price Stability* (Washington, D.C.: U.S. Government Printing Office, January 1969), pp. 79. These findings are generally consistent with those of Weston for an earlier period. See J. Fred Weston, *The Role of Mergers in the Growth of Large Firms* (Berkeley and Los Angeles: University of California Press, 1953), pp. 101–103.

7. See *Studies by the Staff, Cabinet Committee on Price Stability, op. cit.,* p. 45.

8. Betty Bock, *Statistical Games and the "200 Largest" Industrials: 1954 and 1968* (New York: National Industrial Conference Board, 1970).

9. J. Fred Weston, "Business Power over Markets and Consumers," in *Contemporary Challenges in the Business-Society Relationship,* ed. G. A. Steiner (Los Angeles: Graduate School of Management, UCLA, 1972).

10. After an exhaustive review of the empirical evidence concerning the link between the structure of a market and its performance, John M. Vernon wrote, "The overwhelming conclusion would appear to be that solid factual support for public policy in this area does not exist." See his *Market Structure and Industrial Performance: A Review of Statistical Findings* (Boston: Allyn and Bacon, 1972), p. 117.

11. *Studies by the Staff, Cabinet Committee on Price Stability,* p. 58.

12. Stanley I. Ornstein, "Concentration and Profits," *The Journal of Business,* Vol. 45, No. 4 (October 1972), p. 528.

13. See Chapter 2.

14. J. S. Bain, *Barriers to New Competition* (Cambridge: Harvard University Press, 1956). See also Caleb A. Smith, "Survey of the Empirical Evidence on Economies of Scale," in *Business Concentration and Price Policy: A Conference* (Princeton: Princeton University Press, 1955), pp. 229–230.

15. Oliver E. Williamson, *Corporate Control and Business Behavior* (Englewood Cliffs, N.J.: Prentice-Hall, 1970).

16. See Lars Engwall, "Industrial Concentration in Different Economic Systems" (ms., Carnegie-Mellon University, 1972).

17. See Joseph A. Schumpeter, *Capitalism, Socialism and Democracy* (New York: Harper, 1942); also J. M. Clark, *Competition as a Dynamic Process* (Washington, D.C.: Brookings Institution, 1961). The author first adumbrated the elements of a multi-vectored, dynamic theory of competition in 1951. See Neil H. Jacoby, "Perspectives on Monopoly," *Journal of Political Economy,* Vol. 59, No. 6 (December 1951), 523–537. Harold Demsetz presented a multi-dimensional model of competition in "The Nature of Equilibrium in Monopolistic Competition," *Journal of Political Economy,* Vol. LXVII, No. 1 (February 1959). Recently, Yale Brozen stressed the many variables in the competitive process and showed that, in the real world, advertising is a productive and pro-competitive activity, substituting cheaply provided information for expensive costs of search by buyers and sellers. See his "An Ivory Tower (Chicago) View of Advertising," read to the Eastern Conference of the American Association of Advertising Agencies, June 5, 1972. See also J. Fred

Weston, "Pricing Behavior of Large Firms," *Western Economic Journal,* Vol. 10, No. 1 (March 1972), pp. 1–18. Weston shows that dynamic multi-vectored competition, under uncertainty, reduces the probability of effective collusion and increases the probable gains from independent action by a firm.

18. Weston, "Business Power over Markets and Consumers."

19. Galbraith, *The New Industrial State.*

20. Neil H. Jacoby, "Professor Galbraith's *The New Industrial State,*" *California Management Review,* Vol. 11, No. 3 (Spring 1968).

21. A. D. H. Kaplan, *Big Enterprise in a Competitive System* (Washington, D.C.: Brookings Institution, 1954), pp. 243–245. Also A. D. Kaplan, Joel B. Dirlam and Robert F. Lanzillotti, *Pricing in Big Business* (Washington, D.C.: Brookings Institution, 1958), pp. 286–290.

22. Yale W. Brozen, "Competition, Efficiency and Antitrust" (Address to the Business Economists' Conference, University of Chicago, May 1, 1969).

23. Jacoby, "Perspectives on Monopoly," 527.

24. See the *Congressional Record,* Vol. 118, No. 115 (July 24, 1972).

25. Yale W. Brozen, "Significance of Profits for Antitrust Policy," *Antitrust Bulletin,* 14 (Spring 1969).

26. F. M. Scherer, "Firm Size, Market Structure, Opportunity and the Output of Patented Inventions," *American Economic Review,* Vol. 55 (December 1965).

27. F. M. Scherer, *Industrial Market Structure and Economic Performance* (Chicago: Rand McNally, 1970), p. 408.

28. Weston, "Business Power over Markets and Consumers," p. 24.

29. Edward F. Denison, *The Sources of Economic Growth in the United States* (New York: Committee for Economic Development, 1962).

# CHAPTER 7

# Corporate Political Power: Involvement or Detachment?

D^OES American corporate business hold inordinate political power? This question is raised as persistently as whether it possesses undue economic power. Indeed, critics often fail to make a clear distinction between the political and the economic powers of business. Here, we distinguish the two by defining "political power" as the ability of a corporation to influence *government,* and "economic power" as the corporate ability to control *markets.* For example, there was widespread public concern over the charge that International Telephone and Telegraph donated money to the Republican Party for its 1972 convention in order to procure the dismissal of antitrust charges against it. Although the allegation was never proved, and ITT subsequently withdrew its gift, the suspicion remained that the company had excessive political influence and was prepared to use it.

The fundamental question of corporate political power is: What are the proper limits of business influence upon government? And there are related issues: Should profit-seeking enterprises be activists or passivists in the nation's political life? When does corporate involvement in public affairs become an improper intrusion into spheres alien to the purpose and competence of business? Does business lobbying corrupt public officials, pervert the law, and damage the public welfare? Given the many "interest groups" in American society, each putting pressure upon government to promote its special projects, should public policy seek to curtail the

I am indebted to my graduate students for resarch on many subjects covered in this chapter; the work of James M. Carbonne, III, was especially helpful.

influence of business alone or should it curtail the influence of trade unions, professional organizations, and other groups of producers as well? How can an equitable balance of political power be created? These have become pressing issues at a time when the business corporation is called upon to become more involved in solving social problems at home and abroad.

The overweening influence of big business upon government is an ancient complaint, dating back to the days of the freewheeling entrepreneurship of the nineteenth century. Even today, many believe that business dominates elections through campaign contributions, controls legislatures by lobbying, influences regulatory agencies by favors and promises of lucrative positions, and even sways the courts. "Major corporations are the prime institutions of power in our society," wrote one observer, echoing the sentiments of this school of thought.[1] Some compare the modern corporation to an "estate" of medieval times. Just as medieval society was organized around the four "estates" of nobility, church, bourgeois, and peasantry, so, critics say, American society is organized around the corporation, the government, the labor union, and the university. Admittedly, the large company does have a feudal aspect, with its own welfare system, intelligence network, security apparatus, private air transport system, and even, in the case of the multinational company, its own foreign policy! But whether we can conclude from this that the corporation in America has the great power ascribed to it by its critics is a matter we must investigate.

## POLITICIZATION AND SOCIAL PLURALISM

In assessing the significance of corporate political power, we must recall the traditional antigovernmental bias of American political thought. The founders of our republic were individualists who sought to curb the authority of the state over the citizen. They designed a government of limited powers, divided into three branches, each checking and balancing the others. They wrote a constitution guaranteeing the individual's right to associate freely with others. These factors, the federal structure of American government, and the wide ethnic diversity of the country encouraged the formation of all manner of private organizations to which the state has delegated elements of its authority. The inevitable consequence is a pluralistic society, composed of many institutions, each competing with the others for the time, attention, and resources of the public, and each seeking the favor of government in its effort to expand its role in the society. Family, school, church, trade union, farmers' association, university, and business corporation vie for political influence. All are "politicized" in the sense of being involved with and seeking to influence the government. *In a pluralistic society, every institution has a right—if not a duty—to do what it can to survive. Pressure upon government for this purpose is a legitimate expression of a fundamental drive.*

In this situation of institutional competition it was expected that each social organ would be restrained by the actions of the others. Countervailing power would prevent any single institution from dominating the others, or from controlling the government and using it to elevate its special interests above the public interest. The general aim was to maintain a felicitous balance.[2] Should a serious disproportion develop, balance could be restored either by limiting the dominant institution or by creating additional countervailing power to oppose it. In political democracies the latter course is usually easier and tends to be the most frequently used. Thus, Franklin D. Roosevelt's New Deal, in the 1930's, gave powerful encouragement to labor and farmers' organization in order to offset the political influence of corporate business. But it also cut back business power directly.

Institutional pluralism would seem to require institutional politicization. If only to assure its survival, each institution is compelled to involve itself with government. Thus, the church must continually fight a political battle to maintain its immunity from taxation. The university tries to maintain its academic freedom and insulation from politics, despite a heavy dependence upon state and federal governments for financial support. The labor union has its Washington lobby and its political action committee to elect senators and representatives pledged to foster the interests of organized labor. The profit-seeking corporation likewise has no choice but to be as politically influential as the law—and its resources—permit. Hedged in by a multiplicity of local, state, and federal regulations affecting building, zoning, health, safety, insurance, employment, workmen's compensation, social security, wage and hour standards, equal opportunity rules, securities issuance, financing, fees and taxes, product and advertising standards, *et cetera,* corporate business naturally takes political action to defend the freedom of action that remains to it. While Charles E. Wilson overstated the point when he remarked, "What is good for General Motors is good for the country," there *is* a large commonality between the corporate interest and the public interest; much corporate involvement with the government simply expresses and supports values widely accepted in the society.

Indeed, corporate political action is protected by the Federal Constitution, the political foundation of the United States. The First Amendment guarantees to all citizens the right to petition the government "for a redress of grievances," a right later extended by the Supreme Court to corporations.[3] The complete insulation of the corporation from political affairs, long demanded by social observers who feared and still fear the "money power" of corporate interests, would be unconstitutional.[4] The salient issue is not *whether* corporate business should play a political role, but *how extensive* that role should be. It is idle to demand the insulation of business from politics so long as American society maintains its present institutional structure. This does not mean, however, that reasonable restrictions should not be imposed upon corporate political activities.

## INSTRUMENTS OF CORPORATE POLITICAL ACTION

The big corporation endeavors to influence all phases of politics, including elections, legislation, and executive actions. To this end it employs a variety of instruments. It makes contributions—indirectly—to political candidates, joins trade and industry associations, maintains a Washington office, operates a Public Affairs Department at its headquarters, gives to charities whose sponsors' goodwill it seeks, lends its executives for tours of duty in government, and lobbies in federal, state, and municipal corridors for governmental actions that will lighten its burdens and expand its opportunities. Let us quickly review the nature of this political activity.

According to recent surveys, three-quarters of all large American companies maintain a Public Affairs Department, advisory to the chief executive, whose broad mission is to shape public attitudes congenial to the company. This department typically conducts relations with governments, reviews proposed legislation, and campaigns for or against bills affecting the company. It contributes time, money, and facilities to projects in the communities where the company operates. It also sponsors programs of political education for employees. The programs are generally nonpartisan —business must exist under both Democratic and Republican administrations![5]

Because so many crucial decisions affecting business are made by the federal government, more than four hundred companies maintain full-time Washington representatives with supporting staffs.[6] The Washington "rep" maintains liaison with the Congress and the executive agencies, informs his company about pending legislation, feeds information and opinion to the Congress and the federal agency staffs, and often helps to sell his company's products to the government. Indeed, it is not unknown for the Washington representative's office to offer, without charge, research, report writing, and speech writing services to members of the Congress. The profession of the Washington representative is a sophisticated one, dependent upon tact, imagination, and personal contacts. Thousands of smaller companies, unable to afford full-time representation in Washington, retain part-time counsel; some four thousand Washington lawyers are said to serve in this capacity. Only a minority of corporate representatives are registered under the Federal Regulation of Lobbying Act of 1946 because lobbying is not the "principal" business of the majority.

Membership in business "interest" groups and trade associations has been a traditional instrument of corporate political action. Four business "interest" organizations stand out: the National Association of Manufacturers, founded in 1885, is composed of some 14,000 corporate members; the United States Chamber of Commerce, founded in 1912, is a federation of municipal and state chambers of commerce and of trade associations; the Business Council, founded by President Roosevelt in 1933, is a small group of top business leaders that meets twice a year with high federal officials to review the status of the economy and economic policies; and the Committee for Economic Development, which was established in 1942, is a group of high-level executives from two hundred major corporations and universities, who work together to design public policies that will promote the general welfare. In addition to these major business interest organizations, there are several thousand trade associations representing particular industries, regions, and types of business. These normally focus upon the narrower and more specific issues that directly affect their members, whereas the interest groups deal with broader questions of fiscal, monetary, tariff, subsidy, and other federal actions affecting most or all business enterprises.

The appointment of corporate leaders as high government officers— and vice versa—is often cited as a potent source of business influence upon government decisions. The Pentagon has usually been directed by tycoons, as the cases of William S. Knudsen, Charles E. Wilson, Neil McElroy, Robert McNamara, and David Packard illustrate. However, studies show that the number of businessmen in public service is relatively low. And, there is little evidence that businessmen in public service are biased toward business. On the contrary, to take an important example, the military hardware industry realized very low profits during the 1960's as a result of the tough procurement policies of the businessmen who headed the Department of Defense.

Contributions to the election campaigns of candidates for public office represent the most controversial and publicized form of corporate political action. The Tillman Act, passed by the Congress in 1907, prohibits corporate contributions to political parties and candidates in national elections —a prohibition extended to labor unions in 1947—but the law is evaded by a myriad of stratagems. Corporations—and unions—make payments to public relations firms working for candidates; their executives make "personal" donations, later recouped in a salary payment; they lend their aircraft, personnel, and other facilities to candidates without charge; expensive "testimonial" dinners are held at $1,000 per plate; gifts are made to individuals or committees who serve as intermediaries; *et cetera.* Numerous efforts have been made to amend the Tillman Act, and the law now does require the reporting of some political contributions. But, *there is probably no truly effective way of preventing political contributions by unions, corporations, and other producer organizations.*

It must be emphasized that the arsenal of weapons for political action possessed by American labor unions, farm organizations, and professional groups, such as the American Medical Association, are quite as formidable as those of corporate business. It would be both unfair and unwise to limit one without at the same time limiting the others.

# THE DECLINE OF
# CORPORATE POLITICAL POWER

There can be little doubt that the relative political strength of business has fallen dramatically during the past century. Business' political influence rose rapidly after the Civil War and reached a pinnacle in the 1880's. In that era, railroads spread rapidly across the nation without hindrance because their promoters had state legislatures "in their pockets." Stock speculation was unregulated and knew no bounds. John D. Rockefeller put together his Standard Oil trust, and other entrepreneurs emulated him in other industries. This was the golden age of corporate political power and freedom of action—golden to those who wielded the power, but something less than golden to the underprivileged who suffered from its exercise.

The first strong checkrein upon untrammeled *laissez-faire* was the Interstate Commerce Act in 1887; it was followed shortly by the Sherman (Antitrust) Act in 1890. For the first time, the Federal government began to constrain corporate behavior, and state regulations were also tightened. Nevertheless, business continued to have relatively wide freedom of operation for the rest of the nineteenth century and the first quarter of the twentieth century. Government then imposed little restraint on the processes of production, the products, the employee relations, the marketing tactics, or the financing methods of corporations.

But not being exempt from Lord Acton's maxim, "Power tends to corrupt and absolute power corrupts absolutely," business corporations often abused their privileges. The record of the railroads and of the electrical utility industry is replete with examples of corruption. The history of unsanitary meat packing, adulterated foods, dangerous drugs, false advertising, "blue-sky" securities, and collapsible corporations has often been told and need not be repeated here. These episodes of business misbehavior should be viewed in the context of a turbulent period of economic expansion that was also marked by great achievements. Judicial remedies, such as pretrial discovery and class action lawsuits, were not invented until a later era.

A second drastic reduction in the political power of American corporate business occurred during the Great Depression of the 1930's. This crisis shook the faith of the American people in the capability of its industrial and financial leaders, even in the enterprise system itself. Roosevelt's New Deal Congresses imposed a big network of governmental regulations upon business, administered by such new federal agencies as the Securities and Exchange Commission, the National Labor Relations Board, the Federal Power Commission, and the Federal Communications Commission. Corporate income taxes were raised sharply; new payroll taxes were levied to finance old age pensions and unemployment insurance. Roosevelt sought to make political capital of the popular disillusionment with business; and he made business a scapegoat for errors of federal economic policy that had deepened and prolonged the depression. As we have seen, the Democratic Congresses also weakened the relative political influence of business by nourishing the countervailing power of labor unions and farm groups.

The generally good performance of the American economy during World War II as "the arsenal of democracy," and its postwar avoidance of large-scale unemployment, served to restore popular confidence in corporate business. But it did not bring any reduction in regulation and taxation. On the contrary, taxation rose and regulations multiplied. And later, during the 1960's, new political interest groups emerged, and developed growing influence in Washington and the state capitols. Environmentalists, civil rights leaders, and consumer advocates—all criticized corporate behavior and sought new constraints upon it. As the 1970's began, the *relative* political influence of corporate business was probably less than it had been since the dark years of the Great Depression; certainly, it was far less than during the halcyon days of the 1920's.

## PRESENT CORPORATE
## POLITICAL POWER

Notwithstanding a long-term decline, the question remains whether corporate political power remains excessive. What is the extent of corporate influence upon government today? By what criteria should the proper limits to the political power of the corporation be judged?

Epstein has suggested that the political influence of corporate enterprise should be judged excessive if it persistently threatens to deny other social institutions effective access to, and influence upon, centers of governmental decision-making. Judged by this standard, he concluded: "Corporate political power does not presently constitute a danger to the American pluralistic democracy, which continues to produce legislation, rulings, decisions and programs that are contrary to the desires of significant corporate interests." [7]

The validity of Epstein's conclusion might be tested by compiling a year-by-year scorecard of the successes and failures of business in obtaining from the Congress the kind of legislation it favored. If business persistently had a large margin of successes over failures in getting favored legislation enacted and in getting undesired measures defeated, we might conclude that it did, indeed, possess formidable political power.

Unfortunately, such a scorecard does not exist—and cannot easily be made. The primary difficulty is the problem of determining what *the* interest of business is. *At any given time, business corporations are split on many national issues; there does not appear to be a monolithic "business interest."* Thus, petroleum companies have opposed liberal oil import quotas, while petrochemical companies have favored them in order to obtain less expensive feedstocks; steel companies have sought restraints upon imports of foreign steel, whereas automobile companies and other large users of steel have fought them; and even with respect to such matters as labor union legislation or antipollution regulation, businessmen are far from presenting a united front because firms in some industries are much more deeply affected than those in other industries.

All of this notwithstanding, it is still possible to identify some sort of general business stand on certain public issues of recent years. Business did succeed in obtaining the accelerated depreciation and investment tax credits that it desired, and it defeated labor union efforts to repeal the "right-to-work" provision in the Taft-Hartley Act, which permits states to ban union shop agreements. On the other hand, business lost its battle against the Water Quality Standards Act in 1965, the Air Quality Act in 1967, the Fair Packaging and Labeling Act in 1966, the Highway Safety and Motor Vehicle Safety Standards Acts in 1966, and the Consumers Protection Credit Act in 1968. All of this "consumerist" legislation was passed against the determined opposition of business "interest" organizations and of some of the largest companies in the nation. The record leaves the distinct impression that, during the 1960's, business was fighting a defensive rearguard action against other interest groups in the Congress—and that it failed more often than not.

There is also abundant evidence that, during the 1960's, corporate business was generally unable to bend the administrative agencies of the national government to its will. The Antitrust Division of the Department of Justice laid down restrictive guidelines for business mergers and filed many suits against conglomerate mergers. The Federal Trade Commission promulgated tough new rules regarding false and deceptive advertising. The Federal Power Commission continued, against strong protests, to hold down the well-head price of natural gas. The Federal Communications Commission tightened its requirements for the renewal of radio and television broadcasting licenses. The Securities and Exchange Commission compelled diversified companies to disclose their sales and profits by product lines, and deepened its inquiries into the accounting and financial reporting practices of publicly held companies. All these actions refute the position of the conventional critics that corporate business has "captured" its regulators and that federal agencies have become passive agents in defending their business "clients" before the Congress and the public. While most experts present at a conference convened by the Brookings Institution during 1971 agreed that "much of business regulation in the United States is in deep trouble," their consensus was that the causes were complex and went far beyond undue solicitude for business interests.[8]

There has been a strong trend in judicial decisions, during the past decade, toward increasing the liabilities of business for the performance of products under warranty, for damage to third parties, for pollution of air and water, and for other causes. The potential costs of such liabilities have been multiplied by the rising incidence of class-action suits, in which one person may sue in behalf of thousands of others who stand in a similar relationship to a company. Stockholder suits alleging misrepresentation or misbehavior by corporate officers and directors have become more frequent as Securities and Exchange Commission regulations have become more strict. This continuing judicial enlargement of business responsibilities reflects the influence of public opinion upon the courts; and it clearly demonstrates the weakness of corporate political influence.

Finally, the general acceptance of Keynesian economics must be mentioned. It led to the passage of the Employment Act of 1946 and to an active role for government in guiding the level of economic activity. When prosperity became a *political* responsibility, the views of businessmen on economic affairs became less influential. Business dependence upon government deepened.

Thus, the weight of evidence supports Epstein's conclusion that corporate political power is not a danger to American pluralistic democracy. Even more, it suggests that corporate *influence* upon government continued to wane significantly during the 1960's, despite increasing corporate *involvement* with the government. A survey of readers of the *Harvard Business Review* in 1968 revealed that most of those who responded believed business political activity to be limited or moderate in extent and to have been ineffective in its efforts.[9] *The notion that corporate enterprise "dominates" or unduly influences the American government simply does not withstand examination.*

Indeed, case studies of the political decision-making process show that it is extremely complex. Many interest groups are involved. Business interests are frequently divided—and politicians in the end decide by whom they will be influenced! [10]

## CORPORATE VERSUS UNION POLITICAL POWER

Businessmen generally contend that corporate political activity is essential to counterbalance the awesome political influence of the labor unions. An inquiry into the proper limits of corporate political action thus requires a consideration of the relative political strength of organized labor.

Certainly the political assets of American labor organizations are formidable in both manpower and money. Unlike corporations, eighteen million union members vote. With the union shop prevailing in most states and union dues being deducted from members' paychecks, labor unions have a steady inflow of funds, estimated to be around $700 million per year in 1963.[11] Usually, local unions retain 60 percent and transmit 40 percent to the international unions, providing the latter with ample resources to influence government. The political strength of labor is shown by the powerful role it has played on labor-business-public federal bodies dealing with production and wages, such as the Federal Pay Board, established by President Nixon in 1971.[12] It is also implied by the strenuous efforts of American politicians, from presidents downward, to cultivate the favor of trade union leaders and their members. *Indeed, many a businessman seeking a favor from government has found that his most effective course was to get the support of the leaders of the unions representing his employees!*

Organized labor has consciously used its political assets to elect candidates and to foster legislation supporting its interests. Among registered lobbyists, the AFL-CIO, the Letter Carriers, and the Postal Workers are among the largest spenders. The former Political Action Committee of the CIO and the more recent Committee on Political Education (COPE) of the AFL-CIO have been major instruments of labor's political aims. Ever since the passage of the National Labor Relations Act in 1935, organized labor has had an informal political alliance with the Democratic Party, which has become known (inaccurately) as "the party of labor," just as the Republican Party is often described (equally inaccurately) as "the party of business." Unlike their European counterparts, however, American trade union members have traditionally exhibited an independence of party affiliation that has distressed union leaders, who have been unable to deliver a solid union vote to candidates of their choice.

Notwithstanding the ability of organized labor normally to counter the political influence of corporate business, the relative strength of both in governmental affairs has fallen since World War II. *Both the union and the corporation have lost political power in the postwar era as new environmentalist, consumerist, civil rights, and other organizations have come to the fore.* Evidence of the relative slippage of labor unions is impressive. Union membership has declined sharply in relation to the size of the labor force, as the economy has moved from blue collar to white collar worker dominance. Better educated union members have become increasingly critical of union leadership, which, in some large unions, such as the United Mine Workers, has been torn by dissension. Growing affluence has moved many union members toward a conservative social ideology. Recently the record of union success in electing friendly legislators has been no better than that of corporate business. We can concur with Epstein's judgment, "Labor no more controls the political order of the United States than do business corporations." [13] The corporate executive's fear of union domination of government is no more justified than the union chieftain's concern with corporate invincibility.

## POSTWAR SHIFTS IN POLITICAL ALIGNMENTS

Henry Simons pointed out a profound truth when he wrote: "All the grosser mistakes in economic policy, if not most manifestations of democratic corruption, arise from focusing upon the interests of people as producers rather than upon their interests as consumers." [14] *The basic flaw in the distribution of political power among American economic institutions is that producer interests rather than consumer interests tend to dominate and shape the actions of government.* The basic problem now is not how to achieve balance between corporate and union influence upon government; it is how to assure that producer interest groups, taken collectively, do not wield so much political power that the needs of people as consumers are ineffectively represented to government. Basically, the American economy exists to satisfy the demands of people as consumers, and all economic institutions should be subservient to that end.

Historically, the influence of consumer organizations upon American government has been overshadowed by the well-organized and richly financed political activities of producer organizations. The American consumer has had to depend for the protection of his interests upon competition among contending producer groups. Thus, it was expected that the level of farm subsidies would be limited by the opposition of business to the higher taxes needed to finance them. Higher minimum wages would be restrained by the political pressure of the farmers and small businessmen, who were adversely affected by them. Import quotas on steel would be opposed by the automobile, railroad, and construction industries that were heavy users of steel.

Unfortunately, competition among producers in the political arena proved to be an unreliable protector of consumer interests. Producer groups found that collaboration brought them more benefits from government than did competition. If one group supported other groups in exchange for their support of its interests, a compliant Congress would bow to the combined pressure of the coalition. Such logrolling tactics, used in the Congress over many years, resulted in the proliferation of subsidies, quotas, tariffs, loans, loan guarantees, price-supports, union shops, the Davis-Bacon Act (raising the labor costs of public construction), minimum wage laws, and other governmental favors. Congressional solicitude for producers' demands has cost the American consumer dearly in high prices and high taxes.

The damage inflicted on consumers when producer interests fail to restrain each other, even if they do not collaborate, is illustrated by the price inflation of the period from 1965 to 1971. The traditional theory has been that the pressure of employers to keep down wage rates in collective bargaining agreements would check labor union pressure for inflationary pay increases. Collective bargaining presumed a rough balance of power between organized labor and management. It was believed that the cost of a strike to workers in lost wages would restrain the demands of their union, just as the cost of a strike to the employing firm in lost profits would cause it to raise its wage offer. A noninflationary agreement would, according to the theory, emerge without a work stoppage.

During the postwar years, however, the balance of bargaining power shifted sharply to the side of labor. The cost of a strike to employees fell as they accumulated savings, and as a generous government often provided unemployment benefits or welfare payments if they struck. At the same time, the cost of a strike to employers rose as capital investment per worker increased, and the burden of fixed costs of an idle plant became very onerous. In addition, the shift to an inflationary federal fiscal and monetary policy after 1965, and the mounting expenditures of the Southeast Asian war that were not matched by higher taxes, made it easier for employers to pass on higher wage costs to the public in higher prices. As a consequence, employers' opposition to the higher wages that workers demanded to keep up their real incomes was weakened. Labor peace at any price became their aim. By this process, the great wage and price inflation of the 1965 to 1971 period got under way and accelerated, until, in August, 1971, President Nixon, under the Economic Stabilization Act of 1971, ordered a six-month wage-price "freeze." This was followed by a second, and then a third, phase of flexible federal restraints upon pay and prices.

As a public member of the Pay Board during Phase II, the author had the difficult duty of passing upon collective bargaining agreements. Nearly all agreements that came before the Pay Board called for inflationary wage boosts, and were supported by the employers as well as by the unions. At its public hearings, the Board rarely heard the view of any consumer group, although consumers had to pay the higher wages in higher market prices of products. The public lost when labor unions and corporate business ceased to restrain each others' demands.

During the 1960's, the balance of consumer/producer power had begun to change somewhat, as consumer-oriented organizations burgeoned in number and influence. Belatedly, consumer weakness in dealing with government was recognized. The Urban Coalition, Common Cause, Ralph Nader's "Raiders," the Sierra Club, and a host of other environmental and consumerist organizations raised voices in behalf of consumers' and citizens' demands. (A "citizen" is a consumer of governmental services!) Their political potency was proved by their success in persuading Congress to pass a succession of important measures for consumer and environmental protection in the years between 1965 and 1972.

This recent emergence of organized citizen and consumer political action groups marks a salutary change in the American political scene. It is part of the postwar trend toward an increasing pluralization of American society, to which has been allied a trend toward greater individual participation in the activities of social institutions. The consequences of growing pluralization and democratization are bound to be both important and, for the most part, favorable. One result, already noted, is a relative reduction in the political power of older institutions like the corporation and the labor union. Another is a reduction in the probability of a polarization of business and labor interests. With these come a great reduction in the chance that American society will ever be dominated by any single interest bloc.

# TOWARD A CONSUMER-ORIENTED POLITICS

*The key to an effective public policy for enhancing the general welfare is further elevation of the political power of citizen and consumer interest organizations, reinforcing the movement already under way.* Although measures can also be taken to limit the political influence of producer organizations, the main thrust toward a better political balance must be to create more countervailing political power for consumers. Just as a public policy for more effective competition and less corporate *economic* power should rely mainly upon *positive* actions to reduce barriers to entry and to expand markets, so a public policy to hold corporate *political* power within proper bounds should consist primarily of affirmative measures rather than negative actions to dismember or to forbid. A general de-politicization of all producer organizations would be neither constitutional, politically feasible, nor necessary.

We propose five reforms:

## Basic Public Financing of Elections

There is a mounting consensus that, in the era of television, the high cost of political campaigns financed by private contributions is not only a source of corruption of elected officials, but also a means of deterring the poor from running for public office. Expenditures on all American campaigns have been estimated at around $300 million per year, of which half goes for television, radio, and printed advertising.[15] That the high costs of successful campaigning lead public officials to grant favors to donors or even to engage in corrupt practices is illustrated by the cases of Senator Thomas A. Dodd of Connecticut, Mayor H. D. Addonizio of Newark, and the former members of the Los Angeles Harbor Commission.[16] *Basic election campaign financing should be provided from public funds to all* bona fide *candidates.* President Lyndon B. Johnson proposed in 1966 that all citizens add a $1.00 assessment for this purpose to their income tax returns. Whether this is the best method we need not decide here; the principle is sound and should be put into practice.

## Reporting of All Campaign Contributions

With basic public financing of election campaigns, the need for private financing would diminish markedly, yet it would continue to some degree. Private contributions should be reported and disclosed, so that the public would be able to know the individuals and interest groups providing major support of each candidate. To simplify administration, only total contributions to a candidate in a particular election of, say, $100 or more should be reported by the contributor, whether or not the candidate was aware of them. The Federal Election Campaign Act of 1971 moved in this direction by requiring all political committees disposing of $1,000 or more to register, to elect officers, and to report for publication the names of all contributors of more than $100 each year, as well as expenditures made in behalf of candidates in Federal elections. While prohibited from making *direct* contributions, corporations and labor unions were authorized to establish voluntary political funds to which their employees or members could contribute.

## Reporting of All Lobbying Expenditures

The Lobbying Act of 1946 should be amended to require *all* social interest groups and corporations, to register and to report all of their expenditures made for the purpose of influencing legislation. At present, only those persons whose "principal purpose" is to influence legislation must register and make such reports. Full public reporting would at least lift the veil on the magnitude of producer interest group financing, which is now shielded from public inspection.

## Merging the Departments of Commerce, Labor, and Agriculture

President Lyndon B. Johnson recommended that the federal Departments of Commerce, Labor, and Agriculture be merged into a Department of Economic Affairs. While the recommendation was based mainly on considerations of economy and efficiency, the reform is even more desirable for the purpose of eliminating departments whose primary mission is to promote the interests of particular *producer groups* in society. Integration of the present three producer interest departments would greatly reduce producer influence on the Congress. Economic policies could more easily be studied for their effects upon the *public welfare,* rather than simply upon business, labor, or farm interests.

## Establishing a Department of Consumer Affairs

The present Advisor on Consumer Affairs in the White House staff should be elevated to a full-fledged Secretary of Consumer Affairs, with a Department able to provide adequate representation of consumer interests on all pending federal legislation and to initiate proposals of its own. The remarkable public support of Ralph Nader's efforts in behalf of consumers is attributable to the void that has existed in governmental organization.

While the preceding program involves actions by the federal government, it is equally desirable that concurrent actions be taken, where appropriate, by the legislative bodies of states and municipalities. Reorganization of the government at all levels to recognize the primacy of the citizen as taxpayer, and of the consumer as buyer, would go far toward establishing a consumer-oriented politics in the future. It would more effectively establish a felicitous balance of power in American government than would new measures to curb the already waning political influence of corporations and labor unions.


## *NOTES*

1. Theodore J. Jacobs, "Pollution, Consumerism, Accountability," *Center Magazine,* Vol. 5, No. 1 (January/February 1972), a paper presented to the Conference on the Corporation and the Quality of Life, Center for the Study of Democratic Institutions, Santa Barbara, California, September 28, 1971.

2. The process is described well in Robert A. Dahl, *Pluralist Democracy in the United States: Conflict and Consent* (Englewood Cliffs, N. J.: Prentice-Hall, 1969). See also Frank Tannenbaum, *The Balance of Power in Society* (New York: Macmillan, 1969), and Arnold M. Rose, *The Power Structure* (New York: Oxford University Press, 1957).

3. In *Santa Clara County* v. *Southern Pacific Railway Company,* 118 U.S. 394 (1886), the U.S. Supreme Court held that the word "person" in the Fourteenth Amendment included corporations.

4. See, for example, such works as W. B. Munro, *The Invisible Government* (New York: Macmillan, 1928); Gaetano Mosca, *The Ruling Class* (New York: McGraw-Hill, 1939); Robert Brady, *Business as a System of Power* (New York: Columbia University Press, 1945); and Andrew Hacker, ed., *The Corporation Takeover* (New York: Harper and Row, 1964).

5. See *The Role of Business in Public Affairs,* Studies in Public Affairs, No. 2 (New York: National Industrial Conference Board, 1968).

6. Robert W. Miller and Jimmy D. Johnson, *Corporate Ambassadors to Washington* (Washington, D.C.: American University, 1970).

7. Edwin M. Epstein, *The Corporation in American Politics* (Englewood Cliffs, N. J.: Prentice-Hall, 1969), p. 303.

8. See Roger G. Noll, *Reforming Regulation* (Washington, D.C.: Brookings Institution, 1971). This monograph evaluates the proposals for reorganizing the federal regulatory agencies made by the President's Advisory Council on Executive Organization in *A New Regulatory Framework: Report on Selected Independent Regulatory Agencies* (Washington, D.C.: U.S. Government Printing Office, 1971).

9. Stephen A. Greyser, "Business and Politics, 1968," *Harvard Business Review* (November–December 1968), p. 4.

10. See Raymond A. Bauer and Kenneth J. Gergen, eds., *The Study of Policy Formation* (New York: Free Press, 1968).

11. See Edward H. Chamberlin, *The Economic Analysis of Labor Union Power* (Washington, D.C.: American Enterprise Institute, August 1963), p. 2.

12. Originally a fifteen-member tripartite body, the Pay Board was reconstituted by President Nixon into a seven-member, all-public body after AFL-CIO President George Meany and three other labor representatives resigned in March of 1972. On January 10, 1973, however, President Nixon abolished the Pay Board

and appointed the five labor leaders to a Labor-Management Advisory Committee.

13. Epstein, *The Corporation in American Politics,* pp. 132–33.

14. Henry C. Simons, *Economic Policy for a Free Society* (Chicago: University of Chicago Press, 1948), p. 123. The same basic thesis has been advanced recently by John C. Reis, "Interest Group Power and American Democracy," in Werner C. Hirsch and Sidney Sonenblum, eds., *Governing Urban America in the 1970s* (New York: Praeger, 1972).

15. *Voters' Time: Report of the Twentieth Century Fund Commission on Campaign Costs in the Electronic Era* (New York: Twentieth Century Fund, 1969), p. 9.

16. During September, 1971, Secretary of Agriculture Hardin raised government price supports for "manufacturing" milk used to make butter and cheese. There was public speculation that this would trigger perhaps one million dollars of support from a grateful dairy industry for President Nixon's 1972 election campaign. See *Wall Street Journal* (September 29, 1971).

# CHAPTER 8

# Corporate Government: Autocratic or Democratic?

Along with the problems of economic and political power, the third critical problem of the interaction of the corporation with society that we will examine concerns the adequacy of corporate government. American corporate government is often branded as antidemocratic, irresponsible, and ineffective.[1] Complaints are made about all its major organs: the board of directors, the shareowners, and the management. Many hold that there is a grotesque contrast between the legal theory of corporate government and the realities.

State corporation laws are said to make excessive delegations of authority to the corporations they charter. Some critics assert that charters should have a limited duration, should specify permissible lines of business, and should require a public review of corporate performance before being renewed. Other observers note that the states are unlikely to tighten their laws because they compete for corporation fees. They call for federal chartering of all interstate corporations.

Criticism is also directed at the concept that the board of directors should represent only the shareowners. The consumer's interest in products of good quality, the employee's interest in a good job at fair pay, and the supplier's interest in reasonable prices for his products or services, are all assumed by American jurisprudence to be protected by market com-

I am grateful to my graduate students for research on the subjects of this chapter, including again, the work of Mr. Carbonne. And, Dean Harold Williams gave valuable assistance in improving the formulation of some of the ideas presented here.

petition. The critics argue, however, that competition is not effective for these purposes. The remedy, they contend, is to make corporate government representative of consumers, employees, and suppliers. Boards of directors should be elected by, and represent, the several groups affected by corporate activities.[2]

*The functioning of the board of directors has been a target of rising criticism during recent years. Perhaps no single recent event in the business world raised sharper questions than the bankruptcy of the Penn Central on June 21, 1970,* only twenty-eight months after this $4.5 billion transportation giant came into existence as the product of the largest corporation merger in history. As the chroniclers of this debacle observed:

> Penn Central's directors seem to have done very little to earn the $200 each received every time he attended a board meeting. They sat around the big polished table as representatives of the railroad's stockholders, whose interests they were supposed to represent. With few exceptions, they appeared to be blind to the onrushing events that sent the Penn Central hurtling off the tracks. . . . The Penn Central bankruptcy also raised questions about the inherent conflicts of interest that arise as a result of the incestuous, interlocking directorates between financiers who supply money, managers who borrow money, and brokers who traffic between them.[3]

These criticisms were reiterated in the staff report of the House Committee on Banking and Currency, which spent more than a year investigating the Penn Central tragedy. The report censured the Penn Central board for the narrow range of backgrounds of its members, their excessive involvement in other corporate boards, and their subservience to the interests of the financial institutions of which many were officers. The board's "rubber-stamping" of excessive cash dividend payments, and its cavalier approval of disastrous investments in real estate and professional sport teams, revealed the directors' ignorance of the precarious financial condition of the railroad.[4]

Former U.S. Supreme Court Justice Arthur J. Goldberg, referring to the Penn-Central fiasco, has noted that "the board is relegated to an advisory and legitimizing function that is substantially different from the role of policy-maker and guardian of shareholder and public interests contemplated by the law of corporations."[5] Goldberg resigned from the board of directors of Trans World Airlines in October, 1972, following a dispute over his efforts to establish an *independent* committee of outside directors to review the actions and recommendations of the management. While one may heartily agree with Goldberg's criticism of the corporate board, the wisdom of his remedy is open to question. To create a committee of outside directors with its own staff of auditors and experts would have the practical effect of splitting the board into two factions, of blurring management's line of responsibility, and of duplicating controls of corporate operations. The reforms proposed later in this chapter would enable the board to reestablish its role as an independent auditor of managerial performance, without adverse side effects.

Professor Mace, a longtime observer of the corporate board, also found large discrepancies between accepted doctrines about directorial behavior and what directors actually do.[6] His interviews with many top corporation officers led him to conclude that board members generally advise management, help to discipline their behavior, act as a "corporate conscience," and make decisions in the event of a crisis. Few board members establish business objectives and policies, ask discerning questions, audit managerial performance, or even select the president—except in a crisis—which are their classical functions.

The weak influence of stockholders upon corporate behavior is another standard subject of censure. The stockholder is seen as a faceless and impotent character, ignorant of corporate problems, who sells his shares when he loses confidence in the management rather than raises his voice to demand reforms. The annual stockholders' meeting, the proxy statement, the election of the board of directors, are all seen as a meaningless facade behind which the top management of the company manipulates the board.

Finally, the top managers of big corporations are seen as a self-perpetuating and irresponsible "power elite." This group, the critics say, has seized control of the company from apathetic and unorganized shareowners and from the board of directors that it selected and which it dominates. It runs the company to serve its own selfish interests in emoluments, power, and security, rather than to serve the interests of the shareowners.

All of these criticisms reflect a belief that the American corporate constitution is defective and that government should intervene to correct its faults. The real "constitutional crisis" of the corporation is whether the actual power and authority relationships in today's big companies are radically different from those contemplated by legal theory.[7]

We shall first examine some radical proposals for reform, made by those critics who call for a "new social contract" based upon new values and ideologies. Because we find them faulty in conception, we shall propose another set of reforms designed to make the corporation a more responsive social institution. The author's experience in directing corporations leads him to conclude that corporate government is not as defective as the

radical critics contend. Yet there is both an urgent need and an opportunity to improve it.

## CONTEMPORARY CORPORATE GOVERNMENT

*The evolution of corporate chartering by the American states is a
tale of progressive permissiveness.* Until 1837, companies were individually
charted by *ad hoc* legislation. In that year Massachusetts enacted the first
general corporation law, which was comparatively stringent in limiting
corporate powers. Subsequently, motivated by the philosophy of free
enterprise, as well as by competition among the states in charter-mongering,
state corporation laws were progressively relaxed.[8]

The "constitution" of the American business corporation consists of
the general corporation law of the state plus the charter issued under that
law.[9] Because statutory grants are highly permissive, the incorporators are
allowed to define the authority they wish to exercise in the "articles of in
corporation" which, after state approval, become the charter. Most laws
permit companies to be organized "for any lawful purpose"; the states
do not draw a boundary line around the potential business activities of the
corporations they charter.

Most corporation laws provide that charters are perpetual. Time
limits are set only by Arizona (25 years), Mississippi (99 years), Montana
(40 years), and Oklahoma (50 years), and their laws do not contain
any criteria to be met as a condition of the renewal of charters. A charter
normally contains a statement of the capital structure of the proposed
company, the location of the principal office, the number, names, and
addresses of directors, the powers of directors to assess shares, and the
preemptive rights of shareowners to purchase additional shares. There are
also standard provisions authorizing the company to borrow money, to
merge with other companies, and to do all things "reasonably necessary to
carry out its purposes."

The management and direction of companies is vested by law in
a board of directors, elected annually by a vote of all shareowners on the
principle of "one-share-one-vote." Boards are generally authorized to fix
their number, within limits approved by law or by shareowners, and to
fill vacancies between board meetings. Directors generally need not be
shareowners. Cumulative voting for directors is optional in twenty-eight
states, mandatory in twenty-one—and is *prohibited* in Massachusetts! This
diversity reflects a long-standing controversy over the merits of this

electoral practice, which fosters minority representation on a board by permitting a shareowner to concentrate all of his votes on a single director.

Corporation laws authorize the board to delegate to appointed officers the day-to-day operation of the company, but require it to supervise the general course of the business. The board is required to use "that degree of diligence, care, and skill which ordinarily prudent men would exercise under similar circumstances in like positions." The extent of the board's delegations is generally proportional to the size of the company. In the large industrial corporation, the board hires and delegates authority to major executives, reviews their reports, sets major policies, acts on plans and budgets, and approves all matters involving shareowners, external financing, and the compensation of employees.[10]

Although the corporate charter fixes precisely the powers of shareowners and of boards of directors, and thereby determines the relationship between them, it leaves open the relationship between a board of directors and the management. Corporation laws require simply that the board appoint specified officers. They leave it up to the board to decide how much authority to delegate to those officers. Of course, the board always remains responsible to the shareowners for results. The structure of American corporate government is shown in Figure 2.

A 1969 survey of twenty-two large industrial corporations revealed that the typical board of directors had fifteen members and met once a month for a half day.[11] Most companies had boards with a majority of "outside" (nonofficer) members; but full-time officers played a prominent role in all boards. All boards had a compensation committee that dealt with salaries, stock options, and pensions. One-third of the boards had an executive committee empowered to act on matters between board meetings. Although the by-laws generally permitted the chief executive to make organizational changes, the establishment or discontinuance of departments or changes in senior management assignments were usually presented to the board for its approval. In order to appraise management's performance, directors were supplied with much information, including monthly reports on each division of the company.

The board of directors is required by law to approve all changes in the stock of the corporation and all external financing arrangements. Directors must individually sign corporate statements to the Securities and Exchange Commission and are legally liable for the use of "due diligence" in verifying their accuracy.

Manifestly, the responsibilities of the director of a big company are onerous. While some companies carry insurance against the legal liabilities of their directors, its coverage is partial and leaves a director exposed to

FIGURE 2
*Structure of American Corporate Government*

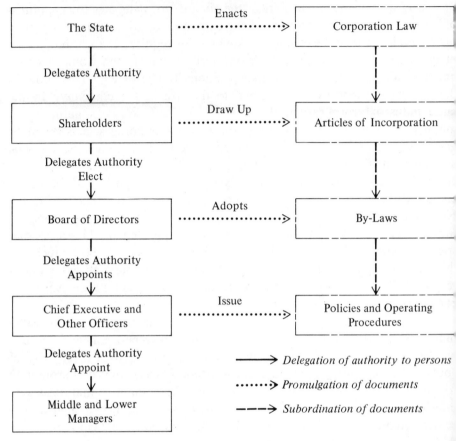

heavy personal damages if it can be shown that he was careless in making a bad decision.

# CONSTRAINTS ON CORPORATE GOVERNMENT

The business corporation is a task-oriented, efficiency-seeking, profit motivated institution, operating in an unstable environment of rapid technological and social change. The outcomes of the decisions made by its board of directors or its managers are usually laden with great uncertainty. The ability of the enterprise to sell its products profitably in competitive markets is tested every day. It confronts instabilities in market demand that threaten its survival and create a need for great internal flexibility.

These characteristics dictate a form of corporate government that is capable of producing decisions quickly in order to avoid pitfalls and to seize opportunities. The pressures of time simply do not permit extensive deliberation, lengthy consultation, or widespread participation in the making of most corporate decisions. *Corporate government must permit rapid responses to changes in the business environment.*

Instability of the business environment requires that the government of corporations be different from that of other social institutions, for which stabler environments allow more leisurely decision-making processes. This instability is the reason why authority to govern the company is concentrated in a board of directors, representing a single constituency—the shareowners —and able to make decisions on one criterion—the shareowners' interests. It is why there is a chain of command from the chief executive officer down the line, with a progressive partitioning of tasks and authority. It is why responsibility is focused upon specific managers, rather than diffused among the members of a committee who cannot be removed, in the event of failure, because personal accountability cannot be fixed.

Many behavioral scientists question the authoritarian mode of corporate government. They see it as overcentralized and autocratic. They believe that wider participation by employees would enhance productivity and psychological satisfactions. The employee-elected board of directors of the Yugoslavian enterprise is often cited with admiration.

Rising levels of education and affluence have undoubtedly changed employees' attitudes and motivations; and a participative style of corporate management is more appropriate today than it would have been in the past. Yet business enterprises require hierarchical order and discipline if they are to survive in a competitive world. These qualities in moderation are not inimical to the morale of employees. On the contrary, human beings have a psychological need for structure and leadership as well as for freedom and self-determination. *The never-ending task of corporate managers is to find the optimum balance between individual freedom and organizational order.*

## RESTRICTIONS ON THE CORPORATE CHARTER

Although the corporate charter traditionally has been considered to be perpetual, questions have recently been raised about the validity of this concept. Should corporation laws fix the life of a charter at twenty or twenty-five years and require the company to show that it has operated in the public interest in order to obtain a renewal? Some believe that this would make enterprises more responsive to the public interest. They note that licenses to television and radio broadcasting companies by the Federal Communications Commission now run for three years, and that the holders must show adequate service to the public to get them renewed.

Persons who oppose unrestrained business diversification would restrict the corporate charter in another way: they would require that potential incorporators set forth the particular lines of business the new company intends to enter. If, later on, a company wished to enter additional industries, it would be obliged to seek an amendment to its charter. No longer would incorporators be able to write into articles of incorporation the phrase "all other lawful activities," which has been the "open sesame" to diversification.

Those who would limit the duration and the activities permitted by the charter appear to overlook the fact that market competition and governmental regulation now tend to assure that enterprises serve the public interest. Competition can assure the public the products it demands at the lowest prices. It can provide employees the jobs they desire at the highest wages. It can provide suppliers with the best prices for their products. When competition alone does not adequately protect the public interest, government regulates business through a battery of boards and commissions. If business still fails to serve the public interest, the proper response of government is to strengthen competition or to extend functional regulation. The alternative of reviewing businesses case by case would be an administrative nightmare. What criteria of "adequate" performance should be applied? With 1,600,000 active business corporations in the United States, how would the task ever be completed?

To limit the permissible types of business activity in the charter would be to restrict freedom of enterprise and to impair the vigor of competition. "Freedom of enterprise" means that any nonfinancial corporation which is not a natural monopoly is free to enter whatever lawful activity it believes it can carry on profitably. To hamper a firm in entering another industry is to shelter existing firms in that industry from new competition, thus tending to create or to perpetuate monopoly power. We have already seen that business diversification through conglomerate mergers has invigorated competition.[12]

Those who would restrict corporate charters misconceive the function of corporation laws, which is simply to define the conditions under which persons may associate for common business activities. Such laws are not intended to be—and should not be made into—omnibus regulatory statutes. The aims and the machinery of business regulation are best dealt with in laws dealing with that subject. We conclude, therefore, that the present liberal grant of power in corporate charters is in the public interest.

# THE MULTI-INTEREST
# BOARD OF DIRECTORS

Whether the board of directors should be elected by and represent only the shareowners or should also represent other interest groups in society is undoubtedly the most controversial issue of corporate government.[13] The issue was raised sharply in Europe after World War II, when socialist parties were strong in many countries. The issue was also raised in the United States by the Managerialist school of corporate critics, which gained a considerable following in the 1950's.[14] The strong upsurge of public demand for corporate action to help resolve social problems during the 1960's led to renewed proposals to broaden the formal constituency of the corporate board.[15] Ralph Nader's Project on Corporate Responsibility, for example, has had among its major aims the addition of "public" directors, the "democratization" of the corporate system, and "public interest" proxy contests.

The case of the multi-interest board of directors was first stated uncompromisingly by Scott Buchanan.[16] The basis of Buchanan's reasoning was Hobbes' observation in *The Leviathan* that corporations are "chips off the block of sovereignty." Buchanan understood this to mean that corporations are private governments. As such, he argued, they should meet the tests of all healthy governments, namely, republican form and democratic process. In his view, American corporation laws fail to prescribe a proper constitution, being silent on the internal administration of companies. Corporate managers are, thus, autocratic and free from public control. The state, he held, should establish democratic control of corporate enterprises in order to protect the public interest. The board of directors should be elected by employees and the public. The government should be democratized, so that the company could play its role legitimately and function as a center of political power resting on the "consent of the governed." In proposing this reform, Buchanan rejected the alternatives of vitalizing competition or of nationalizing private enterprises. In his view, competition could not be made into an effective regulator of corporate behavior in an economy of giant firms. Nor was nationalization an attractive cure in view of the industrial authoritarianism of the Soviet Union.

Buchanan's concept of "democratized" corporate government must be rejected on several grounds. It denies the principle that organizational "form follows function." It ignores the strong discipline of market competition upon corporate behavior. And it is inconsistent with private enterprise. Its adoption would destroy the concept of the enterprise as an association of investors who pooled their capital in a business venture, because investors would share authority over their funds with those who had invested nothing.

If businesses were governed by boards that formally represented many social, economic, ethnic, or other interest groups in society, they would lose singularity of motive and competitive vitality. The corporation would change from a cost-conscious, profit-motivated entity into a political organ pursuing conflicting values. Members of a multi-interest board would be chosen for their political appeal to various groups in society, rather than their competence to make good business decisions. Such a board would be a debating society, incapable of reaching the timely decisions that are essential to efficiency. Managements would be even freer than now from rigorous audit by their boards of directors.[17] *Although the present corporate board is defective, society would be better off to improve it rather than to adopt the special-interest approach.*

## THE EUROPEAN CORPORATION BOARD

The principle of the multi-interest board has been applied, but in a very limited way, to the government of European corporations. (See Figure 3.) The corporation laws of France and of West Germany draw a distinction between the board's functions of *overseeing and advising,* on the one hand, and of *managing,* on the other hand; and they assign them to separate boards. In Germany, two-thirds of the Aufrichtsrat (the Supervisory Board) is elected by the shareowners and one-third is elected by the council of employees of the company. The Aufrichtsrat then appoints the Vorstand (the Managing Board), which is composed of one or more full-time executives who direct the day-by-day operations of the enterprise. A French law of 1966 gave companies a choice between the one-board and the two-board organizations.[18]

The Proposed Statute for the European Company, under consideration by the Council of Ministers of the European Economic Community, also embodies the idea of the two-tier board, with the election of one-third of the Supervisory Board by the council of employees of a company.[19] However, disagreement within the EEC has held up adoption of the statute. The principle of "co-determination," as it is known in Europe, continues to be controversial. It conflicts with the concept that only owners should choose the managers of their property. While German experience with this form of corporate government apparently has been satisfactory, it is important to note that employees play an indirect minority role in choosing top management and are not *directly* represented on the Managing Board.

FIGURE 3

*Structure of European Corporate Government*

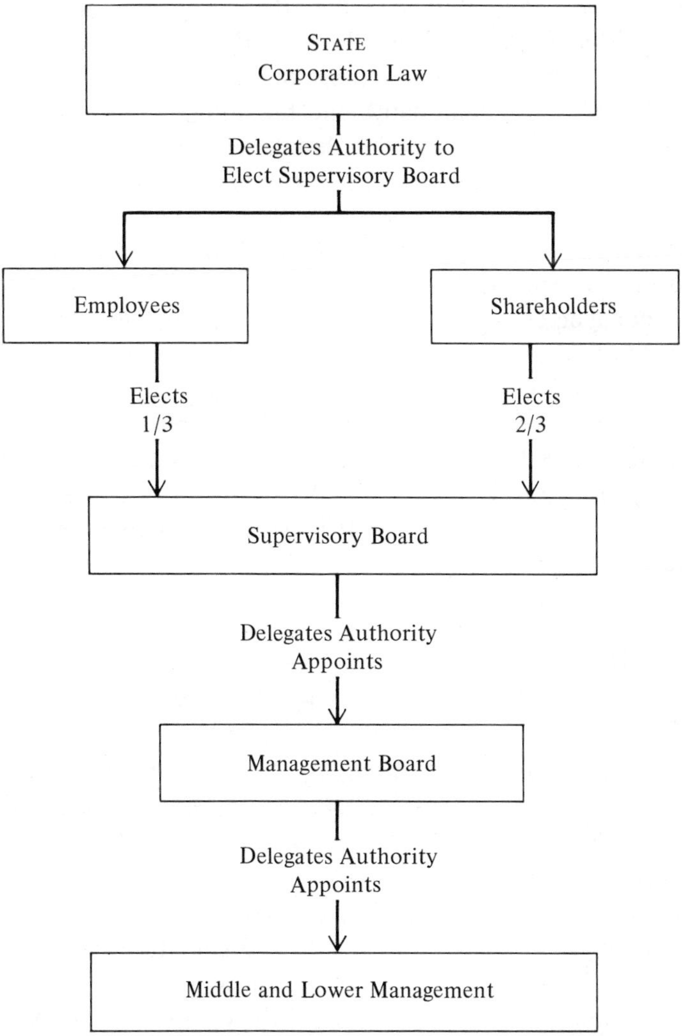

```
┌─────────────────────────────────────┐
│               STATE                  │
│          Corporation Law             │
└─────────────────────────────────────┘
              Delegates Authority to
              Elect Supervisory Board

┌──────────────────┐        ┌──────────────────┐
│    Employees     │        │   Shareholders   │
└──────────────────┘        └──────────────────┘
       Elects                     Elects
        1/3                        2/3

┌─────────────────────────────────────┐
│          Supervisory Board           │
└─────────────────────────────────────┘
            Delegates Authority
                Appoints

        ┌─────────────────────┐
        │   Management Board   │
        └─────────────────────┘
            Delegates Authority
                Appoints

┌─────────────────────────────────────┐
│     Middle and Lower Management      │
└─────────────────────────────────────┘
```

# THE YUGOSLAVIAN ENTERPRISE BOARD

Proponents of employee representation on corporate boards often claim success for the "self-management" of Yugoslavian enterprises by their employees. Beginning in 1950, the government of Yugoslavia began to decentralize the management of industrial enterprises in the interest of greater operating efficiency. At present, the employees of a company elect a

Workers' Council, which elects a Governing Board and a chief executive (the Director) of the enterprise. The Director appoints his department heads and staff assistants, but with the advice and consent of the various committees of the Workers' Council. A distinction is drawn between the governing, or policy-making, functions of the Workers' Council and the Governing Board, on the one hand, and the administrative activities of the Director and his aides, on the other hand. However, nearly all decision-making authority—even the hiring, firing, and disciplining of employees—lies in the hands of the Council and its Committees.

Intensive studies of the operation of Yugoslavian enterprises have shown that the Director lacks the power to carry out his heavy responsibilities.[20] Self-management apparently results in less efficient performance than a more traditional style of management. After a time, Council membership lost its attraction for employees because it made heavy demands on their time, and involved them in problems for which they were unprepared and in which they lacked real interest. We conclude that the Yugoslavian model of corporate government probably is a transitional form—an experiment in an industrializing country. It is not an attractive prototype for the United States.

## STRENGTHENING THE AMERICAN CORPORATE BOARD

*The American corporate board of directors should be reformed to cure its three most frequent weaknesses: a restricted social perspective, domination by the company's management, and conflicts of interest with financial institutions.* There is merit in the complaints of consumers, ecologists, women, ethnic minorities, and other critics that the governing bodies of many great companies lack diverse expertise and are insensitive to changing social values. There is substance to the charge that many boards are dominated by the executives of the companies they are supposed to govern. And, as the example of the Penn Central revealed, many boards have too many directors from financial institutions who have conflicting interests to serve.

Corporate boards must look farther afield for good directors if they are to expand the range of their competence. Some have begun to do so. In 1970, General Motors elected to its board Dr. Leon Sullivan, a black theologian and businessman. This was an affirmative response to Ralph Nader's Project on Corporate Responsibility, although a different one than had been sought. Dr. Sullivan brought new perspective into board discussions. But he did not "represent" black Americans in the sense of being elected by a black constituency. Like all other directors of General Motors, he represented all of the shareowners. Similar comments can be made about the election of Mrs. Patricia Harris, a black woman lawyer, to the Board of the Chase Manhattan Bank in 1972. Corporate boards would exercise more independence and imagination in making up the slate of nominees for directors, if nominations were made by a committee controlled by outside directors.

The board must become more independent, if it is to perform its central function of auditing the performance of the operating management. As Mace found, many directors do little more than rubber-stamp management's recommendations. Outside directors generally lack time to master the information necessary for effective supervision. Inside directors have the knowledge, but are reluctant to challenge their superiors in board meetings. *The key to better corporate government is to increase the power, the independence, the range of competence, and the compensation, of outside directors in public corporations.*

Finally, the number of directors of an industrial company coming from financial institutions should be strictly limited. A partner or senior officer of an investment or commercial bank can have a conflict of interest arising from information he receives as a corporate insider or from opportunities to earn fees from making loans, underwriting securities, or arranging mergers and acquisitions. Mace concluded that representatives of investment banking firms should not serve on corporate boards for these reasons. The Staff Report of the House Banking and Currency Committee recommended a strict limit on the number of directors who are officers of financial institutions.

## THE NEW "MANAGERIAL" STOCKHOLDER

The idea that the stockholders lack influence over the behavior of large corporations is a cliché which, like most clichés, has been much overdrawn. To be sure, stockholders are quiescent so long as a company's affairs go well. When they do not, stockholders can act to unseat the management; and they often do so, notwithstanding the heavy costs involved. The omnipresent threat of a proxy battle—a fight for control—is a powerful discipline to corporate managers.[21] It is a "force in being" which, though rarely used, is continually effective—like the German Navy in World War II.

Even the owner of a few shares in a giant company is not bereft of influence. The fact that most shareowners remain silent endows the active shareowner with disproportionate political power. He can attend the annual shareowners' meeting, interrogate officers and directors, move resolutions from the floor, and require the company to print resolutions in the proxy statements mailed to all shareowners. Because he can act *directly* at stockholder meetings as well as through his representative (the corporate director), he has, as a shareowner, a wider opportunity for the expression of dissent from the corporation's policies than he has, as a citizen, to register with the federal government of the United States, where he can act only through his elected representative. What is often mistakenly called a lack of democracy in corporate government is really the sense of powerlessness that everyone feels in an expanding mass society. It is an inevitable consequence of the growth of all institutions—governments as well as corporations.

Even when a disgruntled shareowner remains silent but sells his shares, his action can influence the company. Selling pressure depresses the price of the stock, and compels the management of the company to finance on less favorable terms. Heavy and prolonged selling pressures may even depress the price to a level where the company becomes a candidate for a takeover bid—or where the directors decide to install a new management.

Social trends are, however, combining to change American shareowners from a passive to an active force in corporate government. Shareowners are steadily becoming more numerous, more professional—and more critical of management. A new "managerial" shareowner has appeared, who is actively participating in the affairs of his company. Concern for the environment and the quality of life has led many of them to use the corporation, and particularly the annual meeting, as instruments of social change. This trend was fostered by a 1970 ruling of the Securities and Exchange Commission, which removed its former ban against "general economic, political, racial, religious or similar issues" in proxy statements. While this ruling opened the door to irrelevance in proxy material, the offsetting advantage of making managers more sensitive to social forces made the risk worth taking. Shareowner democracy costs something; but, in the author's opinion, it is worth the cost.[22]

Another group of managerial stockholders who have appeared are the officers of the financial institutions that now hold about 30 percent of the shares listed on national stock exchanges. When an institution's holdings in a company were comparatively small, they were sold when the officers lost confidence in a company's management. Now, with huge holdings in many corporations, they cannot sell without depressing the price. So they put pressure on the managers of the companies in their portfolios to make desired changes.[23] The large amount of time spent by corporation presidents addressing security analysts and maintaining good relations with institutional investors attests to the power of these stockholders. Beyond doubt, *American shareowners are beginning to play the role in corporate policy-making contemplated by legal theory.*

## STEPS TOWARD BETTER CORPORATE GOVERNMENT

We now propose reforms of American corporate government intended to make the corporation a more sensitive and responsive institution in our complex society. The general thrust of these reforms is to expand the authority and involvement of stockholders and boards of directors. Although top managements have never been the irresponsible oligarchies portrayed in critical dogma, the weakness of boards of directors has left them more power than is in the public interest. As an experienced management consultant has said, "The board's role is what the chief executive makes of it, and there aren't very many who want a strong board." [24]

The following reforms are proposed to apply only to those business corporations whose stock is publicly traded, and which, therefore, interact closely with the society. These comprise the 10,000 of the 1,600,000 operating companies that collectively account for 80 percent or more of all corporate business.[25]

### A Uniform Corporation Law

A uniform corporation law in the United States would end competition among the states to trade liberal charters for revenues and would reduce the cost of doing business. This country should be able to achieve what the nations of the European Economic Community may soon achieve —a common law of corporations.

### A Majority of Outside Directors

The law should require that a majority of the board of directors shall not be officers of the company. This is the current practice of most large companies, and it should be followed by all public companies. No board can evaluate management if most of its members are managers and owe their jobs to the chief executive officer. Nor can a board provide necessary perspective on business-societal relationships, if most of its members are preoccupied with internal management problems.

## Nonofficer Majorities on Standing Committees

The law should require that every board of directors shall have a Committee on Nominations, a Committee on Management and Financial Audit, and a Committee on Public Affairs, a majority of whose members in each case shall not be officers of the company. The independence of the board should be reinforced by assuring that the functions of nominating new members, auditing, and attending to societal relationships are in the hands of committees controlled by outside directors. A legal requirement for the appointment of such committees would give better assurance that the prescribed functions are performed by the board.

## Limitations on Directors from Financial Institutions

The law should limit to 10 percent, or not more than three, whichever is less, the number of directors who are concurrently officers of financial institutions, that a nonfinancial corporation with assets of more than $10 million may have on its board. This recommendation was made in the Staff Report of the House Banking and Currency Committee on the Penn Central bankruptcy. It would reduce conflicts of interest of directors.

## Shareowning Directors

The law should require that all directors shall be shareholders of the company. This requirement would be consistent with the theory that directors are members of the constituency of shareowners they represent, and have at least a minimal financial interest in the prosperity of the company.

## Increased Compensation of Outside Directors

The law should require that outside directors be compensated at a rate per day not less than that of the highest paid officer. A recent survey of large American corporations revealed that three-quarters of the companies paid their outside directors less than $6,250 a year and 37 percent of the companies paid them less than $3,125 a year. This rule would increase the compensation of most outside directors substantially, thus making it possible to obtain directors of great ability who would be willing to spend more time on corporate matters. Better remuneration is much needed to compensate directors for their rising legal liabilities.[26] (If the chief executive of a company were paid an annual salary of $100,000, for example, his per diem pay would be $400, based upon 250 working days in a year, and this would be the daily pay of outside directors.) The obligation to pay directors higher fees would also lead to smaller and harder-working boards. Outside directors should be expected to devote material parts of their time to directorial tasks.

### Cumulative Voting

The law should permit cumulative voting by shareowners for directors. Like "intensity voting," it will enhance the political strength of shareowners. Although it carries a risk of factionalism on the board, the greater shareowner democracy makes this risk worth taking.[27]

---

The combined effect of these reforms would be to make boards more active and effective agencies of corporate government, and corporations themselves more socially sensitive and useful institutions.

## NOTES

1. See, for example, Andrew Hacker, ed., *The Corporation Takeover* (New York: Harper and Row, 1964).

2. See Scott Buchanan, *The Corporation and the Republic* (New York: Fund for the Republic, 1958).

3. See J. R. Daughen and P. Binzen, *The Wreck of the Penn Central* (Boston: Little, Brown, 1971), pp. 12, 17.

4. See *The Penn Central Failure and the Role of Financial Institutions*, Staff Report of the Committee on Banking and Currency, House of Representatives, 92d Congress, 1st Session, January 3, 1972 (Washington, D.C.: U.S. Government Printing Office, 1972), pp. vi, ix.

5. Arthur J. Goldberg, article in the *New York Times*, October 29, 1972.

6. Myles L. Mace, *Directors: Myth and Reality* (Boston: Division of Research, Graduate School of Business Administration, Harvard University, 1971), Ch. 9.

7. Richard Eells, *The Government of Corporations* (New York: Free Press of Glencoe, 1962), Pt. 1.

8. For an authoritative account of this development, see John W. Davis, *Corporations* (New York: Capricorn Books, 1961). Widening corporate powers under charters has, of course, been accompanied by a progressive narrowing of corporate authority by federal, state, and local governmental regulation.

9. See Dow Votaw, *Modern Corporations* (Englewood Cliffs, N.J.: Prentice-Hall, 1965).

10. See *Survey of Boards of Directors—Practices and Procedures* (New York: General Electric Company, December 1969).

11. *Ibid.* The findings of the General Electric Company *Survey of Boards of Directors* were, in general, confirmed by an independent survey of the boards of

directors of 1,500 American corporations by Heidrick and Struggles and reported in *The Director*, October 1971. (London)

12. See Chapter 4.

13. Charles de Hoghton, ed., *The Company: Law, Structure and Reform in Eleven Countries* (New York: Macmillan, 1969).

14. See, for example, Edward S. Mason, ed., *The Corporation in Modern Society* (Cambridge: Harvard University Press, 1959).

15. Specifically, the Project on Corporate Responsibility of the Ralph Nader organization proposed to add two "public" directors to the board of General Motors Corporation.

16. Scott Buchanan, *Essay on Politics* (New York: Philosophical Library, 1953); also his *The Corporation and the Republic*.

17. Professor Harold D. Koontz has emphasized the weakness of corporate boards built from a conglomerate of special interests. See his *The Board of Directors and Effective Management* (New York: McGraw-Hill, 1967), p. 235; also "Should There Be Special Interest Representation on Boards of Directors?" *Business Horizons* (Winter 1972).

18. De Hoghton, *The Company: Law, Structure and Reform,* pp. 141–163.

19. Published by the Commission of the European Communities Secretariat (Brussels: June 24, 1970).

20. See Ichak Adizes, *Industrial Democracy: Yugoslavian Style* (New York: Free Press, 1971), p. 130.

21. David Karr gives a vivid description of stockholder power and its use in proxy battles for control of the New York Central, Bank of America, Twin City Rapid Transit, United Cigar-Whelan, Minneapolis and St. Louis Railroad, Twentieth-Century Fox, and Montgomery Ward in his *Fight for Control* (New York: Ballantine Books, 1956).

22. The policy of the Securities and Exchange Commission has been to encourage stockholder participation in corporate affairs.

23. Abuse of the proxy privilege could be reduced by requiring that the holding of a specified minimum number of shares be required in order to place a name or a proposition on the ballot. See *The Corporate Secretary,* American Society of Corporate Secretaries, Inc., No. 184 (September 28, 1971).

24. Everett E. Smith of McKinsey and Company, quoted in *Business Week* (May 22, 1971).

25. This estimate results from adding the approximately 1,500 corporations whose shares are listed on the New York Stock Exchange, the 1,000 listed on the American Stock Exchange, the 1,000 listed on regional exchanges, and the 6,500 traded over the counter.

26. The courts have tended to lay heavier burdens on directors to exercise "due diligence." An example is the decision in *Escott* v. *BarChris Construction Company,* 283 F. Supp. 643 (S.D.N.Y. 1968). Rules against the use of inside information for personal profit have also become stringent, as witness the decision in the Texas Gulf Sulfur Case. Vance has noted the severe potential liabilities of directors from derivative suits and the difficulties of insuring against them. See Stanley C. Vance, *The Corporate Director—A Critical Evaluation* (Homewood, Illinois: Dow Jones-Irwin, 1968), p. 4.

27. See Charles M. Williams, *Cumulative Voting for Directors* (Boston: Division of Research, Harvard Graduate School of Business Administration, 1951), Ch. 10.

# PART IV

## CRITICAL SOCIAL ROLES

# CHAPTER 9

# The Corporation
# as Social Activist

O UR SOCIAL assessment of the corporation led us to analyze the issues of corporate concentration and fragmentation, of corporate political involvement and detachment, and of autocracy and democracy in corporate government. Our analysis revealed shortcomings in current corporate and government behavior in each of these areas—and we have proposed reforms. We now turn to an appraisal of three critical social roles of the corporation: helping to solve social problems, improving the environment, and supplying military hardware to the government.

The "social responsibilities" of the business corporation have been a central topic of public discussion in recent years. But what is the meaning of "corporate social responsibility"? The public, it appears, has endowed it with a very broad meaning. Thus, when consumers raise their voices in protest against unsafe, faulty, or misrepresented products; when employees complain of routinized jobs, bureaucratic paralysis, or inhumane working environments; when governmental officials investigate the putative misbehavior of military hardware makers, drug manufacturers, or con-

The underlying thesis of this chapter was originally developed for a conference on "The Corporation and the Quality of Life," held at the Center for the Study of Democratic Institutions from September 27 through October 1, 1971. The paper was presented under the title, "The Business Corporation in Social Service: Problem Solver for Government." This chapter also draws on my article, "What Is a Social Problem?" published in *The Center Magazine,* Vol. 4, No. 4 (July 1971), and an article entitled, "Capitalism and Contemporary Social Problems," published in the *Sloan Management Review,* Vol. 12, No. 2 (Winter 1971).

glomerates; when protests emanate from university campuses over the failure of corporations to eliminate poverty, hard-core unemployment, racial discrimination, crime, and urban decay; when stockholders demand that their companies leave South Africa, boycott Angola, or appoint women, blacks, and youths to their boards of directors; all are complaining in one way or another that business is not discharging its "social responsibilities."

*Such broadside criticism of corporate behavior is to be expected in an age of high public expectations and widespread skepticism, when all institutions are under attack.* From one point of view, it flatters corporate enterprise. Because of its demonstrated success in expanding production and elevating living standards, the public now looks to the American business system to achieve other social goals.

Paradoxically, it is the public belief in corporate capabilities, rather than the loss of confidence in them, that inspires criticism. Chairman James M. Roche of General Motors was wrong when he accused corporate critics of threatening the free economic system.[1] The truth is the contrary; having lost faith in government, the trade union, the church, and the university to bring mankind to Utopia, many critics have turned to the profit-seeking corporation. It becomes very important, therefore, to understand the limitations, as well as the possibilities, of corporate action in the social field.

We propose to present here a general theory of the social role of the business corporation, a theory that takes public opinion and political factors into account. This theory will help to justify what we believe is the ideal level of corporate social involvement, and will reconcile such involvement with the principle of optimizing the long-run interests of the shareowners. Implicit in the theory are also the guidelines and policies that enterprises should adopt in responding to the public demand for social action. First, however, we must examine the nature of "social problems."

## SOCIAL PROBLEMS AS EXPECTATION-REALITY GAPS

*We propose that the designation of some social condition as a "social problem" derives from a gap between a society's expectations about that condition and the present realities—from a disparity between what is and what people believe should be.*[2] Such a designation is basically a subjective rather than an objective phenomenon. The importance of a social problem is therefore determined as much by public expectations as it is by real conditions. Thus poverty is perceived to be a serious social problem in the United States when 11 percent of the population have incomes below the official "poverty" level. Twenty-five years ago the problem of poverty was perceived to be less serious, although 27 percent of the people then lived under the same poverty line! The explanation of the paradox is that public expectations of eliminating poverty outraced realities. Other social problems like inadequate housing, crime, malnutrition, poor health care, drug abuse, and racial discrimination are amenable to the same analysis.

The primary cause in enlarging "social problems" in the United States during the postwar era has been rising public expectations, rather than a failure of real conditions to improve. The quality of life has risen dramatically in many ways since World War II,[3] yet public sensitivity to what are viewed as social failings has become sharper than ever. This is so because American society is structured to enlarge expectation-reality gaps; the political and intellectual communities and the mass media all function as "gap enlargers" by elevating expectations and by depreciating social achievements.

*Of course, for each social situation which is viewed as a problem there is an optimal gap between expectations and realities.* Such a gap performs a useful function—public demands *should* be higher than current realities to provide incentive for improvement. When a gap becomes extremely large, however, and expectations of change have been elevated to unattainable heights, it becomes dysfunctional and leads to public disillusionment and frustration, and, in extreme cases, to violence and other antisocial behavior.

*There are also optimal rates of change in public expectations and in real social conditions.* Thus, the rate of improvement in, say, the nation's housing stock, is dependent upon the rate of increase in the real GNP and upon the priority given to housing by national economic policies. This real increase is constrained within rather narrow bounds—a 4 or 5 percent gain each year. But there is no resource constraint upon public *expectations* of additional housing, which may soar almost as high as the human imagination can take them. Ideally, the rate of change in public expectations would parallel the rate of change in objective possibilities for improvement; and, as mentioned above, expectations should be slightly ahead. It follows that political leaders should try to mold public expectations within constructive limits while they are working to improve real social conditions.

*The "social tension" of a society might be defined as the sum of the expectation-reality gaps of all the social problems within the range of public consciousness.* Because the number of problems that the people of a nation can cope with effectively at any time is limited by their stock of wisdom and energy, as well as by the available economic resources, national leaders and the mass media may, by dramatizing one social deficiency after another, stimulate public expectations so powerfully that multiple social "crises" are created in the public's mind. This process went on under the Johnson administration in the 1960's. It was exacerbated by the mounting American involvement in the unpopular Vietnam war, which upset national priorities and civilian programs. By 1968, public frustration, i.e., "social tension," had reached a dangerous level in the United States. The people demanded immediate social improvements which were far beyond the capability of any society to deliver. Violence and radical activism mounted to a peak.

Three elements of an ideal social policy can thus be identified: maintain for each social problem a *functional gap* between expectations and realities; achieve a *rate of change* in expectations which is proportional to real possibilities for improvement in each social condition; and work to *limit* the social conditions actively in the public consciousness to that number for which available resources permit of significant real gains.[4] These conditions should be established, of course, through the democratic processes of public discussion and representative government.

The expectation-reality gap concept may be used to clarify public perception of the social role of the large business corporation. Public opinion polls make clear that *Americans hold high expectations of the role that business should play in bettering our society, but believe that the realities of business performance have fallen short of their expectations.*[5] Indeed, two-thirds of the people believe business corporations should spend some of their profits for social purposes.

The question then arises: To what extent are public expectations of the social performance of business appropriate and functional, and to what extent exaggerated and dysfunctional? The public rightly expects from business a higher level of socially responsible performance than it has displayed in such problems as air pollution or automobile safety. On the other hand, the public has exaggerated the technical, financial, and managerial capabilities of business corporations, by themselves, to alleviate poverty, hard-core unemployment, poor education, or urban slums. The public tends to forget that profit-seeking business needs profit motivation, and that, in these areas, only government can create such motivation. As Chairman C. B. McCoy of duPont observed recently, the call for business social responsibility has validity; but businessmen should educate the public to the fact that corporation executives are not urban planners or policy-makers and cannot solve all social ills.[6]

# POLITICAL AND ECONOMIC INTERACTIONS IN THE SOCIAL SYSTEM

To understand the social role of business, American society must be visualized as an open and dynamic system in which the political and the economic subsystems interact. Figure 4 depicts the basic elements of this system. The *primary* flow of influence runs from changes in public values, *via* the political process, to changes in governmental regulation of the private sector and in allocations of public resources; and then, *via* the market process, to changes in the relative quantities and prices of business products, and in allocations of private resources.

FIGURE 4

*Dynamic Relationships between Public Values, Governmental Regulations, and Corporate Resource Allocations*

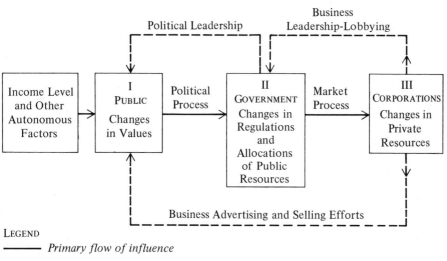

LEGEND

——— *Primary flow of influence*

– – – *Secondary flow of influence*

For example, the rising value placed by Americans upon clean air led to the enactment of federal and state standards limiting emissions of pollutants from automobiles. Manufacturers thereupon modified their cars to meet these standards, recovering their higher costs in higher prices. Essentially, they "internalized," in the purchase price of automobiles, the external costs of avoiding the air pollution which had formerly been thrust upon the public. Because no one manufacturer could afford to internalize these costs by himself, due to the competitive disadvantage he would suffer, government had to enact standards applicable to all automobile makers. And in resolving many social problems, governmental legislation is essential to trigger socially desired business action. Until government acts to create a "market" for clean air, pure water, slum-free cities, or employment of the disadvantaged, the profit-seeking corporation's involvement cannot be extensive. Criticism of business for lack of "social conscience" is pointless if government fails to provide the necessary incentives.

Yet the corporation is not a mere reactor to changes in public values and governmental regulation.[7] As Figure 4 indicates, it is also a secondary source of influence *on* public values and legislation. Corporate advertising and selling efforts help to shape public values, just as they are responses to demands created by those values. Corporate lobbying influences the nature of the public regulation of the private sector. Similarly, political leaders not only respond to changes in public values, they also mobilize and modify these changes.

*If the political and economic subsystems of American society are to interact in the public interest, it is desirable that the business community facilitate rather than obstruct the political and market changes called for by shifts in public values.* Often in the past business has been obstructive, as is illustrated by the initial opposition of American automobile manufacturers to automobile safety and antipollution regulation. But businessmen have a wide scope for initiative in helping government design policies which will facilitate business responses to social demands. Only if the public understands the interaction between the profit-seeking corporation and government will its expectations of corporate social action be realizable. On the other hand, exaggerated public expectations that corporations will quickly resolve all of the nation's social problems can lead to frustration, resentment, and punitive action that could halter American social progress.

## SOCIAL RESPONSIBILITY IN THREE MODELS OF THE ENTERPRISE

Want of an adequate theory of the ideal behavior of the large business corporation lies at the heart of current confusion over the social role of business. The basic difficulty is not so much ignorance of corporate social involvement, but rather the lack of an adequate criterion by which it should be judged. A theory of ideal corporate behavior, having operational validity in the real world, is required.

Many theories have been advanced about the motivation and the behavior of business enterprises, each differing from the others in its emphasis upon particular psychological or economic factors.[8] We will focus our attention upon the two main theories of enterprise behavior. These theories, which have succeeded each other historically, are the Classical Market Model and the Managerial Model. After examining the notion of "social responsibility" in these two models, we shall propose a third theory, the Social Environment Model, which, we hope, avoids the faults of its predecessors and provides a rational explanation of corporate social action that is consistent with the motive of profit optimization. A comparison of the characteristics of the three models is set forth in Figure 5.

## *The Classical Market Model*

The Classical Market Model of enterprise behavior was formulated by members of the Classical school of British economic theory, which began with Adam Smith and was developed mainly through the writings of David Ricardo, John Stuart Mill, and Alfred Marshall. The Classical vision of the mode of operation of the enterprise was, of course, based on observations of the industrial structures and processes that characterized late eighteenth-century and nineteenth-century Britain. That economy was composed of relatively small enterprises, managed by owner-founders or their family heirs, producing relatively simple products. The Classical school held that, except for "natural" monopolies and illegal conspiracies among competitors, large numbers of independent firms tended to make for "atomistic" market structures and for perfect competition. The entrepreneur, in the acquisition of productive factors and in the sale of his products, reacted to information coming to him from markets. Because products and methods of distribution were simple, competition was conducted almost wholly on the basis of price. The limited resources of the enterprise made it necessary for the entrepreneur to maximize his profits in the short run.

Classical theory gave a convincing explanation of the way in which, under perfect competition, the effort of the entrepreneur to maximize his profits concurrently served the interests of society. Competition compelled each firm to produce with maximum efficiency and at lowest cost, to offer its products to the public at prices that covered costs plus profits just sufficient to keep it in business, and to drive inefficient firms out of the market. As Adam Smith put it, the entrepreneur will be "led by an invisible hand to promote . . . the interests of society more effectually than when he really intends to promote it."

*The Classical Market Model did not contemplate involvement by the firm in the solution of social problems, in the sense that we now understand it.* Guided by the rule of profit maximization, the enterprise was considered to have discharged its responsibilities to society if it efficiently met

FIGURE 5

*Three Models of Behavior of the Business Enterprise*

| Characteristic | Classical Market Model | Managerial Model | Social Environment Model |
|---|---|---|---|
| Nature of the Economy | Perfectly Competitive | Monopolistic-Oligopolistic | Effectively Competitive |
| Level of Profits | Normal | Super-normal | Normal |
| Enterprise Goal | Short-run Profit Maximization | Security and Growth of Business Volume | Long-run Profit Maximization |
| Locus of Decision-Making Power | Entrepreneurs | Managers | Stockholders-Board of Directors |
| Nature of Competition | Price | Price Product Variation Selling Costs | Multi-vectored Dynamic Process |
| External Constraints on Enterprise Behavior | Markets | Markets | Markets Public Opinion Political Pressures |
| Determinants of Social Activity | None | Social and Charitable Propensities of Managers | Long-run Profit Maximization |

market demands for its products. Such, essentially, was the view of business social responsibility up through the initial decades of the twentieth century.

## The Managerial Model

During the 1930's economists became aware of the widening gap between the Classical Market Model of enterprise and the then-current nature of corporate business. The catastrophe of the Great Depression precipitated a critical examination of all economic institutions, including the business corporation. In their *Modern Corporation and Private Property,* Berle and Means first analyzed the implications of the widespread separation of ownership from the management of large business corporations.[9] They concluded that this institutional change had altered the goals of enterprise. It had lodged decision-making powers firmly in the hands of hired managers responsible to directors and stockholders only in very limited ways. Later, both Chamberlain and Robinson further challenged the Classical theory of competition by observing that it failed to take into account the phenomena of product variation, advertising, and selling costs.[10] Regrettably, they did not present these factors as new dimensions of competition—which they truly were—but as evidences that monopoly power was pervasive. During the 1930's, there was also much concern about the increasing size of corporations and the concentration of output. The *Studies* and *Final Report* of the Temporary National Economic Committee, made during 1939–1941, emphasized these trends and expressed doubts about the adequacy of competition.[11]

Building on these criticisms and analyses, a number of economists, during the 1940's and 1950's, developed a new view of American enterprise that may appropriately be called the Managerial Model because it emphasizes the central role of professional managers.[12] Managerialists see the giant corporation as the dominant actor in the economy. Because in many industries output is concentrated in a few great companies, the economy is seen to be permeated with oligopoly. Competition being muted, profits are abnormally high. Professional managers hold the reins of power. They are effectively free from control either by the unorganized stockholders or by boards of directors, whose composition they control through the proxy machinery. Hence, the corporation is no longer operated to optimize profits for stockholders. Its goal is to maximize the satisfactions of its managers, who seek security, power, and prestige for themselves through the growth of the firm. An alternative concept, espoused by some Managerialists, is that the corporate executive is essentially a trustee, concerned with an equitable division of corporate gains among owners, workers, suppliers and customers.[13] In either case the behavior of the firm is largely determined by the discretionary power of management and is only loosely constrained by competition.

Clearly, *a considerable involvement of the business corporation in social activities is possible under the Managerial Model.* Once profit-optimization is removed as the criterion of good enterprise behavior, many reasons can be found for spending corporate funds for social purposes. Managers have a wide authority to allocate corporate resources for different purposes. The theory assumes that they have ample monopoly or oligopoly profits to spend on social amelioration and philanthropy. Under this model, a *company's social involvement is limited only by the humanitarian propensities of its management.*

## The Social Environment Model

Historical processes have a perverse habit of overturning popular doctrines. Just as the Market Model of enterprise behavior gave way to the Managerial Model, so the Managerial Model is now being challenged for its inability to depict and explain current realities. We have already seen that large corporations in the highly concentrated industries commonly refuse to behave like monopolists or oligopolists. They continually innovate and bring new products into the market. Their profit rates, far from being abnormally high, have been lower than those of medium-sized companies during recent years. Indeed, competition has expanded along new dimensions, and has come to involve many variables in addition to price.[14]

With the massive institutionalization of shareownership, the rise of stockholder organizations, and the gearing of executive compensation to the profitability of companies through bonuses and stock options, the notion that managers behave contrary to the interests of the shareowners has become obsolete in its application to most companies.[15] Shareowners are reasserting their role as the ultimate arbiters of corporate policy.

The inadequacies of the Managerial Model make it necessary to adopt a new model that more adequately explains enterprise behavior in contemporary society, especially its social involvement. As Kuhn has observed, a model is never abandoned because of its refutation by facts, however damaging, but only when it is replaced by another model.[16] We propose, therefore, a new theory of enterprise behavior which we call the Social Environment Model because its central tenet is that *the enterprise reacts to the total societal environment and not merely to markets.* We offer this Social Environment Model as explanatory of actual corporate behavior, as a basis for predictions of corporate social action, and as suggestive of the norms a profit-seeking enterprise *should* follow in relation to social problems.

*The most important characteristic of the Social Environment Model is the explicit recognition that corporate behavior responds to political as well as to market forces.* Whereas both Classical and Managerial theory ignored the impact of political forces, the Social Environment theory analyzes corporate behavior as a response to both market and nonmarket forces because both affect the firm's costs, revenues, and profits.[17] It has been the pressures of public opinion, the demands of stockholders, the urgings and threats of legislatures and bureaucrats, and the proddings of such enthusiastic ombudsmen as Ralph Nader—all nonmarket forces—that have induced large companies to allocate resources to social purposes. Whether their motives were defensive or offensive, corporations made the allocations basically to enhance their profits in the long run or to defend existing profits against erosion. Large size and greater financial security enable the contemporary corporation to act with reference to a more distant horizon than the relatively small firm of the nineteenth century was able to contemplate. (See Figure 5.)

## RISE OF POLITICAL INFLUENCE ON CORPORATE BEHAVIOR

*The swift increase in political influence on business behavior, of which the burgeoning "consumerism" movement is one example, is an important phenomenon of our times.* It has been discussed by Professor Hirschman in connection with his distinction between "voice" and "exit" as alternative reactions of people to what they consider to be deficient business performance.[18] If a company were deficient in performance, the standard reaction assumed by Classical theory was the customer's exit from market dealings with the firm. His alternative, now increasingly used, is to voice his protest to management in terms ranging from grumbling to violence. Today, *both* exert influence on the firm's behavior. Through the ages, *caveat emptor* has been the accepted rule of law. Consumerism has changed the rule to *caveat vendor!*

Ignored by economic theory, voice can play either an exclusive or a complementary role to exit in disciplining corporate behavior. Voice is the only remedy available to dissatisfied customers in a situation where they cannot exit because the products of *all* firms in an industry have the same deficiency; e.g., until just recently, the bumpers on automobiles of all makers collapsed from impact which occurred at more than three miles per hour! In many instances, voice may be the more powerful instrument because it aims to change an objectionable condition rather than simply to escape from it. Used intelligently, it is a healthy development in American society to which corporate managers must adjust.

People may employ voice not only to express dissatisfaction with products already on the market, but also to condemn corporate failure to develop and offer improved products. An example might be the failure of an automobile manufacturer to make a safe vehicle. Rather than boycott the present products of the company—a market reaction—the public might put strong pressures on the company to install safety devices—a political reaction. If compliance is cheaper than combatting such pressures, the company will comply, thus optimizing profits while improving the product.

The political pressures on an enterprise are *transformed* into market pressures when government enacts laws or regulations compelling all firms in an industry to behave in the socially desired manner. For example strong public pressures to reduce emissions of pollutants from vehicles led to the passage of the Federal Air Quality Standards Act in 1967. All automobile makers were then obliged to produce cars meeting the standards. The new law expressed a social consensus that relieved the dissatisfactions of the public and transformed political pressure into market pressure.[19]

## CORPORATE SOCIAL ACTION AND SELF-INTEREST

The great virtue of the Social Environment Model is that it reconciles the principle of enlightened self-interest with corporate concern for social responsibility. Although sensitive corporate executives have long responded to nonmarket influences, such responses have not found a place in the accepted theory of the firm. Received theory does not take into account the rise in political pressures exerted upon enterprises by groups of stockholders, consumers, environmental protectionists, and others.

Rational enterprise managers judge the yield of outlays for social purposes by their long-run effect upon profits. They measure the return on the "investment" in each social program. Each social outlay is tested by a cost/benefit analysis. Among the benefits may be a reduction in the costs of defending the firm's actions before the legislative or executive agencies of government, an avoidance of onerous governmental regulations or a reduction in property damage at the hands of activists. Social pressures generate costs, the amount of which can be minimized by appropriate corporate outlays. When viewed in the perspective of our model, there is no conflict between profit maximization and corporate social activity. The popular notion that a company which pursues profit must eschew a social role, or that social involvement means a sacrifice of profit, is unfounded.[20] On the contrary, *the contemporary corporation must become socially involved in order to maximize its profits.*

No firm can afford to ignore public attitudes and expectations. Thus Dow Chemical could not be oblivious to the adverse effects, upon its recruitment of college graduates, of widespread student protests of its sale of napalm to the Department of Defense. Nor could General Motors ignore the possibility that Congressional hearings on automobile safety, sparked by Ralph Nader's *Unsafe at Any Speed,* would lead to punitive legislation costly to the company. On the other hand, charitable gifts may cultivate goodwill and generate larger sales from an approving public. Neighborhood rehabilitation can pay off in enhanced business volume or higher property values. Hiring the disadvantaged may enable a company to escape new taxes, repressive governmental regulation, or disruption of business by dissidents.

It is often said that big companies should "legitimate" their great economic and political power by assuming larger social responsibilities. But the premise that big companies possess such power is not correct. Even if it were, the statement that it should mimic the government does not follow. We have already shown that the economic power of even the largest enterprises are closely constrained by market competition and governmental regulation; and we have observed that their political power is more than balanced by that of other interest groups in society.[21] *Should the power of any enterprise become inordinate, the remedy is to curb that power—not to accept it and then ask the firm to become socially "responsible" in using it!* The more important point, however, is that the corporation does, and should, engage in socially ameliorative activity because it serves its enlightened self-interest and not because it is "powerful." Enterprises must balance an equation of social pressure with social action, not an equation of power and "responsibility." The firm's social involvement should be based on political and economic grounds.

The Social Environment theory is congruent with a basic principle which has been advocated by the Committee for Economic Development. It is in the enlightened self-interest of the corporation to devote resources to improving the environment in which it operates, because it "is dependent upon the goodwill of society, which can sustain or impair its existence through public pressures on government." [22]

Professor Friedman has written in a provocative statement that it would undermine the very foundation of a competitive economy if corporate managements generally abandoned the rule of making as much money for their stockholders as possible.[23] Unfortunately, Friedman failed

to add that social involvement is consistent with self-interest, and that cor
porate managers need a sophisticated understanding of business-societa
relationships in order to operate on that principle. Those economists
and businessmen who assert that the purpose of business is "business"
and not social "do-gooding" are as much in error as the radicals of the
New Left who would compel business to concentrate on social improvement.

# THE RATIONALE FOR
# CORPORATE GIVING

Because contributions for charitable and educational purposes were
the earliest form of corporate social action, their pattern enables us to test
the validity of our theory. Corporate giving was stimulated by federal
legislation in 1935 authorizing companies to deduct from taxable income
up to 5 percent on account of such gifts. It was further enhanced by the
decision of a New Jersey court in the A. P. Smith case (1953) that such
gifts were desirable even though a corporate management could not show
that they produced any *direct* benefit to the donor company.[24]

Managerial theory clearly suggests that, as companies grow larger,
gifts will comprise a rising fraction of corporate income. Because monopoly profits are alleged to rise with growing size, corporate managers presumably will seek to gain still greater power and status in society through
corporate gifts. Giant corporations would be expected to donate larger
fractions of their pre-tax incomes to social causes than smaller companies
because they tend to operate in concentrated industries in which monopoly
power and profit rates are alleged to be the highest.

Yet the facts are inconvenient to Managerial theory. A survey of a
thousand corporations revealed that the major companies donated about
0.66 percent of pre-tax incomes in 1968, compared to 1–3 percent for
small concerns. Big corporations have donated *smaller* fractions of their
pre-tax income than have small companies, probably because the owner-
managements of small firms do not have to answer to outside stockholders.[25]
Corporate donations in the aggregate have accounted for under one percent
of pre-tax income—less than one-fifth the amount of allowable deduc-
tions. The percentage of pre-tax income donated has *not* risen during the
past twenty years. Most significantly, the predominant fraction of all corporate gifts is made to schools, hospitals, and welfare and civic agencies of
communities in which the donor firms operate facilities and from which
they derive rather specific benefits. It is likely that donations of the time of
officers, and of equipment and supplies, conform to much the same pattern

as monetary gifts.[26] Evidently, American business corporations have tended to follow the principle of enlightened self-interest, rather than that of pure philanthropy, in making contributions. The Social Environment theory provides a better explanation of corporate behavior than does Managerial theory.

The percentages of gifts from pre-tax income by corporations in different industries throw light upon the factors that determine the level of community involvement by business. (See Figure 6.) The range of philanthropic effort was great. Banks and printing and publishing firms were the most liberal contributors, followed by apparel makers, motion picture exhibitors, department stores, and other retailing and service industries. At the low end of the giving spectrum are oil and gas drilling companies, electronic communications firms, and public utilities.

Taking the percentage of pre-tax income donated by firms in each industry as an index of its social involvement, we find that *corporate giving is generally in proportion to the extensiveness of local public contacts which generate social pressures*. Thus the profitability of a commercial bank is heavily dependent upon the character of its neighborhood and the goodwill and confidence of the local population. A bank is therefore likely to become active in community matters. The profits of an oil-producing firm are far less affected by such factors. (Public utility firms were low because the regulatory agencies have discouraged contributions.)

While gifts have been the means by which corporations have alleviated some of the social pressures of the *communities* in which they operate facilities, changes in products or in production processes have been the means by which they have responded to *national* pressures brought by the public. Thus, while the automobile and petroleum industries stood at the bottom of all industries in the ratio of gifts to net income, they have expended vast sums in rebuilding refineries and automobile engines in order to reduce air pollution.

The degree of social involvement by a corporation appears to be determined by the size of the public's expectation-reality gap in regard to its performance, the amount of public pressure upon it, and, most important of all, by the strength of the incentives to social action provided by government. We now examine public policies for this last purpose.

## PUBLIC POLICIES TO TRIGGER CORPORATE SOCIAL ACTION

Although political pressures can induce social action by business corporations, the most efficient instruments for expanding their social role

FIGURE 6

*Percentages of Pre-tax Net Income of U.S. Business Corporations Donated to Charitable Organizations, by Industry, 1966-67*

| Industry | Percentage of Pre-tax Income Donated |
|---|---|
| Banking, Printing, and Publishing | 2.1 |
| Apparel and Leather Goods Manufacturing | 2.0 |
| Motion Picture Exhibition, Department Stores, Mail-Order Retailing, Furniture Manufacturing, Laundries, Beauty Shops, Photographers, Personal Service Firms | 1.6 |
| Chemical Manufacturing, Photographic Manufacturing, Scientific Equipment Makers, Watchmakers, Textile Manufacturing | 1.4 |
| Specialty Retailing, Stone, Clay and Glass Manufacturing, Wholesaling | 1.3 |
| Construction Contracting, Food Manufacturing, Hotels and Motels, Rubber and Plastic Manufacturing | 1.2 |
| Advertising Agencies, Janitorial Services, Lumber, Paper Manufacturers, Stock and Commodity Brokers, Transportation Equipment Manufacturers other than Automobiles | 1.1 |
| Electrical Equipment Makers, Metal and Steel Fabricators | 1.0 |
| Farming and Fishing, Investment Companies, Insurance Companies, Oil Refining, Real Estate | 0.9 |
| Consumer Financing, Machinery Manufacturers, Mining Companies | 0.8 |
| Automobile Repair Shops, Tobacco Manufacturing, Railroads, Airplanes, Shipping Companies | 0.7 |
| Electric, Gas, and Sewer Utilities | 0.6 |
| Telephone, and Radio and Television Broadcasting | 0.4 |
| Automobile and Truck Manufacturing, Automobile Parts Makers | 0.3 |
| Oil and Gas Drilling Companies | 0.1 |

SOURCE: Study made by C. W. Shever and Company, New York, based on data from the 1966 and 1967 tax returns of 939,846 companies in 42 industries, compiled by the U.S. Internal Revenue Service and reported in the *Wall Street Journal* (January 11, 1971).

are (1) government contracts and *incentives* to produce desired social goods and services, (2) the establishment of environmental or other *standards* to which *all* enterprises must conform, (3) the imposition of *penalties* upon those who damage the public interest. The optimum instrument, or combination of instruments, will vary with the particular social problem on which corporate action is sought.

Such incentives as rent subsidies, governmental leases, low-interest rate mortgage loans, and accelerated depreciation have proved effective in expanding the supply of low- and middle-income housing. Governmental condemnation, clearance, and assembly of land tracts for sale to redevelopers have facilitated urban renewal programs. Contracts for training the hard-core unemployed have been used to good advantage. In reducing air and water pollution, federal or state standards limiting the emission of pollution have been very important. Fines or penalties charged per unit of pollutants emitted, such as the proposed federal tax per pound of sulfur emissions, are further methods of internalizing pollution abatement costs, of making prices reflect full costs. Governmental subsidies, loans, credit guarantees, and tax benefits can also be employed in environmental improvement. These alternatives are examined in the next chapter, which concerns the relation of the corporation to the environment.

Two points need emphasis: *Governmental legislation or regulation is necessary to "trigger" corporate social action.* Governmental regulation of all firms in an industry is superior to private political pressure applied only to some firms in that industry because it can bring about uniform adjustments. To no small degree, criticisms of business derive from a failure to comprehend these truths. The tardiness of the political system in reaching consensus and embodying it in laws and regulations has, more often than not, created "crises" and led to excessive "voice." Business has been wrongly blamed for many faults in American life; but it has been rightly criticized for not facilitating their correction. *Business will only actualize its full potential for improving the quality of life if government creates markets for the socially desired goods that business can supply.*

## CORPORATE POLICIES TO RESPOND TO SOCIAL NEEDS

To assure timely responses to the new demands occasioned by changes in social values, corporations should revamp both their policies and organizations. New organizational structures and managerial processes are required to implement the Social Environmental Model of corporate behavior. Social and political variables should be incorporated into business plans along with economic, financial, and technological factors. Many far sighted companies have already done so. We propose the following specific measures:

## "Social Sensors"

"Social sensors" should be developed to identify and measure changes in public values, attitudes, and expectations that bear upon the company's performance. They must go beyond traditional market research programs that are focused upon consumers' attitudes toward the company's products They should embrace public opinion polls and surveys on a wide range of subjects.

## Feedback Processes

Feedback processes should be established within the company to evaluate and act upon the information acquired. Some corporations meet this requirement with a staff Department of Public Affairs reporting to the President or Board Chairman. To assure consideration of these inputs at the highest policy level, it is also desirable for the Board of Directors to create a standing Committee on Public Affairs. Directors with special knowledge and interests in societal problems should be appointed to this Committee.

## Communication with Social Groups

Two-way channels of communication should be established with consumers, employees, students, and leaders of political, labor, religious, and educational institutions, as well as with the mass media. These channels should be used regularly as sources of intelligence about attitudes and values, and as instruments to transmit information about the company's goals, activities, and accomplishments.

## A "Social Account"

A systematic record should be kept of all company outlays made to improve the quality of life. It will include not only monetary contributions to social agencies, but also the value of employee time and of equipment and supplies loaned or donated for public purposes, the amount of capital and operating expenses incurred to abate pollution, to train hard-core unemployed, or to help resolve other social problems.

## *A "Social Audit"*

A social audit, made under the direction of the Committee on Public Affairs of the Board of Directors, would measure the company's progress toward the social goals it has set for itself. These may include employing minorities and women, meeting pollution standards, improving working conditions, conducting training programs, conserving resources, improving communities, or other goals.[27] Although it would be premature to publish such audits until goals are defined and programs to achieve them are developed, ultimately they should be published. As David Rockefeller has said, "Because of the growing pressure for greater corporate accountability, I can foresee the day when, in addition to the annual financial statements certified by independent accountants, corporations may be required to publish a 'social audit,' similarly certified." [28]

———

The behavior of the business corporation is being ever more strongly influenced by political forces. Increasingly, corporate executives are required to measure, to react to, and to help shape the public attitudes that surround them. The American corporation must be responsive to these forces, while continuing to meet market demands in ways that serve its enlightened self-interest.[29]

## *NOTES*

1. See *Wall Street Journal* (November 15, 1970).
2. See Neil H. Jacoby, "What Is a Social Problem?" *Center Magazine,* Vol. 4, No. 4 (July–August 1971), for a full statement of the concept.
3. See *Toward a Social Report,* A Report to the President by the Panel on Social Indicators (Washington, D.C.: Department of Health, Education, and Welfare, 1969).
4. President Nixon made this point in his State of the Union message to the Congress in January, 1971.
5. See the results of a study made during 1970 by Opinion Research Corporation, cited in *Social Responsibilities of Business Corporations* (New York: Committee for Economic Development, June 1971), pp. 14–15.
6. Address to The Business Council (May 7, 1971), White Sulphur Springs.
7. The *primary* processes of value formation in American society occur in the home, the school, the church, and in the political system of the state. It is here that each person acquires and assigns priorities to his values. Only after values have been so ordered does the business corporation enter the scene as a satisfier of the value-based wants of the public. However, it would be naive to assert that the corporation has not come to play a significant role in the formation of individual and social values. After all, half of the work force spends half of its waking hours within

the business corporation. And all of us spend many of our nonworking hours sur
rounded by the products and services of corporate enterprise, and looking at or hear
ing its advertising, all of which circumscribe our choices and shape the quality o
our day-to-day existence. Clearly, the corporation is, to some extent, a *creator* o
values as well as a responder to them.

8. For a discussion of these theories see Richard M. Cyert and James F. March
*Behavioral Theory of the Firm* (Englewood Cliffs, N.J.: Prentice-Hall, 1963)
J. G. March and H. A. Simon, *Organizations* (New York: Wiley, 1958); Willian
Baumol, *Business Behavior, Values and Growth,* 2d ed. (New York: Harcour
Brace and World, 1967).

9. Adolf Berle and Gardiner Means, *The Modern Corporation and Privat*
*Property* (New York: Macmillan, 1932).

10. Edward S. Chamberlin, *Theory of Monopolistic Competition* (Cambridge
Harvard University Press, 1938); Joan Robinson, *The Economics of Imperfect Com*
*petition* (London: Macmillan, 1938).

11. See especially *Final Report of the Temporary National Economic Com*
*mittee* (Washington, D.C.: U.S. Government Printing Office, 1941).

12. See, for example, Clarence Walton, *Corporate Social Responsibilities* (Bel
mont, Calif.: Wadsworth, 1967) and its extensive footnote citations. Galbrait
has carried the Managerial concept to an extreme in his, *The New Industrial Stat*
(Boston: Houghton Mifflin, 1967).

13. See, for example, Edward S. Mason, ed., *The Corporation in Moder*
*Society* (Cambridge: Harvard University Press, 1959). Also, Ralph Cordiner, *New*
*Frontiers for Professional Managers* (New York: McGraw-Hill, 1956).

14. See Chapter 6.

15. See, for example, Robert J. Larner, *Management Control and the Larg*
*Corporation* (Cambridge: Dunellen, 1970), who concludes, "although control i
separated from ownership in most of America's large corporations, the effects on th
profit orientation of firms and on stockholders' welfare have been minor." (p. 66)
Wilbur G. Lewellen in *The Ownership Income of Management* (New York: Nationa
Bureau of Economic Research, 1971), also produces convincing evidence that pro
fessional managers of large corporations share with stockholders the goal of profi
maximization. (pp. 11–12)

16. Thomas S. Kuhn, *The Structure of Scientific Revolutions* (Chicago: Uni
versity of Chicago Press, 1962).

17. There is a widening perception of the fact that both the Classical and th
Managerial theories provide too constrictive a framework for understanding enter
prise behavior, and that the viability of the firm depends upon its adaptability to it
total environment. See, for example, William R. King, "Systems Analysis at th
Public-Private Marketing Frontier," *Journal of Marketing,* Vol. 33 (January 1969)
pp. 84–89.

18. Albert O. Hirschman, *Exit, Voice, and Loyalty* (Cambridge: Harvard Uni
versity Press, 1970).

19. Daniel Bell contends that this trend will be strong. See his "The Yea
2000—The Trajectory of an Idea," *Daedalus* (Summer 1967), pp. 639–651.

20. This error is frequently made. For example, President B. R. Dorsey of Gul
Oil Company told his shareholders at their annual meeting in 1971 that "maximun
financial gain must now move into second place, wherever it conflicts with the well
being of society." Many stockholders replied indignantly, "Not with my money!
*Wall Street Journal* (March 22, 1971). In their article, "Do We Need a New Cor

porate Response to a Changing Social Environment?" Professors Dow Votaw and Prakash Sethi assert that the "old" concepts of profit maximizing and responsibility to shareholders are "outmoded"! *California Management Review,* Vol. 12. No. 1 (Fall 1969).

21. See Chapters 6 and 7.

22. Committee for Economic Development, *Social Responsibilities of Business Corporations* (New York: June 1971). Founded in 1942, the CED is an influential organization of the top executives of two hundred leading American corporations and universities. It studies important public issues and publishes Statements on National Policy.

23. Milton Friedman, *Capitalism and Freedom* (Chicago: University of Chicago Press, 1962), p. 133.

24. See *A. P. Smith Manufacturing Co.* v. *Barlow et al.,* 13 N.J. 145, 98 A. 2d 551 (1953). For a full history of this subject see Morrell Heald, *The Social Responsibilities of Business: Company and Community, 1900–1960* (Cleveland: Western Reserve University Press, 1970).

25. See Committee for Economic Development, *op. cit.,* p. 41.

26. For a full discussion of the development of corporate gifts to education in the United States, see Kenneth G. Patrick and Richard Eells, *Education and the Business Dollar* (New York: Macmillan, 1969).

27. See *Indicators of Social Change,* eds. Eleanor Sheldon and Wilbert E. Moore (New York: Russell Sage Foundation, 1968).

28. David Rockefeller, Address to the Advertising Council, reported in *Los Angeles Times* (January 3, 1971). See also Raymond A. Bauer and Dan H. Fenn, Jr., *The Corporate Social Audit* (New York: Russell Sage Foundation, 1972).

29. George A. Steiner reached a similar conclusion, but through a somewhat different argument. See his *Business and Society* (New York: Random House, 1971), p. 164. Impressive evidence of voluntary responses to social needs was furnished by the 181 companies that responded to a request made to the first 300 corporations on the *Fortune* "500" list. See *Initiatives in Corporate Responsibility,* Consumer Subcommittee of the Committee on Commerce, U.S. Senate (Washington, D.C.: U.S. Government Printing Office, October 1972). See also *Profiles of Involvement: A Compilation of Over 500 Case Studies of Corporate Social Action* (Philadelphia: Human Resources Corporation, 1972).

# CHAPTER 10

# The Corporation
# as Environmentalist

O F THE MANY social problems recently laid at the door of American corporate enterprise, the most complex and insistent is the problem of improving the physical environment. It merits special attention because it teaches important lessons about business-government cooperation to improve the quality of life.

Public concern about the environment mounted with astonishing swiftness in the late 1960's. Suddenly, it was discovered that the nation was running out of clean air and water. Suddenly, everyone saw that smog, noise, congestion, highway carnage, oil-stained beaches, automobile graveyards, and ugliness not only offend the senses, but can threaten our health and our very lives. Having belatedly come to a realization of environmental degradation, we have begun to identify the sources and to take corrective action. It is timely, therefore, to ask some central questions. What caused environmental deterioration, and why did the problem emerge so swiftly? What are the merits of the many diagnoses of, and prescriptions for, this problem? How can the environment be improved and who should pay the costs? What should be the respective roles of business and of government in restoring environmental amenities? Above all, what lessons can this issue teach about the functioning of our political and market systems and the reforms needed to avert similar problems in the future?

An early version of this chapter was published under the title, "The Environmental Crisis," in *The Center Magazine*, Vol. 3, No. 6 (November–December 1970). Parts of it were subsequently reprinted in *Ecocide—and Thoughts Toward Survival*, eds., Clifton Fadiman and Jean White (Palo Alto, Calif.: James Freel, 1971), and elsewhere. I gratefully acknowledge the helpful comments of Professors Fred E. Case and Michael Granfield.

# FOCUS ON THE URBAN
# PHYSICAL ENVIRONMENT

We will focus our attention upon the physical environment of our cities and urbanized areas, that is, upon the aesthetic and life-sustaining qualities of the land, air, water, and physical facilities that surround the three out of four Americans who live in towns and cities. It is this milieu, in particular, that has become less and less desirable and humane through air and water pollution, excessive noise, industrial and household waste, deteriorating homes and neighborhoods, congestion, loss of privacy and recreational facilities, accidents, slower transportation, and—not least— drabness and ugliness. It is the combination of these symptoms of environmental deterioration that has aroused the American people.

The urban environment can only be understood adequately when it is viewed as one aspect of the entire global ecosystem, which also embraces rural lands, the oceans, the atmosphere surrounding the earth, and some aspects of outer space. It has also become clear that, since all parts of this system are organically related, human interaction with it must be analyzed, planned, and managed as a whole.

Of course, the physical environment is only one dimension of man's well-being, of the quality of human life. In focusing upon the physical environment, we put to one side important factors of our social and psychological "environment," such as order and security, social mobility, and the individual's opportunity for social participation. All of these factors, along with per capita income, wealth, health and education, it goes without saying, need enhancement.[1]

The urban physical environment, nevertheless, merits special study because it affects so seriously such a large majority of our population, and, by general assent, many of its qualities have sunk below the threshold of tolerability. In addition, physical factors powerfully influence the health, mental attitude, and life-style of urban residents, so that the enhancement of the physical environment may be counted on to elevate the social and psychological qualities of American society.

# ROOTS OF THE
# ENVIRONMENTAL PROBLEM

The deterioration of the physical environment of American cities can be attributed, in large measure, to the combined effects of three powerful social forces: *population concentration, rising affluence, and the develop-*

*ment of technology.* During the sixty years between 1910 and 1970, the percentage of Americans living in urban areas of 2,500 or more rose from 45.7 to 73.5, and the number of urbanites more than tripled from 42 to 150 million.[2] Urbanization clearly has brought important benefits to people —wider job opportunities, richer educational and cultural fare, more individual freedom from social constraints—had it not, it should hardly have been so powerful and enduring a movement. But this overwhelming tendency of people to concentrate in cities has worsened the environment through crowding, traffic congestion, delays and loss of time, and the overloading of transportation, marketing, and living facilities. These, along with rising levels of air, water, and noise pollution, have been among the social costs of urbanization. Obviously, beyond some levels of population size and density, the costs of urbanization begin to exceed the benefits. Discovery of the optimum size and density of urban populations is a vitally important task confronting national planners.

A second prime mover in environmental deterioration has, paradoxically, been rising affluence—the expansion of annual real income and expenditure per capita. Real personal income per capita (measured in 1958 dollars) nearly doubled during the twenty-year period from 1950 to 1970, going from $1,810 to $3,017.[3] As real incomes have mounted, each person has bought more tangible goods, used what was bought more quickly, and has, thereby, generated more waste. Each person has travelled more miles per year, expanded his usage of energy, and augmented air and noise pollution, crowding and congestion—and traffic accidents. With both the number of urbanites and per capita real incomes tripling about every forty years, the problem of maintaining urban amenities has been exploding.

It is often overlooked that the rising per capita income of city dwellers has resulted in an increased demand for the amenities of the urban environment. People naturally have wanted better public goods, more comfort, convenience, and beauty in their communities, to match the better private goods and services their rising real incomes were enabling them to buy. *The overall physical environment of large American cities has not degenerated absolutely, but relatively to contemporary demand.* We easily forget the amenities taken for granted today that were lacking half a century ago: air-conditioned offices, restaurants, and homes; thermostatically controlled electric and gas heat; underground utility wires; paved boulevards and freeways. These have widely replaced the steaming miseries of unrefrigerated summers, the drafty cold water flats and belching chimneys of winter, and the ruts and mud of unpaved streets. Even in the inner city, people today live longer, healthier, more comfortable—and, perhaps, happier—lives than they did before World War I. The problem has been that the supply of urban amenities has fallen far short of the rising demand for them; and the supply of certain critical goods, such as pure air and water, has virtually vanished.

Environmental degradation is not, of course, *inherent* in rising affluence. With a proper use of currently known science and technology and a reallocation of economic resources much of it could be avoided today. Rising affluence can—and should—be a source of environmental enhancement.

The third major cause of the environmental problem has been the phenomenal rate at which discoveries in the physical sciences have yielded to practical application, to the development of new technologies. These technologies have expanded the variety of products available for consumption, made them more complex, raised rates of obsolescence, frequently made them non-biodegradable, and thereby added to both the quantity and permanence of waste. They have added to the per capita consumption of physical materials and energy, with consequent increments of air and water pollution.

*The growth of technology is, however, like rising affluence, a two-edged sword; it can be used to improve as well as to degrade the environment.* We can use our current technologies and develop new technologies for reducing our wasteful use of many materials; and we can devise methods of recycling what we do use. And we have done this in some areas: bulky vacuum tubes in electronic equipment have been replaced by microminiaturized circuits; sewage has been converted into pure water and fertilizers; discarded newspapers, glass bottles, and metal cans are being recycled. *Environmental preservation calls for a redirection of our technological efforts, as well as a restructuring of the patterns of consumption.*

## THE SWIFT RISE OF THE PROBLEM

The rapid surge of public interest in the environment has been mainly due to the decline in certain amenities below thresholds of tolerability. Although such amenities as pure air had been diminishing for many years, the public became aware very suddenly that severe deficiencies had appeared. For example, the quality of air in the Los Angeles basin deteriorated steadily after 1940. Yet it was only in the mid-1960's—after school children were being advised not to exercise outdoors on smoggy days and when smog alerts were sounded many days of each year—that people saw that the "capacity" of the atmosphere over the basin to disperse pollutants had been overloaded.[4] It was only then that decisive action was taken to reduce motor vehicle emissions, the dominant source of air pollution.

The sudden awareness of environmental failure is analogous to the overloading of any physical facility. After the design capacity of any system or facility has been reached, per capita amenities diminish exponentially with arithmetic increases in the load. For example, when the twenty-first person enters an elevator designed to hold twenty persons, everyone in the elevator suffers loss of comfort, and the percentage loss of amenity is much greater than the 5 percent increase in the number of passengers. Similarly, when the 5,001st automobile enters a freeway designed to carry 5,000 vehicles per hour, the percent of interference with the traffic flow is much greater than the 0.02 percent increase in the number of automobiles.

## ASPECTS OF ENVIRONMENTAL DETERIORATION

A conspicuous aspect of environmental deterioration has been the disappearance of "free goods"—amenities such as clean air, pure water, and open space—that have been in such ample supply relative to the demand for them that they were not economized. But pure air is no longer free. Pure water must now be purchased by the bottle in many localities, where the product of the municipal water systems is hardly potable. Many urban dwellers must now spend large sums of money for travel to gain privacy and recreational values unavailable in their home environments.

A second aspect is the fast-rising awareness of the importance of spatial relationships in the cities. Building heights and densities, street layout, park location, and zoning patterns largely determine the life-styles of urban residents and the supply of amenities available to them. The atrociously bad planning of many American cities and the abject perversion of good zoning and adequate building requirements to serve short-term commercial interests are well-documented facts. The flagrantly overdense building in Manhattan has been permitted only because of popular ignorance and apathy. Now, the public is belatedly recognizing the heavy social costs that its neglect has created. Popular concern with city planning, zoning, and building development is rising, as the large stake of the individual in the physical attributes of his community is finally appreciated.

A third aspect is the multiplication of interdependencies among individuals. Increasingly, the activities of each of us impinge upon others and affect the utilities they derive from their activities. This is so because more people now live more closely in cities, because the scale of each person's activities rises with the amount of his consumption, and because in many of those activities we still seek to pervade surrounding space in a traditional, pre-urban, manner. Thus, no one suffered disamenity a genera-tion ago when his neighbor played a phonograph in his suburban home; but many suffer now when that neighbor's son turns up the volume of his hi-fi in an apartment building!

*Increasing interdependency is one way of looking at what economists call "spillover effects" or external costs.* For example, paper mills emit chemical wastes into lakes and streams; copper smelters inject sulfur dioxide into the air; and electric generating stations throw off carbon monoxide, radioactive wastes, or hot water, depending on their fuels. Motor vehicles cause massive air and noise pollution, traffic accidents, and vast expenditures on medical, legal, and policing services—all borne mainly by the public. External costs, thrust upon society in the form of loss of environmental amenities, total tens of billions of dollars a year.

Another aspect of the high public concern with the environment is the inequity felt because some groups in society gain benefits at the cost of other groups. The automobilist whose vehicle spews out air pollution gets the benefits of rapid and convenient travel; but he imposes part of the costs of that travel upon people who are forced to breathe bad air and hear deafening noise to the detriment of their health, and who must bear the costs of restoring property corroded by pollutants. Because this is manifestly inequitable, upgrading the environment can not only add to aggregate real income, but can also improve its distribution.

## ILLUSORY APPROACHES
## TO A SOLUTION

Deep public concern about the urban physical environment has pro-duced a variety of partial or superficial diagnoses of, and prescriptions for, this social problem. First, there is the Doomsday School, which holds, in effect, that *the environmental problem is insoluble because of population pressure.* Thus, the biologist, Paul Ehrlich, has argued that it is already too late to arrest man's inexorable march to racial extinction through overpopulation, malnutrition, famine, and disease.[5] But, accumulating evidence suggests that population growth in the advanced nations has already slowed appreciably and is starting to do so in many less developed lands. Other criers of doom are the natural scientists who predict changes in the earth's temperature, as a result of accumulating carbon dioxide in the atmosphere, with the consequent melting of the polar ice and flooding disasters. But these issues remain moot among natural scientists as a group and, therefore, call for suspended judgment. In any event, an apocalyptic view of the future should be rejected because it can lead to despair and inaction. If one believes that the future is hopeless, he will not try to improve society.

At the opposite pole is the School of Environmental Minimalism which holds that *the environment is a minor matter in comparison with such contemporary social issues as poverty, civil rights, or arms limitation.* Advocates of this school argue that political leaders calling for a better environment are "eco-escapists," seeking to divert public attention from their failure to resolve these basic social issues. What the Minimalists overlook, however, is that the nation *is* making progress in resolving other social problems, while it has not yet arrested the decline of the urban environment. They also forget that attention to the environment does not mean neglect of the poor. On the contrary, central city areas, populated mainly by low-income families, generally have the worst physical conditions of life. Because the poor stand to gain most from environmental enhancement, an attack on pollution is one battle in the war on poverty; and action on that front need not inhibit other actions.

There is also the Socialist School, which views *environmental deterioration as an inescapable consequence of capitalist "exploitation."* If only private enterprise and profit incentives were replaced by central planning and state ownership of enterprises, they contend, the pollution problem would disappear. *However, it is a stubborn fact that socialist countries have not avoided serious problems of pollution as their per capita GNP's have risen.*[6] Managers of socialist enterprises are judged by the efficiency of their operations. They are under as much pressure to minimize internal costs and to throw external costs upon the public as are the managers of private firms in market economies who seek to optimize profits. *Because the monolithic socialist society lacks an extra-governmental structure for influencing economic processes, it is less likely to internalize the external costs of production than is the market economy with its forces external to the government.* This is not to deny, however, that a socialist country *can* use central planning to improve the environment, just as a capitalist country can combine governmental regulation and enterprise action for the same end.

A large group of environmentalists has adopted the stance of the Zero Growth School. Its thesis is simple: *since environmental degradation is caused by more people consuming more goods, the answer is to stop the growth of population, production, and consumption.* Nature has fixed the dimensions of the natural environment; man should, therefore, limit his numbers and economic activities. We must establish a stable relationship between human society and the natural world.

But zero growth of the GNP is neither practicable nor desirable. It could arrest the process of environmental degradation, but it could not restore an agreeable environment. So long as present patterns of production and consumption continue, a constant GNP would maintain pollution at present levels.

It is possible and—in the opinion of this writer—desirable to arrest the growth of the human population. However, this cannot be achieved in the proximate future. Even if, beginning in 1975, every family in the United States were limited to two children, population dynamics are such that this nation would not stop adding people until about 2050 A.D., when it would have nearly 300 million.[7] American experience suggests that zero population growth would reduce the rate of growth of the GNP about one-third.

Zero economic growth would require not only a stable population but also an end to capital formation and a static technology. A voluntary decline in net savings and investment to zero is extremely unlikely, in view of the savings and investment rates Americans have maintained during the present century in the face of enormous increases in their real incomes and wealth.[8] Nevertheless, heavy taxation of incomes, capital gains, corporate profits, and a sharp reduction in depreciation and depletion allowances could considerably reduce savings and investment, and thereby slow down economic growth. A static technology is, however, almost inconceivable. It runs so strongly against established drives in American society as to be practically impossible. So long as we are thinking beings, we will find new ways to increase the productivity of work!

*The basic point, however, is that economic growth is needed to improve the quality of life.* A rise in the GNP, taken by itself, is neither good nor bad. Everything depends upon what kind of production has increased, its costs to society, and who benefits from it. What people now want and need is resource-conserving, pollution-free growth—growth that does not harm the environment and demands less of the earth's limited resources. Increasingly, growth *is* of this kind. In the advanced nations, economic growth is concentrated in the service industries which, as a whole, use less materials and create less pollution than do the commodity-producing industries. Also, as the cost of materials rises and as technology uncovers new ways to recycle (i.e., reuse) materials, growth becomes less demanding of raw materials. Social policy should encourage technological advances in these fields, thus accelerating the adjustments that market forces are producing. *In short, the environmental problem can be solved by redirecting the economic growth that inevitably and desirably will take place.*

The Austerity School of environmental thought is related to the Zero Growth School. Its members assert that *environmental decline is produced by an excessive use of resources.* They are outraged by the fact that the

United States consumes about 35 percent of the world's energy and ma terials, although it has only 6 percent of the world's population. Believin; that asceticism is the remedy, they call for less consumption in order to con serve resources and to reduce production and pollution. We should conver ourselves from a society of "waste-makers" into one of "string-savers."

The basic error of the Austerity School is, of course, that *it is not th. amount of production and consumption that degrades the environment but the fact that current processes of production and consumption generate pollution.* If government and business act to change these processes, con- sumption can be greatly expanded while pollution is radically reduced The second error of the Austerity School is the position that the worl. confronts a severe shortage of natural resources. Careful studies have revealed, to the contrary, that there are adequate supplies of basic natura. resources, including energy, available at somewhat higher than present cost. for the next generation or two, which is as far ahead as it pays man tc forecast and plan. Those who stress the natural "limits to growth" forge! that technology is continually making substitute materials available (e.g. synthetic rubber and fibers), and lowering the costs of alternative source. of energy (e.g., production of petroleum products from oil shales, tar sands, and coal).[9] Austerity theorists do make a valid point, however. when they observe that governmental regulations to internalize externa! costs can cause enterprises to develop ways of recycling hitherto wasted materials back into useful channels.

Finally, there is the Public Priorities School of environmental thought, which holds that *the environmental problem is one of too much govern- mental spending on defense and space exploration, leaving too little for environmental protection.* The solution, as they see it, is to reallocate pub- lic expenditures. However, public expenditures began to be reallocated in 1969;[10] but the reallocations of *private* expenditures will, over time, weigh far more heavily in a solution of the environmental problem. Federal gov- ernment expenditures for major environmental quality programs rose from $644 million in fiscal 1969 to $2.4 billion in fiscal 1973. While environ- mental restoration requires large increases in *public* expenditures for sewage and water purification, parks, housing, and public transportation, it also calls for a reallocation of *private* expenditures as a result of governmental actions requiring the internalization of external costs. For example, the pur- chase price and operating expenses of an automobile that is pollution-free will undoubtedly be higher than that of the present vehicle because the user will be paying the full costs of his private transportation. (Estimates of the increase range from $200 to $500 per car.) Aggregate spending on private automobile transportation may be expected to decline *relatively.* At the same time, spending on education and housing, which produce external benefits, will increase relatively. In the aggregate, readjustments in patterns of private expenditure will far outweigh reallocations of public expenditure.

## BASIC ENVIRONMENTAL ECONOMICS

Neither socialization, zero growth, austerity, nor new public spending priorities offer a satisfactory solution to the environmental problem; a more basic approach must be made. A good policy for environmental improvement should improve the distribution of income among people as well as the allocation of society's resources. Both governmental and corporate actions are necessary.

We have seen that when environmental degradation occurs, there is usually an externalization of the costs involved in producing or consuming commodities. But a social optimum cannot be achieved when there is a divergence between private costs and full costs. An optimal allocation of society's resources requires that the *full* costs of each good or service be taken into account in its price. The internalization of external costs should be a pivotal aim of environmental policy.[11]

Theoretically, perfectly competitive markets in which there are *no* transaction costs will lead to an optimum reallocation of resources, *via* bargaining between the polluter and the person harmed by pollution, regardless of which party is legally responsible to compensate the other.[12] In practice, however, the transaction costs of education, organization, and litigation are excessively high when pollution affects large numbers of people, as it usually does. For this reason it is much more efficient for government to resolve pollution problems by legislation or regulation, rather than to leave them to bilateral bargaining. For example, government can order air polluters to reduce their emissions by $x$ percent. Polluters then incur (internalize) costs in order to conform to the public regulation, thereby relieving the public of the even greater costs of rehabilitating health and property damaged by pollution.

Governmental action is essential because the competitive market system is incapable, by itself, of internalizing the costs of antipollution measures. Suppose, for example, that the automobile could be made pollution-free by installing a device costing $x$ dollars. Most automobile owners would not voluntarily install the device, because other people would reap most of the benefits of the cleaner air made possible by the installers' expenditures. General Motors proved this during the summer of 1971 by making a well-advertised effort to sell to motorists in the Phoenix area an effective pollution-reducing kit with an installed cost of well under $30.00.

After an intensive two-month promotional campaign, only 528 owners installed the kit, although there were 334,000 owners of pre-1968 cars in the area who could have used it! Texaco and some other petroleum companies also proved it by investing millions of dollars to make and sell low-lead and lead-free gasolines; few motorists bought them, because they were priced slightly higher than regular gasolines.

Nor would an automobile maker voluntarily install an antipollution device because this would add to his costs and put him at a disadvantage in competition with other manufacturers who did not install it. Society cannot reasonably expect him to shoulder the extra cost in the name of "social responsibility"; market competition presses him to minimize his costs in order to survive. Where external costs or benefits are involved, there is thus a conflict between the decision that serves the self-interest of the enterprise and that which serves the collective welfare of the community. *Public welfare can only be given precedence by a governmental regulation of private behavior which requires actions by all enterprises, or all consumers, to modify processes and products so as to conform to the public interest.*

There are usually alternative solutions to pollution problems, and each should be evaluated in order to identify the least costly. Consider, again, the example of smog in the Los Angeles basin. Among possible ways of dealing with this problem are the following: controlling pollution from motor vehicles and stationary sources by public regulation; moving people out of the basin; rezoning to reduce population density; building a rapid mass-transit system; imposing heavy taxes on private automobiles; subsidizing motorists to limit their mileage. The costs and benefits of each alternative, and each combination of alternatives, should be evaluated before an antipollution policy is adopted.

All desirable things in limited supply have a cost, and people may gain more of one thing only by giving up something else. The optimum situation is reached when no additional (marginal) benefits can be obtained by further substitutions. These principles apply to environmental amenities. For example, aircraft engine noise can be reduced with benefits to health and well-being; but only at the cost of larger expenditures for insulation or noise abatement devices, or a reduction in the speed or power of engines. Conceivably, utter silence could be achieved by incurring astronomical costs and by making great sacrifices of mobility, power, and time. The public decides the *optimal* noise level by balancing the benefits of less noise against the costs of attaining it. Government then fixes a noise standard at that point where the costs of reducing noise further would exceed the additional benefits to health and well-being. Although the calculus is necessarily rough, this is the rationale of determining antipollution standards.

## ASSESSING THE COSTS

Governmental intervention is also needed to levy the costs of environmental improvement equitably among individuals and groups in society, so as to improve—or, at least to prevent a worsening of—the distribution of income. There are opposite approaches to cost allocation. By one principle, the public should pay polluters to stop polluting; by a second, polluters should pay the costs of suppressing their pollution. The first principle is defended on the grounds that the public as a whole benefits from the reduction of pollution and should pay the costs of this benefit through tax credits and public subsidies. Libertarians usually favor this approach because of their preference for the "carrot" versus the "stick," and their belief that public regulatory boards are not to be trusted because they are often dominated by those they are supposed to regulate.

Advocates of the second principle argue that society initiates an antipollution policy from a current status of inequity. The problem is to *restore* equity between polluters and those damaged by pollution, not to *compensate* polluters for a loss of their rights. They also observe that persons with large incomes usually generate disproportionately more pollution than those with low incomes, so that a policy of internalizing costs in the polluter will tend to shift income from richer to poorer, with resulting gains in social well-being. The appropriate instruments for dealing with pollution are, in their view, public regulations to reduce harmful activities, or taxes and fines. In the opinion of the author, *equity requires that the costs of suppressing environmental damage be borne by those responsible for it*. Public restraint of private actions harmful to the environment should thus be the dominant instrument of environmental policy.

## INSTRUMENTS OF POLICY

Since the quality of the urban environment is a product of many variables, public policies to enhance the environment will employ many instruments, such as government regulation, guarantees of legal rights, taxes and fines, and public expenditures.

Instances of direct governmental regulation are the laws governing air and water pollution, and the levels of aircraft, construction, and other noises. Assuming that reduction of emissions is the least-cost solution, the main problem is to determine appropriate standards. In fixing standards, the existing technology of pollution control is an important consideration. Where the necessary technology exists and can be applied at reasonable cost, the law should simply *ban* emissions and enforce compliance. This appears to be true of much air and water pollution from fixed sources, such as the smokestacks of manufacturing and power-generating plants. Where a particular pollution technology is in the process of development, as in the case of reducing automobile emissions, government should fix standards that are raised progressively through time. This appears to be more efficient as a general rule, than the alternative of charging fees or prices per unit of pollution, an action favored by some economists because it makes use of markets and the pricing system.[13]

Another way to internalize costs is to guarantee each property owner legal rights to the amenities pertaining to his property. A California court recently awarded substantial damages to home owners near the Los Angeles International Airport to compensate them for demonstrated loss of property values on account of excessive noise. If a constitutional amendment were enacted guaranteeing every property owner a right to environmental amenities, this would induce enterprises to reduce or eliminate pollution in order to escape legal liabilities.[14] However, because judicial processes are so costly, time-consuming and uneven in their results, other solutions to environmental problems are usually preferable.

Governments themselves contribute to air and water pollution, especially by discharging untreated sewage into rivers and lakes. Governments should internalize these costs by making public expenditures on sewage treatment and water purification plants. Such outlays will, of course, ultimately be paid for by a public that, presumably, votes for them because it values the benefits of a clean environment more highly than other things to which it could devote its (tax) money.

Urban planning, zoning, and building regulations are powerful instruments for enhancing the amenities of space, privacy, recreation, housing, transportation, and beauty in our cities. *If American cities are to offer ample amenities for living, much stronger governmental controls of the design, quality, height and density of buildings, and of the layout of transportation, recreation, and cultural facilities will be necessary.* Americans will have to put a much higher priority on urban amenities, if strong enough instruments of social control over property usage are to be forged. Such controls will be opposed by builders, accustomed as they are to permissive public regulation that can be bent to their own purposes. Yet firm public control of land usage under a long-range metropolitan plan is one reason why such cities as London hold a strong attraction for their residents, as well as for millions of foreign visitors.[15]

The California Environmental Quality Act of 1970 is a harbinger of future American public policy. It requires the appropriate local government to make an "environmental impact study," with a finding of no substantial avoidable environmental damage, before authorizing any real estate development project which may have a significant effect upon the environment. Each such study and report must set forth the environmental impact of the proposed project, unavoidable adverse effects, proposed actions to mitigate adverse effects, alternative actions, short-term and long-term consequences, and any irreversible environmental changes that might be involved. In a landmark decision in 1972, the California Supreme Court held that the Act applied to "substantial" *private* building projects as well as to public works.[16] Although the far-reaching consequences of the Act remain to be clarified, it is clearly destined to become a powerful instrument of environmental control. The right of an owner to determine the use of his property has been much more narrowly circumscribed by this Act than by the traditional urban planning and zoning processes. We can expect the nation to move rapidly to strengthen public control of real estate development.

Enlargement of the supply of urban amenities also calls for immense expenditures on recreational and cultural facilities, housing, and public transportation systems. The many programs under the aegis of the Federal Departments of Transportation and of Housing and Urban Development are instruments to this end. Incentives for the participation of private enterprise in these gargantuan tasks will need to be provided, including tax credits, accelerated depreciation, credit guarantees, contracts, and direct governmental subsidies. The naive idea that private corporations can or will undertake urban rehabilitation purely out of a sense of "social responsibility" denies the ineluctable fact that, *in a competitive market economy, the firm cannot devote a material part of its resources to unprofitable activities and survive.* That enterprise responses are swift when incentives are strong is shown by the thrust of the private housing boom after World War II, triggered by liberal FHA mortgage insurance and Veterans Administration home loan guarantees.

## IMPROVING POLITICAL AND CORPORATE BEHAVIOR

The environmental problem raises profound issues about the functioning of our social institutions. Does it signify an institutional breakdown —a failure to respond to new demands of the public? Has the political system been seriously laggard in its responses? Or does the fault lie mainly in the economic system of corporate enterprises?

The most defensible position appears to be that the environmenta problem was generated primarily by tardy responses of the political system and secondarily by faults in the economic system. If society is to attai maximum well-being, its dual set of political and market controls mus operate promptly and in the proper sequence in response to changes i social values. Political action is first needed to create a demand for environ ment-improving products; corporate enterprises competing in markets ca then assure that this demand is satisfied economically. (See Figure 4, ir Chapter 9.) Measures are needed to improve both the political and the market processes.

## Making Government More Responsive to Change

The political system must be made capable of translating change in social values rapidly and accurately into governmental actions. It capacity to sense, record, transmit, and act on countless individua preferences must be improved. The basic requirements for a more efficien political system are a better education and a more sustained participation of the citizens in political affairs. Purchases of public goods and service are now nearly one-third the size of private expenditures on consumption.[1] Yet, only a minute fraction of the time and effort people devote to choosin private goods is spent in making choices of the public goods they "purchase" with their taxes. Rational behavior in allocating resources calls for a con siderable increase in the time and effort devoted to public decisions. We may hope that the present irrationality represents a cultural lag that wil be eliminated. While one may be pessimistic in the light of the past, ther is—in the recent political involvement of the young, women, and minoritie —grounds for hope of improvement.

## Intensity Voting

Changes should be made in the voting process to make it functio more like a market. Just as consumers record the relative intensities o their demands for different private goods by the amounts of their expen ditures in markets, so voters could be enabled to record the relative inten sities of their demands for public goods. For example, each voter could be given, say, 1,000 votes, which he could cast in whatever numbers he chose for different levels of public expenditures and for alternative allocations within the level chosen, among different objects. Such a procedure ough to receive early study and testing in an urban setting. Finally, the establish ment of direct links between public expenditures and the taxes levied to finance them, could help to make the political system more responsive.

## Making Business More Responsive to Social Change

Corporate enterprise must also become more sensitive and responsive to shifts in public values and governmental regulations. The rise of the "consumerism" movement reflects, among other things, a disturbing insensitivity of business corporations to changing public demands and expectations. The foot-dragging behavior of the automobile makers over safety and air pollution, and of the oil companies over air and ocean pollution, are symptomatic. *Enterprises generally have been reluctant—if not obstructive—reactors to new social values, instead of innovative leaders in satisfying them.* Either market researchers have been unable to detect value changes, or else correct market intelligence has not been utilized by engineering, manufacturing, and marketing executives.

## Corporate Organization for Environmental Action

Corporate organizations need to be reoriented, from the board of directors down through corporate and divisional managers to individual plant and store executives. The board should include "outside" directors chosen especially for their knowledge of business-societal relationships. Every policy and action of the firm should be reviewed for its effect upon the environment, and an Environmental Analyst should be assigned to this task as a staff adviser to the chief executive. Standard policy should require all managers to include, in their proposals for new facilities, measures for preventing adverse environmental effects. (See Chapters 8 and 9.)

Many well-managed companies have combined environmental matters with other external concerns in a Department of Public Affairs, headed by an officer reporting to the chief executive. Their boards of directors have standing Committees on Public Affairs, making policy in this area and monitoring corporate operations. Each major facility of these companies also has an external affairs officer reporting to local management. Figure 7 shows a model organization of a large manufacturing company and indicates the locations of public affairs specialists in the structure.[18]

## Business Leadership in Social Change

The secondary influence exercised by business leaders on social values should be helpful rather than obstructive. Whereas corporate lobbyists should be helping legislators to shape new environmental regulations desired by the public, they usually blindly oppose such actions. Most corporate advertising is narrowly focused upon expanding public demand for products without regard to their environmental effects. As Henry Ford II recently advised, corporate managers should "stop thinking about changing public

**Figure 7**

*Organization of the Business Corporation for Environmental Management*

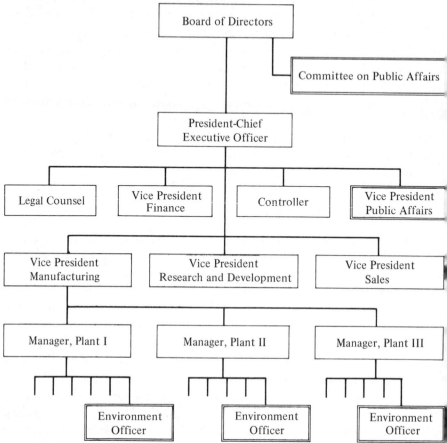

expectations as new costs which may have to be accepted but certainly have to be minimized. Instead, we should start thinking about changes in public values as opportunities to profit by serving new needs." [19] The environment is a new dimension of business and social management, the outer limits of which we cannot yet discern.

The ability of our profit-oriented enterprise system to internalize costs and to improve the environment cannot be doubted, when one recalls its successful assimilation of radical technological changes since World War II.[20] Notwithstanding the great magnitude of the necessary private and public expenditures, which have been estimated by the Environmental Protection Agency at $287 billion over the decade from 1970 to 1980, they will involve only about 2 percent of the GNP for that period.[21] In a growing economy, they will tend to change the growth rates of different industries rather than cause an absolute decline in the output of any one.

Also, new industries are emerging to supply the growing demand for pollution-controlling equipment and services.

———————

A better environment will enable people to reduce many other costs they now incur for health, property maintenance, cleaning, travel to leave uncongenial surroundings, and recreation. Rising social well-being is not in conflict with an expanding GNP, provided that the increments of production are designed to improve the quality of life. As President Nixon pointed out in his State of the Union Message in January, 1970, "The answer is not to abandon growth, but to redirect it." [22]

## NOTES

1. See the listing of factors in "Quality of American Life," in *Toward a Social Report* (Washington, D.C.: U.S. Department of Health, Education, and Welfare, January 1968); also Perloff's tabulation of factors in the urban environment in Harvey Perloff, ed., *The Quality of the Urban Environment* (Baltimore: Johns Hopkins University Press, 1969), pp. 26–29.

2. U.S. Bureau of the Census, *Statistical Abstract of the United States 1971* (Washington, D.C.: U.S. Government Printing Office, 1971), p. 17.

3. *Ibid.,* p. 308.

4. Allen V. Kneese concurs in the view that "ecosystem overload" is the primary explanation of public concern about the environment. See his *The Economics of Environmental Pollution in the United States,* prepared for the Atlantic Council (ms., December 1970).

5. Paul Ehrlich, *The Population Bomb* (London: Ballantine Books, 1968).

6. See M. I. Goldman, "The Convergence of Environmental Disruption," *Science,* Vol. 170, No. 3953 (October 1970).

7. See Stephen Enke, "Zero Population Growth—When, How, and Why," TEMPO Publication 70TMP35 (Santa Barbara, Calif.: TEMPO, June 2, 1970).

8. See *Policies for Economic Growth and Progress in the Seventies: Report of the President's Task Force on Economic Growth* (Washington, D.C.: U.S. Government Printing Office, 1970).

9. See Harold J. Barnett and Chandler Morse, *Economics of Natural Resource Scarcity* (Baltimore: Johns Hopkins University Press, 1962).

10. See *Budget of the United States Government, Fiscal Year 1971* (Washington, D.C.: U.S. Government Printing Office, 1971), p. 17.

11. A trenchant description of the external costs of economic growth is given in E. J. Mishan, *The Costs of Economic Growth* (New York: Frederick A. Praeger, 1967).

12. See R. H. Coase, "The Problem of Social Costs," *Journal of Law and Economics,* III (October 1960).

13. For example, in commenting upon the author's views, Professor F. G. Pennance argues: "Prices, fees or taxes related to the degree of environmental pollution caused by private economic activity allow that pollution to be treated like any other

commodity. The quantity 'demanded' is rationed by price and preferences instead of by administrative rule. At present the 'right' to pollute—if permitted at all—is free. And, as with all free goods, there is no incentive to economise on use." See Neil H. Jacoby and F. G. Pennance, *The Polluters: Industry or Government,* Occasional Paper 36 (London: Institute of Economic Affairs, 1972), pp. 42–43. Allen V. Kneese and Blair T. Bower also take this position. See their *Regional Water Quality Management* (Baltimore: Johns Hopkins University Press, 1968).

14. Such a legal right would remedy a market failure as A. Myrick Freeman III notes in *The Economics of Pollution Control and Environmental Quality* (New York: General Learning Press, 1971).

15. See "If Only Other Cities Were Like London," *Business Week* (May 30, 1970).

16. See *Friends of Mammoth et al.* v. *Board of Supervisors et al.,* Opinion of the Supreme Court of California, filed September 21, 1972. Friends of Mammoth is an unincorporated association of hundreds of owners of lots and mountain residences at Mammoth Lakes. It opposed the issuance of a building permit to International Recreation, Ltd., to construct a group of high-rise condominiums in the High Sierra community.

17. During 1970 government purchases of goods and services were $221 billion and personal consumption expenditures were $617 billion. See *Statistical Abstract of the United States 1971,* p. 306.

18. Figure 7 is taken from the author's paper, "Organization for Environmental Management: National and Transnational," *Management Science,* Vol. 19, No. 10, issue on Ecology and the Quality of Life (June 1973).

19. Address to the Public Affairs Forum of the Harvard Business School. See *Wall Street Journal* (February 17, 1970).

20. We reject the view of Bentley Glass, who argued in his presidential address to the American Association for the Advancement of Science that a new economic system, more responsive to human needs than capitalism or socialism, is necessary. See *Science* (January 8, 1971).

21. See *Wall Street Journal* (August 8, 1972). The estimate includes capital equipment and operating costs for cleaning up air and water, for protection from nuclear power-plant radiation, for solid waste disposal, and for the reclamation of strip-mined land.

22. *State of the Union Message to Congress, January 22, 1970* (Washington, D.C.: U.S. Government Printing Office, 1970).

# CHAPTER 11

# The Corporation as Arms Maker

P ROFIT-SEEKING corporations have, by common consent, performed reasonably well in meeting the civilian needs of American society. But their performance as suppliers of the advanced military products required for national security, as well as space products, has been widely censured. Critics charge that they have diverted national resources into a useless arms race, and that, despite gross inefficiency, they reap unconscionable profits. Military hardware makers are frustrated by work which must be performed under a network of governmental controls, and consider themselves badly rewarded for their efforts. Taxpayers have been troubled because they believe that aerospace companies are, to a considerable extent, responsible for high defense costs. Despite unquestioned technical achievements, defense corporations are accused of loose management and excessive profits. The peculiar and ambivalent public-private nature of the advanced military-hardware business has been difficult to rationalize.

Many of these problems and difficulties were epitomized in the case of the Lockheed loan guarantee. When President Nixon signed an act on August 6, 1971, authorizing the federal government to guarantee up to

In its original form, this chapter was presented to a conference held at UCLA in the summer of 1971, whose proceedings were published in 1972 by the Graduate School of Management under the title, *Contemporary Challenges in the Business-Society Relationship,* edited by George A. Steiner. His comments, and those of Dudley Browne, Barry Shillito, and Charles Wolf, Jr., were helpful. I have also drawn upon the doctoral dissertation of my student, Herbert Spiro, entitled, *Optimal Organization of the Military Hardware Industry.*

$250 million of bank loans to Lockheed Aircraft, the loans were needed by the company to avoid imminent bankruptcy. The bill had passed the Congress only after bitter debate and by the thinnest of margins. The loan guarantee troubled the conscience of the nation. Government had been asked to save a private corporation, apparently unable to stand the test of market competition, from a stern but just fate. How can the competitive enterprise system serve society, it was asked, if government keeps corporate resources in the hands of an inefficient management?

What was generally overlooked in the public debate was the symbiotic relationship between defense contractors and government. As will be seen, Lockheed's plight was not solely due to inefficient management; it was primarily the product of a government procurement policy that loaded catastrophic risks upon a private company in an economically and technologically unstable environment. Also overlooked was the possible loss to the country of Lockheed's talented scientific and engineering organization, which had authored many of the nation's most potent instruments of defense.

The Lockheed episode, involving the fate of the nation's largest defense contractor, raised fundamental issues. What, in fact, is the corporate role in what has come to be called "the military-industrial complex"? What influence has the aerospace industry had upon defense, and civilian, spending? Is the procurement of advanced military hardware from private corporations inefficient in comparison with the alternatives? Is the proper economic model of the defense industry one of oligopolists extracting monopoly profits from the government; or is it one of a government monopsonist denying normal profits to its suppliers? How might government structure the market so that procurement from private companies would be more efficient? Above all, what lessons does our national experience with military procurement teach about the conditions of successful corporate enterprise?

## THE MILITARY HARDWARE INDUSTRY

During the fiscal year 1968, the federal government purchased about $60 billion of goods and services from private business. Four-fifths of that amount—$48 billion—was spent by the Department of Defense, the National Aviation and Space Agency, and the Atomic Energy Commission.[1] Of that vast outlay, some $24 billion went for advanced-technology defense products—planes, spacecraft, ships, rockets, missiles, ordnance, and electronic and communications equipment. These products embody extensive development and design work, and are based on advanced scientific and engineering knowledge. Their production calls for extremely precise processes, enabling them to meet demanding specifications for performance and reliability. We will refer to them as "advanced military hardware" or "advanced-technology defense products," although some of them are used in the civilian space and atomic energy programs. It is the governmental procurement of these products with which we will be concerned.

The major suppliers of advanced-technology defense products to government are the aerospace companies, notably Lockheed, General Dynamics, Rockwell International, Boeing, McDonnell Douglas, Grumman, Northrop, United Aircraft, and TRW. Other major suppliers include General Electric, General Motors, Ford, Chrysler, and Avco, although their defense sales are a minor part of their total business. Strictly, there is no sharply delineated "defense" industry. According to the Standard Industrial Classification Code, the military hardware industry is composed of producers of "ordnance and accessories" and "aircraft and related components." For the most part, only the latter involve problems of high-technology development. The leading hundred prime Department of Defense contractors are essentially the hundred largest industrial corporations in the United States. For only fourteen of them—the aerospace companies—are military sales more than half of their total sales.[2] However, tens of thousands of prime contractors, subcontractors, and sub-subcontractors in dozens of industries participate in defense production.

The American policy of procuring advanced-technology defense products from private enterprises emerged after World War I. The motives for turning to private industry were to escape Civil Service barriers to the recruiting and rewarding of the talented scientists and engineers needed to develop such products, and to provide incentives to creative performance impossible in a governmental bureaucracy. Some would add that the military services also had the self-serving motive of gaining political support for defense spending from the business community. *In turning to business for its weaponry, government sought to benefit from the flexibility and productivity of the task- and profit-oriented corporation.* As a result of this policy, government-owned arsenals and shipyards languished, while the private defense business expanded. This change went on slowly between the two World Wars; it gained great momentum during World War II and the Korean War buildup of the 1950's. By 1965, about 90 percent of all defense procurement was extramural, including 99 percent of aircraft, 96 percent of communications, 74 percent of ships, and 63 percent of ordnance.[3]

The main purchasers of advanced-technology defense products have been the military services, the Army, the Navy and the Air Force. Although all are branches of the Department of Defense, to some extent they have competed with each other for military missions and for public funds, and deal independently with defense companies in the procuremen of military hardware. Because a given military mission (e.g., interconti-nental transport) can be performed with several kinds of equipment (e.g., fast-deployment ships or giant cargo planes), there is rivalry among the military services in acquiring missions, just as there is among defense con-tractors in promoting their products.

Aerospace companies compete by offering superior performance and prompter delivery of their products, rather than lower prices, because these factors are emphasized by their customer. They are product-quality max-imizers, rather than cost and price minimizers. Their basic competence is invention, discovery, and the organization and coordination of the efforts of huge teams of scientists and engineers. Having few customers, all of which are branches of the Federal government, their marketing activities are designed to influence the customer's selection of technical goals and the hardware to attain them.

## THE MYTH OF THE "MILITARY-INDUSTRIAL COMPLEX"

These industrial contractors and military services, along with their lobbyists and sympathetic Congressmen, compose the well-advertised "mil-itary-industrial complex," against whose undue power and influence Presi-dent Eisenhower warned in his farewell address in 1960. The popular view of the "military-industrial complex" is that of a gigantic combine, operated with a single-minded dedication to unlimited expenditure on weaponry. The picture is one of a monolithic coalition of aerospace executives, Pentagon officers, and hawkish Congressmen, working toward a single end.[4] To a large degree, it is this image of an invincible coalition that became the whipping boy for the nation's discontent about Vietnam, heavy military spending, high taxes, and unresolved social problems.

But myths should be separated from realities. When President Eisen-hower used his much-quoted phrase, he simply intended to point out that a military establishment, then accounting for some 8 percent of the GNP, with thousands of installations and millions of employees throughout the world, could not fail to exert significant influence upon American society—influence which should be watched and checked. He did *not* imply any conspiracy or conscious community of interest among the many disparate elements of the "complex." And, he used the word "complex" in its precise sense, an entity composed of many interrelated parts. The military-industrial complex embraces thousands of enterprises, several military services, and hundreds of legislators, each having their own self-interests and motives, and each characteristically competing with other elements for tax dollars.

If any evidence were needed to dispel the coalition concept of the military-industrial complex, it was revealed at the Congressional hearings on the Lockheed loan guarantee. The chief executives of three of the largest aerospace companies all *opposed* the loan guarantee. Chairman Willard F. Rockwell of Rockwell International predicted the failure of Lockheed's commercial jet airplane program and said that his company would be interested in acquiring some of the divisions of a bankrupt Lockheed. The then Chairman of General Electric, Fred Borch, emphatically objected to a loan guarantee that would expand the market for British Rolls-Royce engines and asked the Congress to insist upon American (i.e., General Electric) engines. And McDonnell Douglas issued a statement promising to generate twenty thousand more jobs in its DC-10 commercial airplane program, if only the Congress would close down Lockheed's competing Tristar program by declining to guarantee the loan. If this is "cooperation" among members of the military-industrial complex, who needs competitors!

Even those critics who concede that there is no conspiracy among the members of the military-industrial complex still contend that industry and the military operate to inflate national defense expenditures. And they consider that the aerospace companies, which produce the "big ticket" items procured by the Department of Defense, form the industrial nucleus of this effort. We must inquire, then, does the United States spend too much money on defense, and if so, are the aerospace companies responsible?

Presumably, the level of defense expenditures is determined by three variables: the size of the perceived threat to national security, the (opportunity) costs of civilian programs foregone because of defense outlays, and the efficiency with which military goods are supplied.[5] If defense expenditures are excessive because of business influence, this may come about because the aerospace companies persistently lead the Congress to exaggerate the foreign threat to our national security; or lead the Congress to underestimate the values of the health, education, welfare, civil works, and other programs that might be expanded with resources devoted to national defense; or are wasteful in designing and producing military hardware. Let us consider each factor in turn.

## THE FOREIGN THREAT TO NATIONAL SECURITY

*The evidence shows that the primary determinant of American defense expenditures has been the Congress's perception of the foreign threat to national security and that the dominant role in forming this perception has been played by the Department of Defense; the influence of the aerospace companies has been negligible.*

The military services naturally propagandize for large military appropriations. Bearing the ultimate responsibility for the nation's protection, they understandably seek the arms that will assure success under all circumstances. Realizing that in war there is no prize for "second best," military officers are risk averters, trained to be intolerant of ambiguity or uncertainty. Although the President and the Secretary of Defense usually reduce the requests for funds submitted by the military services, the latter often persuade the Congress to restore spending programs disapproved by the Commander in Chief. Indeed, more than once, the President has even refused to spend all that the Congress appropriated for defense!

Congressional perception of the threat to the security of the United States is strongly influenced by our intelligence about the weapons and the military plans of foreign countries, particularly of the Soviet Union— but it is by no means always accurate. If the Congress learns that the Russians are building an antiballistic missile (ABM) defense, or are mounting multiple independently targeted reentry vehicles (MIRV's) on their missiles, public pressures for American countermeasures mount. "Doves" often forget that the decisions of the men in the Kremlin weigh as heavily in the American military budget as do those of the men in the Pentagon or in the White House. Of course, the reverse is also true. There is an interaction of military spending programs between the superpowers that produces the upward spiral known as the "arms race." All reasonable men now agree that this madness must cease. The continuance of civilization— let alone its improvement—demands not only limitations upon the production of arms, but arms reduction as a next step and ultimately the control by a world government of all military forces, which would then be used solely in keeping the peace. (As an economic advisor to the United States Arms Control and Disarmament Agency, the author has long worked to that end.)

Because they lack sources of world military or political intelligence, expertise in international relations, or skill in military affairs, aerospace firms exert relatively little influence on Congressional perceptions of the threat to our national security. Essentially, such companies are pools of engineering and managerial talent that, in the main, *respond* to the demands of the military services for advanced weaponry. Although it may be true, as Adam Yarmolinsky asserts, that the decision-making processes in the Pentagon bias spending decisions toward over-procurement and costly new technologies, this bias derives primarily from the military staffs.[6]

*A fact that cannot be reconciled to the claim that aerospace companies control the defense budget is the instability in the composition and in the total of defense expenditures.* The up-and-down movements in total defense expenditures mainly reflect changes in the Congress's perception of the threat to national security. Thus, the nation passed successively through the mobilization for World War II, the postwar disarmament from 1945 to 1949, the Korean build-up from 1950 to 1953, the post-Korean letdown from 1954 to 1957, the post-Sputnik and Vietnam escalations from 1958 to 1969, and the subsequent "winding down." Rapid technological changes have brought shocking shifts in the composition of aerospace outlays. The federal government has repeatedly cancelled large aerospace programs, causing severe distress to the companies and to the communities in which they operate; examples include the Skybolt, Navaho, Dynasoar, and Valkyrie projects, and the Supersonic Transport plane. In fact, the Pentagon has listed sixty-eight major weapons systems that were cancelled after a total expenditure of $10 billion.[7] Because market instability imposes extremely difficult problems upon them, aerospace companies have powerful reasons for trying to stabilize their markets; their inability to do so reveals their limited influence. (See Table 9.)

## THE VALUE OF CIVILIAN EXPENDITURE PROGRAMS

Have aerospace companies brought about excessive defense spending by depreciating the worth of federal spending for health, education, welfare, public works or other civilian purposes? There is even less evidence to support an affirmative answer to this question than there is to bear out the contention that they exaggerate the foreign threat to national security.

Admittedly, aerospace companies do their full share of lobbying in Congress and in the Pentagon. Their efforts are normally focused upon gaining support for their own projects, rather than enlarging the military budget as a whole. To a considerable extent, therefore, in terms of the absolute size of the military budget, the lobbying efforts of different firms with competing weapons systems tend to cancel each other.

Furthermore, an aerospace company is not competent to weigh the social benefits from spending an additional $1 billion on defense against spending an equivalent amount on, say, education. Any representations it made to the Congress on this subject would be greeted with incredulity, if not resentment. Only the Congress has the information, the expertise, and the ultimate responsibility to weigh competing claims for public funds. After 1968—the peak of the Southeast Asian war—it allocated a diminishing proportion of federal funds to defense and a rising proportion to human

TABLE 9

*Federal Expenditures for National Defense and for Aerospace Products and Services Compared with U.S. Gross National Product, 1948-1971*

(Amounts in billions. Calendar years for GNP, Fiscal Years for Expenditures)

| Year | Gross National Product | National Defense Expenditures | | Expenditures for Aerospace Products | |
|------|------|------|------|------|------|
| | | Amt. | Percent of GNP | Amt. | Percent of GNP |
| 1948 | $ 257.6 | $12.0 | 4.7 | $ 0.9 | 0.3 |
| 1949 | 256.5 | 14.0 | 5.5 | 1.5 | 0.6 |
| 1950 | 284.8 | 13.0 | 4.6 | 2.1 | 0.7 |
| 1951 | 328.4 | 22.4 | 6.8 | 2.9 | 0.9 |
| 1952 | 345.5 | 46.0 | 13.3 | 6.1 | 1.8 |
| 1953 | 364.6 | 50.4 | 13.8 | 9.2 | 2.5 |
| 1954 | 364.8 | 47.0 | 12.9 | 11.2 | 3.1 |
| 1955 | 398.0 | 40.7 | 10.2 | 10.5 | 2.6 |
| 1956 | 419.2 | 40.7 | 9.7 | 10.5 | 2.5 |
| 1957 | 441.1 | 43.4 | 9.8 | 12.5 | 2.8 |
| 1958 | 447.3 | 44.2 | 9.9 | 13.2 | 3.0 |
| 1959 | 483.7 | 46.5 | 9.6 | 13.3 | 2.7 |
| 1960 | 503.7 | 45.7 | 9.1 | 13.3 | 2.6 |
| 1961 | 520.1 | 47.5 | 9.1 | 13.9 | 2.7 |
| 1962 | 560.3 | 51.1 | 9.1 | 15.3 | 2.7 |
| 1963 | 590.5 | 52.8 | 8.9 | 16.2 | 2.7 |
| 1964 | 632.4 | 54.2 | 8.6 | 17.9 | 2.8 |
| 1965 | 684.9 | 50.2 | 7.3 | 15.7 | 2.4 |
| 1966 | 749.9 | 57.7 | 7.7 | 17.8 | 2.5 |
| 1967 | 793.9 | 70.1 | 8.8 | 20.2 | 2.5 |
| 1968 | 864.2 | 77.4 | 9.0 | 21.4 | 2.5 |
| 1969 | 929.1 | 77.9 | 8.4 | 20.5 | 2.2 |
| 1970 | 974.1 | 76.5 | 7.9 | 18.8 | 1.9 |
| 1971 | 1,046.8 | 71.2 | 6.8 | 17.6 | 1.7 |

SOURCES: GNP from *Economic Report of the President, 1971* (Washington, D. C.: U.S. Government Printing Office, 1971), p. 200; expenditures from *1971 Aerospace Facts and Figures* (New York: Aerospace Industries Association, 1970), p. 13.

resources. Despite the continuing American military engagement in Southeast Asia, the 6.8 percent of the GNP spent on national defense in the fiscal year 1971 was lower than in any year since 1951.[8]

After 1968 the American people began to assign a higher priority to domestic, civilian needs and to place a relatively lower value upon national defense. The Nixon Administration pursued a policy of reducing American political commitments and military forces throughout the world. Moreover, it began to subject the defense budget to independent review by the federal Office of Management and Budget.[9] It was 6.4 percent of GNP in 1973.

There is another important consideration. *Within the past decade, American society has developed an "educational complex," a "health complex," a "welfare complex," and a "housing complex." These politically potent interest groups have been successfully challenging the waning "military-industrial complex" for taxpayers' dollars.* They form a strong counterpoise to military interest groups. Skyrocketing federal expenditures on these civilian programs show that they are succeeding. Will their political power be the subject of some future president's farewell warning to the people?

## THE COST OF MILITARY HARDWARE

Aerospace companies supply the United States government with advanced-technology defense products costing around $20 billion a year. Do we spend more than is necessary on these products because procurement from private corporations results in extravagant costs and profits?

As the technology of warfare has become more sophisticated and complex, the task of producing military hardware has been fraught with rising risks. Like show business, the advanced weaponry business became "like no business." It called for the production of incredibly complex devices, many of which had never been made before. The risks of producing such products at a predetermined price became so enormous as to be beyond the capability of any private company to accept. Only the prospect of extremely high profit rates, in the event of success, could justify a private enterprise in assuming such risks—if they could be assumed at all.

However, American public opinion has never tolerated more than "moderate" or "fair" profit rates on defense work. In practice, this has meant a percentage of profit on sales or net worth no more than that which the contractor could earn in civilian business carrying a much lower level of risk. The Congress limited the maximum profit rate by law. It required that all defense contracts be renegotiated *ex post facto* to recover any "excessive" profits. Given this condition of very high risk combined with a limited low profit rate, the production of advanced weaponry by private enterprises would not have taken place at all unless government had limited the contractor's risk. Government did this by assuming a good part of the risk, both by writing cost-plus (fee) contracts and by supplying the contractor with much plant, equipment, and working capital.

"He who pays the piper calls the tune." Government naturally retained for itself a wide range of authority over defense business. The

Pentagon thus makes many decisions normally within the purview of the enterprise management. What Melman has called the "military-industrial firm" operates differently from its civilian counterpart.[10] The Department of Defense has much to say about the nature of the products, quantity to be produced, production processes and schedules, prices, conditions of employment, fixed investment, working capital requirements, sources of finance, and methods of accounting and reporting. This process of governmental supervision expanded in the 1960's during the regime of Secretary of Defense Robert McNamara.

But close governmental supervision has not resolved the industry's problems. Congressional hearings have made the public aware of enormous "cost overruns" in producing the C5A military transport plane and the F-111 fighter-bomber, to take two examples. Also, it is known that advanced weapons programs such as Dynasoar, Skybolt, and Navaho have been cancelled after huge sums had been spent on them. Aerospace companies are said to have "bought in" contracts with low bids, in the expectation of obtaining upward adjustments later on. They are accused of hiring retired military officers, who are alleged to use their friends in the Pentagon to secure favorable contracts.

Studies have shown that cost overruns in the production of complex military products are not mainly due to bad contractor management; they arise primarily from great uncertainty in estimating the cost of producing products that have never been made before, from changes in specifications and designs as technology advances, from inflation of costs and interest rates during the project, and from optimistic biases of estimators.[11] Cost overruns have been characteristic of complex civilian and military engineering projects throughout man's history. A Roman aqueduct is reported to have cost more than twice its original estimate.[12] Notable examples of large overruns on civilian projects include the construction of the Rayburn House Office Building and the John F. Kennedy Center in Washington, D.C., Lincoln Center for the Performing Arts in New York City, and the refurbishing of the Queen Mary in Long Beach, California.

The allegation that retired military officers in aerospace employment pervert contract awards by "influence peddling" has been deflated by Yarmolinsky. He showed that the 2,072 retired officers on the payrolls of the hundred largest military contractors in 1969 represented only 8.8 percent of retired officers of top rank, and that many of them did not work in defense-related activities.[13] In any event, federal law forbids them from engaging in defense-related activities for a period of two years after separation from military service.

Granted that there are inefficiencies in the present system of military supply, most of them are inherent in the task. There is "organizational slack" in all business firms, and it may be greater than normal in the aerospace industry because of the unusual fluctuations in demand for its products. But aerospace managers have been ingenious in inventing methods of monitoring progress and controlling costs. Such concepts as statistical cost control, critical path scheduling, and value engineering originated in the defense industry. The Pentagon, too, has been cost-conscious. Secretary McNamara made cost reduction a primary objective of his administration. By the application of advanced management techniques, he succeeded in wringing between $2 and $3 billion a year out of the defense budget.[14]

Whether there is a less expensive way of obtaining advanced defense products has been the subject of extensive study by the RAND Corporation.[15] Efforts to push out technological frontiers, whether military or civilian, are inherently hazardous and involve false starts that appear wasteful in hindsight. As in the petroleum industry, the cost of technological "dry holes" must be counted an unavoidable part of the total costs of successful projects. Knowledge gained from abandoned efforts has only the negative value of showing what cannot be done. In all nations, advanced military products have been enormously expensive. It is reasonable to conclude that *aerospace costs cannot be greatly reduced, given the highly unstable demand by the Pentagon for advanced products.*

## PROFITS IN THE MILITARY HARDWARE BUSINESS

Have aerospace contractors been too liberally rewarded with high profits? Two recent and authoritative studies provide an answer. The General Accounting Office studied the profitability of the defense business and the comparable commercial business of the 154 defense contractors that accounted for about 60 percent of Department of Defense prime contracts from 1966 to 1969. Its *Report* to the Congress stated that "when profit is considered as a percent of equity there was little difference between the rate of return for defense work and that for commercial work." When profit was figured on total assets, including government-furnished facilities, it was 11.2 percent for defense and 14 percent for commercial business.[16]

The Logistics Management Institute—of which the author was formerly a director—studied the profits, over the period from 1957 to 1969, of all companies whose defense sales were over $25 million a year and constituted at least 10 percent of their total business.[17] It found that while defense business had a higher profit rate on total capital investment than commercial business during the years from 1958 to 1962, it was distinctly *less* profitable during the years from 1963 to 1968. In 1968, after-tax defense profits were 6.8 percent of total capital investment, whereas the commercial business of defense firms produced a return of 8.3 percent, and the return to all manufacturing companies was 10.2 percent. *Since 1962, the military hardware business has been less profitable than civilian business!*

Confirming these negative findings we may note the unsentimental verdict of Wall Street. The investment community has consistently valued aerospace equity securities at a low multiple of earnings because of the wide fluctuations in their sales and earnings, high uncertainties, and the ever-present possibility of catastrophic loss. Small wonder that these companies have almost desperately sought to diversify into civilian business by merger. Some have succeeded, but only at the cost of surrendering control, as was the case with the North American Aviation merger with Rockwell Standard Manufacturing or the Ramo-Woolridge merger with Thompson Products. Others, like Lockheed and General Dynamics, failed to achieve substantial diversification in nondefense business and became financially troubled. Rarely do firms with great political power fail to earn normal profits. The subnormal profitability of the aerospace industry casts doubt on the claim that it possesses great political strength.

## ALTERNATIVE SOURCES OF DEFENSE PRODUCTS

Could the nation obtain better defense products at lower prices from other sources than profit-seeking corporations? One alternative is to produce all military hardware in government-owned and government-managed arsenals. For example, ordnance is now produced in the Rock Island Arsenal in Illinois and missiles in the Redstone Arsenal in Alabama. A second possibility is to buy defense products from government-owned companies, such as the Aerospace Corporation, which now supervises private American aerospace companies. This is the practice of the Soviet Union and, to a considerable degree, of France. A third arrangement would be to procure from private corporations, but to regulate them like public utility companies. Still another option is to make more extensive use of universities and other nonprofit organizations for research and development work, such as the Lincoln Electronics Laboratory operated by the Massachusetts Institute of Technology and the Jet Propulsion Laboratory operated by the California Institute of Technology.

A close examination of these alternatives reveals grave drawbacks in each and leads to the conclusion that *the country will be better off by improving the present system of military hardware procurement than by adopting a new system.*[18]

Nationalizing the military hardware industry and reverting to an arsenal system would probably restore the rigidities and bureaucratic attitudes from which the present system was a salutary escape. The arsenal approach also abolishes the market mechanism and, thereby, shields the government's problems from public exposure and correction.

The use of public corporations as military suppliers overcomes some of the limitations of arsenals; but, lacking profit incentives, they do not provide the competitive stimulus to efficient and technically advanced solutions of hardware design and production problems.[19]

Nor does the privately owned public utility company appear to be an attractive source of high-technology military products. Its essential characteristics are a guaranteed market and a limited return on investment. Although public utilities *use* the results of advanced technology (e.g., nuclear power, microwave transmission), they have not been tested as *developers* of such technology. (The Bell Laboratories—the research and development arm of American Telephone and Telegraph—is *not* subject to normal public utility regulations.) Moreover, a monopolist is less likely to advance technology as rapidly as will a number of competing enterprises, each generating a unique solution to a problem. A leading student of this subject has dismissed the public utility concept, particularly in view of the dismal record of the public regulation of transportation and other industries.[20] As Clair Wilcox has written: "Regulation, at best, is a pallid substitute for competition. It cannot prescribe quality, force efficiency, or require innovation." [21]

Finally, the strong trend of public opinion is opposed to more extensive use of universities in carrying out military tasks, even when they function primarily as managers of governmental installations. Such responsibilities can dilute their primary duties to society. Although universities and other nonprofit agencies should continue to be used in performing some defense tasks, none has the capabilities of the profit-seeking corporation in marshalling resources for development and production operations.[22]

## A NEW STRUCTURE OF PROCUREMENT

*While the profit-seeking corporation should continue to be the primary source of advanced military hardware, its performance should be improved by changes in the procurement policies of the government.* Two reforms are crucial: restructuring the contracting process and establishing a better reward/risk ratio.

The production of advanced-technology defense products embraces three kinds of tasks: research, design-development, and production. Thus, a new military aircraft will probably require research in metallurgy, propulsion, and electronic systems, followed by the design and development of prototypes, followed by the production of the planes in quantity. The government has encouraged defense suppliers to *integrate* operations, by calling for bids to perform both research and design-development. Indeed, when Secretary of Defense McNamara introduced "total package procurement" (TPP) in the 1960's, contractors were obliged to perform *all three tasks,* requiring complete vertical integration. TPP was supposed to inhibit the practice of "buy-in" bidding by contractors, who sometimes deliberately underbid research and design-development contracts in order to be in a favorable position to compete for profitable production contracts later on. TPP also avoided the need to transfer technology and design concepts from one contractor to another.

However, over time, it became clear that this kind of structuring of military procurement involved unanticipated difficulties. The vertical integration of defense companies limited competition among them. When combined with a fixed price, as in the case of the C5A contract, it thrust catastrophic risks upon the supplier. And, American experience in transferring advanced aerospace technology has demonstrated that technology can be transferred from one to another American contractor—even to firms in foreign countries—without serious difficulty.

*Government could enliven competition among defense suppliers, if it clearly separated research, design-development, and production contracts, and opened each to competition.* Since 1939, the Soviet Union has organized its military aircraft supply into a three-tiered structure of research institutes, design bureaus, and manufacturing plants, each separately administered and each internally competitive.[23] The research institutes produce data on aerodynamic forms and structures, materials, and manufacturing processes. Design bureaus evolve designs and build prototypes. Manufacturing plants produce large numbers of aircraft from selected prototypes. The system has been technologically successful, although we do not know at what costs.

There is a growing appreciation among students of military industrial firms that their faulty past performance has been mainly due to existing market structures; and that the key to better performance is governmental action to restructure the demand for military hardware and, thereby, its supply. Thus, Professor Walter Adams—long a severe critic of the industry—in 1972 rejected both nationalization and public-utility type regulation of the military hardware industry, and called instead for reforms in defense procurement similar to those advocated here.[24]

# IMPROVING THE REWARD/RISK RATIO

*A central problem in aerospace procurement is to establish an optimal ratio between reward to the contractor and the amount of risk he assumes.* At any given level of risk, prospective profits must be high enough to induce companies to continue to bid on and to produce defense products. It is in the public interest that profits be high enough to maintain a viable defense industry. In theory, the Department of Defense could either balance a high level of contractor risk with a high prospective return on investment, or it could equate a low risk with a commensurably lower profit rate. Since American public opinion and policy has permitted contractors to earn no higher a profit rate on defense than on civilian business, the Department of Defense has had to assume the major risks, by supplying much plant and equipment to the contractor and by writing cost-plus types of contracts.

During the 1960's, the terms of their "partnership" with the government worsened considerably for the aerospace companies. Under the regime of Secretary McNamara, a higher level of risk was forced back on defense contractors. Cost-plus type contracts were widely replaced by fixed-price type contracts; and, as we have seen, the TPP concept was applied, which made the contractor responsible for the complete sequence of research, development, design, production, and maintenance of the product.[25] The Pentagon also wove a thicker web of regulation over military contractors, further hampering their freedom of management.

While fixed-price contracts for major military "packages" might have worked in a stable environment without profit ceilings, they were simply not viable in a situation of price inflation, rapid technological change, and a low ceiling on profits. This is the basic lesson of Lockheed's experience with the C5A. Skyrocketing costs were mainly due to wage and price inflation, and to engineering changes made at the initiative of the Pentagon to increase the capacity and reduce the weight of the aircraft. Lockheed settled the government's claim by paying a sum equal to more than half its equity capital. This so debilitated the company financially as to make necessary a governmental loan guarantee in order to forestall bankruptcy.

The steadily worsening profit position of the military hardware industry during the 1960's is dramatically shown in a tabulation of after-tax profits as a percentage of total capital investment for defense contractors and for a sample of 3,500 other comparable American corporations.[26] (See Table 10.)

After 1962, as a result of McNamara's policies and increasing unused capacity in the industry, the reward/risk ratio in the defense business

TABLE 10

*Comparison of After-Tax Profits of Defense Contract and Other U.S. Corporations, 1958-1968*

| Year | Profits as a Percent of Total Capital Investments | |
| --- | --- | --- |
| | Defense Companies | Other Companies |
| 1958 | 10.1 | 7.1 |
| 1959 | 9.5 | 9.3 |
| 1960 | 8.7 | 7.8 |
| 1961 | 7.5 | 7.4 |
| 1962 | 7.4 | 7.3 |
| 1963 | 6.5 | 9.8 |
| 1964 | 6.3 | 10.8 |
| 1965 | 7.6 | 12.6 |
| 1966 | 7.0 | 12.4 |
| 1967 | 7.3 | 10.0 |
| 1968 | 6.8 | 10.2 |

SOURCE: See Logistics Management Institute, *Defense Industry Profit Review: 1968 Profit Data.*

became steadily worse in comparison with civilian business. The financial difficulties of many defense companies and their low standing in the investment community raised the question, by the end of the 1960's, whether the United States would maintain a viable military hardware industry. Corporate enterprise cannot function with unlimited risk and restricted reward. *The national welfare would be enhanced if the present low ceilings on the profits of defense business were raised or eliminated, and if contractors were given adequate incentives for efficient performance and for the assumption of high risks, along with less governmental regulation.*

Spiro has pointed out that the evidence refutes the conventional criticism of the military industrial firm as an oligopolist, extracting monopoly profits from a compliant government. On the contrary, it supports the concept of the federal government as a monopsonist (single buyer) that, during the 1960's, increasingly exerted its market power to exploit its contractors.[27] Weidenbaum also has noted "the adverse effects on private industry of governmental involvement and regulations, notably on the science-based enterprises that look to the federal government for their basic markets."[28]

The unfavorable current position of the defense contract corporation in comparison with the civilian market corporation and the public utility corporation is shown in Figure 8. The typical civilian market company makes products with conventional technology and sells them in competitive markets. Its risk level is relatively low, its managerial discretion relatively

FIGURE 8

*Comparison of Civilian Market and Public Utility Corporation with the Defense Contract Corporation*

| Characteristic | Civilian Market Corporation | Public Utility Corporation | Defense Contract Corporation |
|---|---|---|---|
| Product: Technology | Conventional | Conventional | Advanced |
| Market Structure: | | | |
|   Supply | Competitive | Monopolistic | Competitive |
|   Demand | Competitive | Competitive | Monopsonistic |
| Prices | Constrained by Market Competition | Maxima Fixed by Government | Constrained by Market Competition |
| Outputs | Constrained by Market Competition | Constrained by Market Competition | Negotiated |
| Risk and Uncertainty: | | | |
|   Level | Relatively Low | Relatively Low | Relatively High* |
|   Borne by | Corporation | Corporation | Divided between Corporation and Government |
| Managerial Discretion | Relatively Wide | Mildly Constrained | Severely Constrained |
| Profit Rate | Unlimited-Constrained by Market Competition | Maximum Limited by Law | Maximum Limited by Law |

*Under fixed-price or fixed-price-incentive type contracts.

wide, and its profits are limited only by competition. The typical public utility company also produces a product by conventional technology carrying relatively small risks. Because government has granted it a monopoly, government imposes a maximum profit rate and regulates prices to prevent excessive profits. The defense contract corporation, in contrast, has no monopoly and produces advanced technology products at great risk; nevertheless, its managerial discretion and its rewards are severely constrained. The system is viable only if government takes over most of the risks.

## TOWARD AN EFFICIENT CORPORATE ROLE IN DEFENSE

Our analysis of the corporate role in national defense has not unmasked a villain or a military-industrial conspiracy. Rather, it has revealed a very complex problem of business-governmental relationships in which fallible men in both government and business have often erred. It has shown that government holds the key to improvement of business performance in supplying military hardware. It has also shown that the aerospace companies are an essential component of the national security system. By reforming its procurement policies, government can reshape both the structure and the behavior of the industry. *Government should aim to make the defense contract corporation more like the civilian market corporation.* Then, the public will reap the full benefits of competition—greater innovation and better cost-effectiveness—which are now being partly lost in the present ambiguous system of oppressive public controls combined with a subnormal reward/risk ratio.

We now recapitulate the specific measures needed:

### Separation of Research, Design-Development, and Production Contracts

Government should divide all advanced defense projects into research, design-development, and production contracts, and call for competitive bids on each. Successful bidders on one phase should not be permitted to bid on subsequent phases of the same project. This would limit the risks borne by the contractor; and it would also foster specialization and competition in the industry.

### Elimination of Defense Profit Limits

Government should repeal the present ceilings on defense profits and eliminate the renegotiation of defense contracts to recapture "excessive" profits. These reforms would create incentives to managers of defense companies to control costs and raise efficiency, incentives that are now lacking.

## Reduction of Government Regulation

Government should reduce its detailed regulation of defense contractors and its provision of plant, equipment, and working capital to such firms. This reform would be consistent with the aim of expanding the contractors' managerial authority to complete his contract.

## Reliance on Fixed-Price Contracts

Government should mainly use fixed-price and fixed-incentive contracts for defense products. This policy would be consistent with that of expanding prospective rewards to the contractor for successful performance. The idea would be to balance risks with rewards at a higher than current level.

## Stabilization of the Economic Environment

Finally, government should stabilize the economic environment, and reduce cost and price inflation. This action would greatly reduce the risks of the military hardware industry and the costs of defense products.

---

Taken together, these policies would enable defense companies to become more like vigorous market enterprises and less like governmental bureaus within corporate shells. The nation would get more for its defense dollars.

The really large opportunities to reduce the burden of national defense inhere, of course, in new American foreign policies and in the negotiation of progressive disarmament agreements. We may hope for implementation of President Nixon's call to "reduce our involvement and our presence in other nation's affairs." [29] We should also work unremittingly for international agreements that will progressively reduce national armed forces of all kinds and which will ultimately lead to the control of all military forces by a world government.

## NOTES

1. Murray Weidenbaum, *The Modern Public Sector* (New York: Basic Books, 1969), Ch. 2.

2. A. E. Lieberman, "Updating Impressions of the Military-Industrial Complex," *California Management Review*, Vol. 6, No. 4 (Summer 1969).

3. Frederick M. Scherer, "The Aerospace Industry," in *The Structure of American Industry*, 4th ed., Walter Adams, ed. (New York: Macmillan, 1971).

4. See, for example, Donald McDonald, "Militarism in America," *Center Magazine*, Vol. 3, No. 1 (January 1970). See also, *Anti-Ballistic Missile: Yes or No?*, A Special Report from the Center for the Study of Democratic Institutions (New York: Hill and Wang, 1969). The author's observations on the influence of the military-industrial complex appear on pages 90–95. Also, General David M. Shoup, "The New American Militarism," *Atlantic Monthly* (April 1969).

5. See Charles E. Wolf, Jr., "Military-Industrial Complexities," *Bulletin of the Atomic Scientists* (February 1971), pp. 19–22.

6. Adam Yarmolinsky, *The Military Establishment: Its Impacts upon American Society* (New York: Twentieth Century Fund, 1971), p. 17.

7. See John S. Baumgartner, *The Lonely Warriors: The Case for the Military Industrial Complex* (Los Angeles: Nash Publishing Company, 1970), p. 3.

8. *Budget of the United States Government, Fiscal Year 1971* (Washington, D.C.: U.S. Government Printing Office, 1970), p. 20.

9. See *National Security Strategy of Realistic Deterrence, Secretary of Defense's Annual Defense Department Report for FY 1973* (Washington, D.C.: U.S. Government Printing Office, 1972), p. 203.

10. See the *War Economy of the United States*, ed., Seymour Melman (New York: St. Martin's Press, 1971), Chapter 1. Melman, and other authors in his book, exaggerate the degree of governmental control of the defense enterprise and unduly minimize the discretionary sphere of its management. Although closely supervised, the motive of aerospace managers *is* long-run profit maximization within the statutory limits, and they do retain a material amount of discretionary authority in carrying out defense contracts.

11. Whether Lockheed "bought in" the C5A contract is doubtful. While its original bid was 15 percent under Boeing's and 10 percent under that of McDonnell Douglas, it was 27 percent under the midpoint of the U.S. Air Force's range of estimates. *All three companies* substantially underbid the Air Force's estimates.

12. David Novick, *Are Cost Overruns a Military-Industrial Complex Specialty?*, Paper P-4311 (Santa Monica, Calif.: RAND Corporation, March 1970).

13. Yarmolinsky, *The Military Establishment*, Chapter 5.

14. A primary instrument of McNamara's policy was the Logistics Management Institute, founded in 1962 as an independent nonprofit corporate research entity, financed by the Department of Defense and governed by a board of trustees composed of industrialists and management experts.

15. See *A Bibliography of Selected RAND Publications: Weapons Acquisition* (Santa Monica, Calif.: RAND Corporation, June 1971) containing a listing of over 150 books, reports, and papers.

16. *Defense Industry Profit Study: Report to the Congress by the Comptroller General of the United States* (Washington, D.C.: U.S. Government Printing Office, March 17, 1971), pp. 8–9 and Summary on page 1.

17. *Defense Industry Profit Review: 1968 Profit Data:* LMI Task 69-27 (Washington, D.C.: Logistics Management Institute, March 1970), pp. 8–19.

18. This conclusion was reached by Herbert Spiro in his *Optimal Organization of the Military Hardware Industry* (Ph.D. Dissertation, Graduate School of Management, University of California, Los Angeles, 1972).

19. See U.S. House of Representatives, *Hearings before the Committee on Armed Services on the Aerospace Corporation*, May 1965.

20. George R. Hall, "Defense Procurement and Public Utility Regulation," *Land Economics* (May 1969); also I. N. Fisher and G. R. Hall, *Defense Profit Policy in the United States and the United Kingdom,* RM 5610-PR (Santa Monica, Calif.: RAND Corporation, October 1968).

21. Clair Wilcox, *Public Policies Toward Business* (Homewood, Ill.: Richard D. Irwin, 1971), p. 476.

22. See *Report* of the Committee appointed to advise the President on the use of government contracts (Washington, D.C.: Bureau of the Budget, April 30, 1962).

23. Arthur J. Alexander, *R. and D. in Soviet Aviation,* R-53-PR (Santa Monica, Calif.: RAND Corporation, November 1970).

24. See Walter Adams and William James Adams, "The Military-Industrial Complex: A Market Structure Analysis," *American Economic Review,* Vol. 62, No. 2 (May 1972), pp. 279–287.

25. See *Risk Elements in Government Contracting* (Washington, D.C.: Aerospace Industries Association, October 1970) for a comprehensive treatment of this trend. See also, Dudley Browne, "The Risk/Reward Relationship in Military Procurement," *Management Accounting* (March 1971).

26. *Defense Industry Profit Review,* p. 14.

27. See Herbert Spiro, *Optimal Organization of the Military Hardware Industry* (Ph.D. Dissertation, Graduate School of Management, University of California, Los Angeles, 1972), pp. 49–52.

28. Murray Weidenbaum, *The Modern Public Sector* (New York: Basic Books, 1969), pp. 34–35.

29. *State of the Union Message to the Congress, January 22, 1970* (Washington, D.C.: U.S. Government Printing Office, 1970).

# PART V

## THE FUTURE

# CHAPTER 12

# The Future of the Corporation in Society

THE CORPORATION has long played a stellar role on the American social stage, and our assessment shows that it continues to be a vital institution, despite insistent criticism of its performance. And while corporate enterprise is of central importance in the economy, the notion that the United States has become a "corporate state" is pure myth. Even the idea that giant corporations dominate the economy is simplistic. Government occupies the center of the social stage and wields expanding power over an American society that grows ever more pluralistic. Over the years, corporate business has lost both economic and political power relative to other groups in society. Nevertheless, the corporation continues to demonstrate a remarkable adaptability to a dynamic social and technological environment. Since World War II, it has rationalized its management and has conglomerated and multinationalized its operations. Under the pressure of public opinion and, particularly, of new "managerial" stockholders, corporate directors and managers have become more responsive to social needs. Although the corporation was laggard in its response to the public outcry for a better physical environment, government was even more tardy in enacting regulations requiring all corporations to internalize costs. Similarly, corporate performance as a maker of arms has been less than satisfactory, mainly because government had failed to structure the market properly and to offer adequate incentives to efficiency.

With this understanding of salient trends, we may now probe the corporate future. What will be the nature of American and world society a generation hence, and what roles will corporations play in them? What new tasks will corporate managers face, and how will they perform them? Above all, what new relationships are likely to develop among corporate enterprises, governments, and other social institutions? [1]

## PERSPECTIVES ON SOCIAL PREDICTION

Our perspective on the future of corporate business in society is based upon the belief—supported by strong historical evidence—that modern society is an open, adaptive, learning, innovative system.[2] Therefore, we reject equally the fatalistic view that no matter what man does about his future, he is apocalyptically doomed, and the messianic vision that his salvation will suddenly appear. Instead, we hold the attitude that history is shaped mainly by human will—be it good or evil—and intelligence—be it much or little; it is, in short, shaped by the actions of men. As the physicist Dennis Gabor has written: "Man cannot predict his future; he can invent it." [3]

Man's progress through time, his social evolution, John Platt has suggested, should be likened to a wagon train of settlers moving across some unknown country in search of a better home, confronted during their journey by a succession of choices of the best path; it is not like a railroad train running on fixed tracks to a preordained destination.[4]

If we see man's future in this way as a series of choices, we might ask: What choices are open to us? Where can we expect to influence the world we have inherited? Here, again, Platt is helpful. He has proposed that the future can be scanned in terms of three different periods of time, with respect to which the relationships of prediction, choice, and planning are quite different. For a few years ahead, the "inertia period," events are determined mainly by previous decisions, and little can be done to change their course. Predictions can therefore take the form of simple projections of existing trends and patterns.

This interval shades into the "choice period," twenty-five or so years distant, within which present decisions are important in attaining intended results. Predictions for this period require both a statement of expected social decisions and an assessment of their effects; they cannot be mere extrapolations of the past. Since predictions of such decisions are likely to reflect, in some measure, the forecaster's own preferences regarding the future shape of society, they will necessarily have a prescriptive as well as a scientific quality. Let the reader be forewarned!

Still farther ahead is the "uncertainty period," in which the shape of things is too dependent upon unforeseeable events and responses to make de-

tailed predictions and planning profitable.[5] Much of the "doomsday" literature of futurology falls into this category.

Accepting Platt's tripartite division of the future, we will focus our
attention on the developments we anticipate during the next twenty to
thirty years, and especially on the last decade of this century.

The evolution of human societies and their institutions can be seen
as a combination of continuities and discontinuities. Successful prediction
presumes, of course, the existence of much continuity; and our study of
corporate-societal relationships in the United States over the past quarter-
century has confirmed the validity of this presumption. Yet, the persistence
of a social trend may never be lightly assumed, as the demographers have
recently discovered in regard to the human population. Thus, recent down-
turns in birth rates in many countries have confounded the experts and
have led to estimates of world population in the year 2000 that range
everywhere from 4.5 billion to 7.5 billion people!

We rule out the most radical "discontinuities" from our scenario of
the future. We shall assume that a major military conflict among the
advanced nations will be avoided during the next quarter-century, and that
the period will be marked by a progressive relaxation of tensions between
West and East. The industrialized nations will recognize that the best
route to the realization of their national goals is through cooperative
economic growth, rather than military adventurism. While local wars are
probable, especially among the less developed countries, their scale will
not be large enough to disrupt world social evolution.

We shall also exclude the possibility of a catastrophic economic depression, such as the one that devastated the United States, Germany, and
other countries in the 1930's. The probability is negligible that such an
event will recur, given contemporary knowledge of the use of monetary
and fiscal policies to control aggregate demand. However, the problems
of price inflation and unemployment will continue to plague nations in the
decades ahead.

We shall assume that the economies of the Western nations will
continue to be based mainly on the institutions of private property, free
enterprise, open markets, and profit incentives. The manifold drawbacks
of socialist economies are serious enough to allow us to assume that people
will not support the replacement of capitalism by socialism.

Finally, we shall take the view that racial or ideological differences will
not polarize the advanced nations and lead to civil war. Wider participation
by citizens in public affairs will doubtless foment bitter debates in the future.
Politicians will, at times, pump up popular expectations of social gains
beyond any hope of fulfillment, and this may lead to public frustration
and even violence. Yet, most people want the same things from their so-

ciety; and most will be too sophisticated to fall prey to demagogic promises. Reason, we expect, will usually prevail.

Our perception of the next quarter-century is one of orderly change rather than sudden mutation, of evolution rather than revolution, of more continuity than discontinuity, at least in the advanced countries. We see the youth "revolt," the communal family, the drug culture, the free-form university, and the leaderless enterprise as intriguing experiments of passing interest, but of little enduring significance. In the less developed regions of the world, the struggle to modernize economies and to build nations will be accompanied by much local turbulence and discontinuity.

## THE GLOBAL BUSINESS ENVIRONMENT IN THE 1990'S

It is likely that many long-term social trends will continue into the 1990's. In general, the world's societies will become increasingly populous, urban, industrial, affluent, secular, pragmatic, democratic, bureaucratic, technological, literate, and dynamic.[6] However, the amount of change in these different aspects of society will differ materially as between the more and the less developed nations, and also as between the East and the West.

World population will probably mount from 3.3 billion people in 1970 to nearly 6 billion at the end of the century. Population growth will slow appreciably as a result of popular education in contraceptive techniques, but zero population growth will still be far from realization. By the 1990's, populations are likely to be rising about 1 percent a year in the advanced nations, and about 2 percent a year in the less developed countries. By permitting increased saving, and by lightening the economic burdens of rearing so many children, slower population growth will have accelerated the rise in real income per person.

During the 1960's, the "gross world product" rose by 70 percent, or more than 5 percent a year, and the rise was as rapid in the less developed as in the more developed countries.[7] World population grew by 22 percent during the same decade, or at the rate of 2 percent a year. Thus, the worldwide gain in real output per person averaged 3 percent a year. However, the population of the world's less developed "South" rose 3 percent a year, reducing the annual gain in output per person to 2 percent; whereas in the world's more developed "North" a population growth of about 1 percent made it possible for production per person to increase 4 percent a year—twice as fast. The widening gap between living standards in the rich and the poor nations has resulted from the high birth rates that prevailed in the poor countries.

During the 1970's and 1980's, the annual growth of GNP will probably continue to average 5 percent or more in the less developed nations. (However, the 6 percent annual growth target set by the United Nations for the Second Development Decade might be attained.) And their birth rates are likely to fall, so that they will be able to elevate the living standards of their peoples more rapidly than in the past. In contrast, the economic growth of the developed countries as a group is likely to be less rapid than during the 1960's. Shorter hours of work, a slower rise in productivity, and a new emphasis upon humanistic values and a better quality of life will reduce their annual gains in GNP to between 4 and 4.5 percent.[8] *The relative economic gap between the less- and the more-developed countries will begin to close.*

In the United States and Europe, the era of suburbanization that followed the automobile age will have ended, and many people will have returned to the central cities. The formerly decrepit central cores of large cities will have been redeveloped, and they will once again have become the meccas of civilized living. The cities will have clean air and water, ample parks, better schools, greater personal security, and more beauty.

By the last decade of this century, advanced farming and industrial technology will be in wide use around the world, postponing food and fiber shortages well into the future. Major advances will have been made in structural materials, transportation, and the automation of households and trade and service enterprises. Economical processes for converting plentiful deposits of coal and oil shales into petroleum will be widely used. Unlimited power from nuclear fusion will be in clear prospect, if not a reality. A biological revolution, predicated in the 1920's by Haldane, will long since have supplanted the physical revolution in natural science.[9] Among biological wonders will be the development of new species of plants and animals, the widespread transplantation of human organs, the choice of sex for unborn children, human hibernation, and increases in life expectancy.

By the last decade of this century, there will be more evidences of international cooperation and of a stronger sense of world community. Agreements will have been reached by the nuclear powers—which may then consist of more than a dozen nations—concerning the reduction of stocks of nuclear weapons as well as concerning the limitation of their production. Conventional military forces will also have been reduced by mutual agreement. Defense spending will be a much smaller element in national budgets. Although nationalism will remain strong in the younger, less developed countries, the economically advanced nations will have delegated some of their authority to regional and international organizations, which will be better able to cope with the problems of an interdependent world.

The European Economic Community will have become a political community as well. Common markets will be thriving in Central and South America and other regions of the world. A supranational government of the deep oceans will hold sovereign power over two-thirds of the world's surface. The United Nations probably will have become a more potent force in world affairs as a result of charter reform. The voting strengths of nations will have been made more congruent with their populations by grouping small states into blocs. The permanent membership of the Security Council will have been enlarged to include Japan and India.

By the 1990's, fairly liberal international trading and investment practices will prevail. The incipient protectionism of the early 1970's will have been overcome. Special Drawing Rights (SDR's) of the International Monetary Fund will have replaced the American dollar as the dominant international reserve currency. National currencies will be more loosely linked to SDR's than at present, affording each country more freedom to adjust its internal policies. By stern measures, including structural reforms to foster competition in labor and other markets, the United States will have overcome the debilitating price inflation that afflicted its economy during the period from 1966–1971. Other advanced nations will have done likewise, in order to protect their balances of international payments, so that the currencies of the leading trading nations will have attained reasonably stable purchasing powers and exchange rates. Nations will ultimately find ways to stabilize their price levels, simply because the evil effects of inflation—social and moral as well as economic—subject economically advanced societies to unendurable strains.

The ending of the Cold War will have been followed by increasing cultural and economic intercourse between East and West; and, by the 1990's, trade between the two blocs will have reached a high level. The socialist countries probably will have become members of the International Monetary Fund and the World Bank. As the Soviet economy passes from scarcity to abundance, its central planners will have found it necessary to decentralize many economic decisions to the managers of enterprises, and to use markets for pricing and capital allocation. Market socialism in the East and the further diffusion of the ownership of private enterprises in the West will propel the two economic systems toward convergence—although differences will remain.[10]

By the last decade of this century, the Pacific Basin will have emerged as the most dynamic theater of world events. Following Japan's lead, Taiwan, Korea, Hong Kong, and Malaysia, and—at a greater distance—the People's Republic of China and Indonesia will have become centers of rapid economic development. The Japan Economic Research Center has forecast that the per capita GNP of Japan will *surpass* that of the United

States after 1980! Thrust forward by large interjections of American and Japanese management skills, technology, and credit, the People's Republic of China will have become a formidable economic power by the 1990's, with an annual GNP of something like $300 billion. (If the policies of the People's Republic of China continue to foster economic growth, this nation could well become the world's leading economy before the end of the twenty-first century.)

The stimulus of modernizing the Asian nations will be an important element in the continuing dynamism of the American and Japanese economies. However, the two nations could find themselves engaged in a contest for economic dominion which could lead to hostilities. The hope is that both sides will avoid this contingency by making necessary and timely accommodations.

## AMERICAN SOCIETY OF THE 1990'S

How may we most aptly characterize the emerging American society? Without doubt, it will differ from contemporary society in many ways. Daniel Bell has called it the "post-industrial" society, but this is a deceptive phrase; the society of the future will remain profoundly "industrial." The "service" society would be more meaningful because it names the economic sector that will continue to replace agriculture and industry as the dominant employer of people. Robert Hutchins has termed it the "learning" society, emphasizing the heightened role that education will play. Japanese economic planners have proposed naming it the "information" society, stressing the explosion of the volume of information in modern life. Dennis Gabor has written of the "mature" society; but one wonders whether he intended, by his biological analogy, to imply that senescence lies ahead! Alvin Toffler insists that it will be a "new" society, not merely a changed society; he writes, "we are simultaneously experiencing a youth revolution, a sexual revolution, a racial revolution, a colonial revolution, an economic revolution, and the most rapid and deepgoing technological revolution in history." [11]

Certainly, the powerful forces of population growth and urbanization, of scientific and technological change, and of rising affluence will continue to reshape the values of American society into the 1990's. One may foresee serious social strains as institutions adapt to major shifts in social values. A more complex society, dependent upon the proper intermeshing of many parts, will become more vulnerable to breakdown by reason of the noncooperation or acts of sabotage of dissident elements. To protect itself against this contingency, American society will probably impose constraints upon the exceptionally wide individual freedoms that have existed, as B. F. Skinner has suggested.[12] Thus, essential workers may lose the right to strike.

A United States population of about 280 million is clearly in sight by the year 2000, even though family size, hitherto a matter of private decision, will come under firmer control by the state and population growth will slow significantly. Accommodating another 75 million Americans will require a staggering effort; and the impending shift in the age-structure of the population will complicate the problem. As biological science extends the period of mature life, the proportion of the people over fifty will rise dramatically. This, together with a lower birth rate, will radically reduce the proportion of the population below sixteen. An aging population will change market demands from youth-oriented to age-oriented goods and services. The health care, travel, and leisure goods markets will burgeon.

Greater affluence for more people will bring a relaxation in the work ethic that has been, historically, a dominant value for Americans. The four-day workweek and the one-month paid vacation will become standard. People will enter the labor force later and leave it earlier than at present. Income and wealth will become less potent incentives to effort and symbols of social status. In a society of general affluence, based upon the possession and use of knowledge, the individual's occupation and professional standing will become the significant symbols of social status. Nobel Laureates will outrank multimillionaires in public esteem.

Nevertheless, Americans will remain in the 1990's a predominantly work-oriented people. They will continue to believe that work is more than a source of income—that it provides social status, human interaction, personal dignity, and a sense of achievement. Utopian movements calling for freedom from the work discipline will never gain a significant following. Although there will be more leisure time for most people, those who lead and administer our social institutions—including corporations—will continue to work full time. For them, the distinction between "work" and "play" will not have much meaning.

Still the most productive nation in the world—although with a lessening margin of leadership—the United States will continue to grow in the 1990's. With a population and a labor force expanding about 1 percent a year, and with productivity rising about 3 percent a year, the real GNP will expand about 4 percent a year. By 1990, the nation's GNP will rise to nearly $2,200 billion (measured in 1971 prices) from the $1,027 billion in 1971. GNP per person will expand from $4,875 per person to something like $8,864 in 1990. People will spend a larger part of their income on housing, education, and services; less on food, clothing, and transportation. The comparative advantage of the United States in world trade will lie increasingly in the realm of ideas and sophisticated technologies rather than commodities.

By the turn of this century, however, the concept of economic growth will no longer figure heavily in the thinking of the country. People will emphasize improvements in the physical environment and the quality of life. By the 1990's, the external costs of producing and consuming goods will have been largely included in their prices. The public will be reaping the gains from an improved environment in better health, lower burdens of maintaining property, and lessened social tensions.

During the last third of the twentieth century, government will continue to expand its economic role at the expense of the corporate sector. Whereas in 1970 government *produced* only 11.6 percent of the GNP, and produced or purchased 22.6 percent, by 1990 these percentages may well rise to 15 percent and 30 percent, respectively. A slow, but steady, expansion of the governmental sector is assured by the enormous long-term public commitments already made to health, education, welfare, public works, and environmental improvement.

Government will also weave a wider web of regulation over business, in response to public demands for higher standards of health and safety, for honest representation, and for pollution-free production of goods. On the other hand, government will contract with private or mixed corporations to provide many health, education, welfare, transportation, and other services formerly performed by governmental bureaus. By the 1990's, governments will offer incentives of many kinds to corporations to induce them to train the unemployable, rebuild the slums, educate the young, and deliver medical and health services to the public. The entry of the aerospace and other advanced-technology companies into urban transportation, policing, fire protection, and other civilian government services will create a new "social-industrial complex." While there will be more governmental control of private activities, the notion that governmental planning will "replace the market" will be refuted by history. Already, those eastern European countries with the longest experience of central planning are turning to *market* socialism. Paradoxically, those who know central planning best appear to have more confidence in markets than do the American critics who predict their demise!

American society will continue to be pluralistic in the 1990's. Because blacks will account for about one-fifth of the future increase in the population, and will predominate in many central cities, their political influence will grow. Equality with the white community, not further integration, will probably be their goal. The rise of citizen, consumer, civil rights, environmental, feminist, and other new blocs to political power will further restrain the political influence of corporate business and of labor unions.

Our society will have a more diverse balance of political power than it has known for a century. Antitrust laws will be applied to labor unions, cooperatives, professional associations, and other private groups, as well as to corporations. It seems probable that the family and the church, beleaguered and disintegrating institutions during most of this century, will mount a revival during the next generation. The inability of the state and the school to carry out well the tasks of educating and socializing the young, which have also been traditional functions of family and church, will stimulate both public and private action to strengthen the latter institutions.

Technological changes will continue to open up new options to people —to create new social values, opportunities, and problems.[13] But American society will take these changes in stride. They will not require a "radical reexamination of attitudes and a vast restructuring of institutions," as some have suggested. They will call upon individuals and institutions to make continual adjustments. Continual evolutionary change is a way to avoid the trauma of violent revolution. While it does not make for a comfortable society, it does produce a vital and stable one.

# THE EMERGING AMERICAN
# BUSINESS SYSTEM

Expansion of the corporate population in the future is assured by the recent validation of "professional corporations" of medical doctors, lawyers, dentists, and engineers by the courts and by the Internal Revenue Service. Incorporation enables such professionals to shelter more income from taxation and to limit their liabilities. Considering that more than 600,000 professionals are in private practice in the United States, most not incorporated, the effect of their incorporation upon the company population can be large.[14]

Whereas the postwar era was marked by a slow rise in the concentration of corporate business among the giant firms, *it is likely that there will be little, if any, further concentration of business during the next quarter-century.* One reason is that economic expansion will be greatest in the service industries, now composed mainly of small- and medium-sized firms. Another is that the relatively low profitability of the largest industrial companies after 1965 will hamper their further growth. Indeed, the adequacy of corporate profits will be a persistent problem into the 1990's.

The next generation will probably witness *a further diffusion of corporate shareownership,* and the passage of more shares into the hands of investing institutions. Inflation has made many Americans equity-minded; this will not change even if inflation ends. While the total number of direct shareowners may increase at a less rapid rate than during the past twenty years, it is sure to increase. History shows that dips in the stock market only temporarily dampen the ardor of Americans to own corporate shares.[15] The spectacular expansion of employee retirement plans and of periodic investment plans in the past assures a huge inflow of funds for investment in corporate equities in coming years, and new plans will be adopted in the future.[16] It has been credibly estimated that the share holdings of financial intermediaries will rise from about 30 percent of the total in 1972, to 55 percent in the year 2000.

# NEW THRUSTS OF CORPORATE MANAGEMENT

We have seen how the application of economics, behavioral science, and quantitative analysis added to the scientific component of corporate management after World War II. This transformation was facilitated by, and fostered, the evolution of electronic computers and data processing technology. Corporate planning, and management to attain planned objectives, became standard operating procedures. The corporate headquarters staff was enlarged to provide the chief executive with the expertise he needed to deal with complex problems. The speed of intra-company communications increased by several orders of magnitude. The use of task forces, specially assembled to carry out particular projects, became common in the advanced-technology companies. Programs to develop executive talent, and to gear managerial compensation to profits through profit-sharing and stock option plans, were widely adopted. Indeed, a 1972 survey of large companies showed that three-quarters had regular bonus or incentive compensation plans, and more than four-fifths granted stock options to executives.[17]

Concomitantly, graduate education for management emerged as a professional academic discipline in American universities. An operationally useful, general theory of management was developed. More of the brightest students flocked to the graduate schools of management. The strong demand for managers by *all kinds* of organizations widened the opportunities open to the graduates of these schools. Many schools substituted "management" for "business administration" in their names, thus identifying themselves with their basic discipline rather than with one institution in which it is applied.

Most of these trends will persist into the future. By the last decade of this century, management will be mainly a "people-oriented" process. The automation of many routine business operations will enable managers to spend more time on the development of the people in their organizations. An affluent working force will be less tolerant of impersonal direction; it will require more motivation and identification with enterprise goals.

As Kozmetsky has observed, more of the manager's time will be occupied by the task of solving complex problems.[18] He will call upon *ad hoc* teams of professionals with the requisite talents to assist him. Increasingly, he will be a mobilizer of intellectual resources, whose chief function is to define problems and methods of solving them. He will need high intelligence, broad education, and a capacity for systematic thinking. He will spend a large part of his time studying technological and social developments throughout the world in an effort to identify profit-making opportunities for his company. Some of his study will be done in "refresher" courses offered by universities, to which he will return for periods of several months every five years or so during his career.

Competition in the 1990's will generally be based upon the comparative cost/effectiveness of different commodity systems throughout their useful lives, rather than upon the selling prices of discrete "products." Emphasis will be placed upon what Madden has called "a holistic mode of business planning," aimed at providing want-satisfying *systems* meeting the functional needs of people. As the concept of competition as a dynamic, multi-vectored process comes to prevail, antimonopoly authorities will increasingly turn from a sterile preoccupation with "concentration" and "market shares" to attacks upon artificial barriers to entry into occupations and lines of trade. Increasingly, global will replace local markets.

Corporation managers, in the 1990's, will be deeply involved in the measurement of social attitudes and expectations and in designing corporate responses to them. Every substantial business will maintain a "social account" of its outlays for social projects outside of its normal business activities. "Social accountants" will routinely make an annual "social audit" of corporate performance, which will be published along with the company's audited accounts. Although profit optimization will continue to be the central goal of business and the master criterion for judging managerial performance, stockholders will expect managers to act with enlightenment in a long-term framework. They will judge management by the state of a company's relations with the public as well as by the trend of its profits, recognizing that present public relations affect future profits.

We may expect that, by the last decade of this century, the strident criticism of business, which reached a crescendo in the early 1970's, will have abated. Large companies will have become sensitive to changes in the values of the public, will have organized Departments of Public Affairs, and will have equipped themselves to sense and respond rapidly to those values. Also, the public will have come to understand the need to provide incentives for business participation in social activities, and government will provide them.

## MULTINATIONAL BUSINESS PROSPECTS

World conditions during the last decade of this century are likely to form a mixed environment for corporate enterprise. In the developed nations of the world's "North," the environment will be generally hospitable to the expansion of multinational business. Political stability and a large measure of international cooperation will make it easy for companies to move across national boundary lines. Differences in economic ideologies will play a minor role, and East-West trade, technical assistance, and capital movements will have taken on large dimensions.

In many of the less developed lands the environment will be difficult and, in some countries, hostile to multinational business. Political turmoil, civil strife, and local wars will recur, as these younger nations strive to reconcile conflicting internal elements in their societies and fight to establish firm national boundaries. National pride and the quest for autarchy will conflict with their needs for assistance in economic development. Paradoxically, the policies of the nations most needing foreign investment are most likely to repel it!

By the 1990's, nearly all large American corporations and many medium-sized firms will operate multinationally. And American markets will be served by hundreds of foreign-based enterprises manufacturing their products in the United States. Indeed, foreign penetration of the American economy may be more extensive in the next twenty years than American penetration of foreign economies. An outflow of American private foreign direct investment may well be replaced by a net inflow.

Contrary to the predictions of some observers—that multinational business will become concentrated in the hands of, perhaps, a hundred giant companies—ever larger numbers of companies from a rising number of nations will enter the global arena. Among the new entrants will be many from Japan, the Western European countries, and even some from the socialist nations of Eastern Europe. By the last decade of this century, multinational companies will account for a significant proportion of the production in all of the industrialized nations. But concentration in the global market probably will be no greater in 1990 than it was in 1970.

The continued growth of multinational enterprise will be a potent force for the development of supranational organizations and the harmonization of national policies and actions. Although some scholars have predicted a sharp clash between the multinational company and the nation-state, resulting in national restrictions on multinational business, a much different course of events is probable. *National governments will find that the most effective way to prevent multinational firms from benefitting from differences in national policies is to harmonize those policies.* We may expect, therefore, to witness a succession of actions to unify the taxation, trade, antimonopoly, labor, and regulatory laws of the industrialized countries. While such reforms will reduce corporate opportunities to profit from differences, greater uniformity in the national regulation of business will reduce the costs of doing business. Even more importantly, it will ameliorate friction between the global firm and the national governments with which it deals.

The coming expansion of multinational enterprise will also be a force for the creation of supranational organizations. As Richard Eells has predicted, nations may be expected more and more in the coming decades to engage in a "search for congruence" of the political with the economic boundaries of "corporate domains," in order to prevent global corporations from leaping across national frontiers in an effort to escape national restraints and burdens.[19] To no small degree, the nations of Western Europe were pushed into the Common Market by multinational companies. On the other hand, the existence of the Common Market has spurred the growth of multinational business. Both corporations and nations were motivated, each by different reasons, to search for a congruence between economic and political boundaries. Similarly, the development of common markets among regional groups of the smaller countries is likely to proceed more rapidly than is now generally expected.

The spread of multinational enterprise will multiply the amount of international travel and of contact between peoples, causing ancient myths and suspicions to decay. Cross-cultural experiences will gradually build understanding and trust. Eells has written that multinational business is "indispensable to the maintenance of a stable civilization and to sustain the hope of a world order."[20] We would suggest that *multinational business is the most powerful human institution in the forging of a world order.* Whereas direct political efforts to enlarge the authority of the United Nations have been unavailing, the imperatives of world economic development provide a more likely means of accomplishing that end.

## CORPORATIONS IN A SUPRANATIONAL OCEAN REGIME

Among the tasks that will challenge men's ingenuity during the final decades of this century will be the establishment of a supranational government of the deep oceans which lie beyond national jurisdiction. Although the oceans are indispensable to life on earth, ocean waters and seabeds are now being polluted by the effluents of commerce and industry; their economic resources are being plundered by myopic exploitation; and the resources of ever-larger areas of the oceans are being claimed by nations in a dangerous competition that could lead to war. Only a supranational authority can stop the dissipation of ocean resources and enforce stable relationships between the oceans and human society.

The corporate institution will undoubtedly find important new applications in the ocean regime.[21] Indeed, Eells has suggested that a "corporate sovereignty of the seas" be established.[22] Such a corporation, he has proposed, would be founded with the moral support of the United Nations and would be owned by a consortium of national governments, scientific organizations, and public and private enterprises interested in ocean resources. Despite the interest of this proposal, it would involve much practical difficulty in execution. National governments would be required to delegate to such a corporation their sovereign powers to control pollution and to regulate ocean production; but they would surrender such authority with great reluctance. The allocation of shares of stock in such a corporation among nations and their citizens would also pose knotty problems. Because of these difficulties, a *political* organization, such as has been suggested by Elisabeth Mann Borgese, appears preferable to a corporate one.[23] And although the Borgese proposal was to establish a *regulatory* agency, such a regime might also be an *operating* agency, with controlled subsidiary corporations carrying on ocean activities. Thus, one can readily conceive of:

- An Ocean Science Corporation, conducting ocean research.
- An Ocean Weather Corporation, engaged in making meteorological observations and in providing weather forecasting services, for a fee, to nations and enterprises.
- An Ocean Petroleum Corporation, engaged in exploring for and producing petroleum from the deep oceans, by itself or in joint ventures with national or private oil companies.
- An Ocean Mining Corporation, engaged in prospecting for and producing minerals from the seabeds and developing underwater recovery methods, again, by itself or in joint ventures with other companies.

Conducting ocean operations through such mixed public-private corporations rather than through bureaus of a political organization would have definite advantages. Corporate managements are capable of more rapid decision and action. They would have wide authority to employ the best talent. They could freely establish the fees and prices for the goods and services they produced.

An ocean regime would, of course, also regulate the activities of private enterprises engaged in the petroleum, hard minerals, fishing, transportation, aquaculture, and other ocean-based industries. It would need to establish concession and taxation policies, as well as conservation and antipollution rules.

## THE CONTINUING DECLINE
## OF CORPORATE POWER

Earlier we traced the long decline in the economic and political power of corporate business in American society. The economic power of big business shrank mainly because of the increase of competition associated with the development of national and multinational markets, and the rise of product substitution in an affluent society. Corporate political power diminished as a result of governmental restraints, and of the emergence and growth of countervailing power blocs. Recently, corporate business and union labor both lost political strength, as consumer, civil rights, environmentalist, and other "public interest" organizations gained influence with the government.

These trends will persist, and, by the 1990's, the major *economic* institutions—corporations and unions—will throw still smaller shadows on the political horizon than they do today. As the time-worn goals of production and economic growth are supplanted by the new drive for social well-being, and as the emphasis upon public goods rises, their weight in public policy decisions will lessen. The situation in prospect is one of an increasing pluralism of social values and institutional structures. There will be less public visibility of the "business lobby" and the "labor lobby"; more attention will be paid to the "environmental lobby," the "health lobby," the "education lobby," the "housing lobby," the "urban lobby," and a dozen others. Each will represent politically powerful interests. Each will make a plausible case in the Congress, and in state and local governments, for a larger share of limited public resources.

A well-functioning political democracy requires a balance of power among its institutions. The evolution of the new pressure groups has, up to the present time, served to countervail the disproportionate political influence of producer groups. Yet, the maintenance of balance is difficult; and there are signs that new interest blocs, taken together, may at some point become too influential for the national welfare. For example, a study of federal budgetary trends by the Brookings Institution showed that the "built-in" increases in civilian public expenditures are so large that the budget would run a deficit of $17 billion in the fiscal year 1975, even at full employment and without any important new spending programs! [24]

The tendency of the Congress to run large budget deficits, under conditions of full employment, probably will be stopped by raising taxes and using sharper instruments for controlling expenditures. Fiscal restraint is an essential weapon in the battle to end inflation.

*By the last decade of this century, dominant political power may emanate from the new interest blocs and may need to be curbed in the public interest.* The nation will have to guard against the inordinate influence of health, education, welfare, housing, and other lobbies just as it has had to be vigilant in regard to corporate and union lobbies. The danger of imbalance may come from those who would, in the name of "the public welfare," use the instruments of heavy taxation and massive public spending, which would reduce savings and investment in the economy. At some point in this process, incentives to production and innovation could become dulled, slowing economic and social progress.

## THE RESTORATION OF SHAREOWNER CONTROL

American corporate government, which has been widely criticized as authoritarian, irresponsible, and ineffective, is not as bad as its critics contend—nor as good as it should be. Having been designed to facilitate rapid decision-making in an unstable environment, corporate government involves hierarchical structures and relatively authoritarian decision processes. Corporate charters wisely leave to stockholders and to boards of directors the authority to enter any line of business and to build any kind of organization they choose. Any other public policy would hamper the freedom and adaptability of enterprise.

The key to better corporate government is more independence, competence, power, and compensation for the members of the board of directors. This does *not* mean that boards should be elected by and represent different interest groups in society. A multi-interest board would not be able to act quickly, and would lack the single criterion of profit optimization upon which to base its decisions. It *does* mean that corporate boards should contain members with *diverse* social perspectives and experiences, and that they should not be dominated by managements or by bankers.

By the 1990's, it is likely that all corporations doing business in more than one state or engaged in interstate commerce will be chartered by the federal government. (It is also conceivable that multinational corporations will be chartered by a World Corporation Authority.) The federal corporation law will assign shareowners a more active role as participants in corporate affairs; it will help to make directors more versatile, active, and independent. The law will probably require that a majority of the board of a publicly held company shall be nonofficers; and that the board shall have standing committees on nominations, management audit, and public affairs, a majority of whose members shall also be nonofficers. General Electric, which has authored many managerial innovations, reorganized its board along these lines in 1972, setting a trend that will be followed by other large corporations in subsequent years.[25] Finally, there will be a statutory requirement that outside board members be compensated at per diem rates not less than those paid to the top officer of the company.

These reforms, coupled with the pressure brought to bear by "managerial" stockholders, will have energized the governing bodies of business enterprises. Because nonofficers will nominate replacements for board vacancies, new members are likely to be both more versatile in their capabilities and more independent in their attitudes. Being paid adequately for the onerous risks they must run and the difficult decisions they must reach, directors will devote more time to their jobs. On the average, the quality of their decisions will be higher.

The social sensitivity of corporate boards and managements in the 1990's will be increased by the active participation of sophisticated and articulate shareowners, many of them professional "money managers" in trust companies, investment companies, and pension funds. The stock holdings of these financial intermediaries have been estimated to rise from about 30 percent of the total market in 1972, to a remarkable 55 percent in the year 2000.[26] Annual meetings of shareowners will be forums for the discussion of corporate policies and programs in the social field as well as in product markets. The total performance of the management will receive a searching audit.

## THE NEW PARTNERSHIP BETWEEN GOVERNMENT AND BUSINESS

We have analyzed the relationship of corporate business to government in three different contexts: in the solution of social problems, in the improvement of the environment, and in the production of military hardware. In all three cases one fundamental principle stood out: *Public disappointment in, and disapproval of, corporate performance stemmed primarily from a failure of government to structure corporate tasks properly or to provide adequate incentives for their performance.* Citizens, legislators, and public administrators should bear this basic point in mind. The business corporation is task-oriented and profit-motivated; it functions best when the task is clearly specified and when the prospective profit from efficient performance is proportional to the risks assumed. The neglect of these requirements by governments has led to disappointing corporate performance in the production of advanced-technology military hardware and in the restoration of the environment. The corporation is the servant of society, the junior partner of the state. Depending upon the state for its very existence, and doing business on the terms the state prescribes, the corporation cannot justly be blamed for poor performance when the state fails to give it adequate direction and motivation.

The other side of the matter is that the *corporation has a responsibility to the state and to its citizens to respond promptly to changes in social values and priorities.* In the past many corporations failed to meet this responsibility. H. Bruce Palmer, former President of the Conference Board, put it well, "Throughout this era of breath-taking change, business has always been ten jumps ahead of the world in invention, production and distribution—and ten jumps behind the American people in its awareness of new socioeconomic needs, wants and demands." [27] The solution is to make the corporation sensitive and responsive to social change. This can be done by installing organizations and staff specialists in public affairs. The corporation needs sensory and feedback "social devices" linking it with all sectors of society. It needs continuing contact with all the channels of communication. It must become a practitioner of the political arts. As mentioned earlier, it should establish a "social account" and subject itself to an annual "social audit."

By the final decade of this century, if not well before, the conditions of a new and fruitful business-government relationship can be widely understood and practiced. Public servant and businessman should understand better the role and responsibilities of the other. Both should agree that, in a fiercely competitive world, the United States will achieve neither its public nor its business goals if American business and government work against each other while their foreign counterparts collaborate. Both should appreciate that maximum corporate service to society calls for timely actions by *both* the political and the enterprise systems of society. To improve the operation of both will, however, require more powerful tools of public policy formation than are presently available.

## SYSTEMS ANALYSIS—A FRESH APPROACH TO PUBLIC POLICY

We have often referred to American society as a complex system composed of numerous interacting subsystems. For example, we may think of a *political* subsystem composed of numerous electoral and governmental institutions and processes; an *economic* subsystem composed of .governments, households, and corporate and noncorporate business institutions and markets; a *scientific and technological* subsystem made up of educational, research, development, patenting, and other institutions; and an *environmental and natural-resources* subsystem consisting of stocks, flows, and balances of materials and wastes. Each subsystem is related to all the others in numerous and little-understood ways.[28] As our society becomes more populous, affluent, and scientific, the interdependencies among the subsystems multiply.

But it is not enough to say that "everything relates to everything else." Rather, we must try to say *how* a particular policy action is related to the many variables within the society. It has become immensely difficult to predict the secondary, tertiary, and more distant consequences of any given action, whether by a government, a large corporation, or some other institution. In a provocative essay, "Don't We Know Enough to Make Better Public Policies?," Max Ways asked why man's capacity to use knowledge for social improvement had not increased proportionately to the amount of his knowledge.[29] His answer was that, *while the amount of information about society has grown explosively, knowledge of social relationships has not risen anywhere near as much.* Much as we need it, we lack adequate theories or models of the intricate relationships between the different aspects of our society.

Consider the example of poverty. There is a national consensus that poverty should be eliminated and a willingness to spend a great deal to reach that goal. But where is it most effective to spend money? On stimulating economic growth? On creating wider educational opportunities? On job training programs? On central city redevelopment? On cash payments to the poor? Or on a combination of these purposes? We simply don't know the answers to these questions. Nor do government policy-makers know how to cope with the public problems of drugs, crime, slums, health, race relations, or hard-core unemployment. For want of knowledge of social relationships, many of the billions spent in the "war on poverty" during the 1960's were wasted, according to a study sponsored by the Brookings Institution.

Decision-makers in government and in business must understand the workings of our complex social system in order to allocate resources efficiently and to make wise policies. Whether a policy-maker is responsible for distributing grants to support scientific research, for assessing the consequences of developing technologies, or for constructing budgets for governments or corporations, he needs accurate knowledge of the results of his decisions. In short, he needs access to an integrated, systematic understanding of our society. By the final decade of this century—and probably long before that—American policy-makers will have this available in the form of a *computerized national socioeconomic model system.* Such a model system will comprise data banks and equations describing relationships between myriads of variables, stored in the memories of vast computers. With such a system, policy-makers will be able to make decisions with a sharper and fuller knowledge of the direct and indirect consequences of each alternative course of action.

Some persons oppose the development of a national socioeconomic model system. They perceive it as a powerful nonhuman machine that will control man's destiny, à la George Orwell's *1984.* They fear that it might pass into the hands of an evil dictator, who would abuse its power. Other critics contend that the existence of such a model would substitute mechanical decision-making for the democratic political process of debate among contending groups. Both criticism are misplaced. The model system will be an aid to decision-makers. It will not *make* any decisions. Men will continue to make the strategic choices, in accordance with their values. Nor will the model system be a substitute for the democratic process of making choices. It will only enable that process to be carried on in a more rational way. The rationalization of public and private policy-making will be a boon to mankind because it will enable us to obtain a higher level of welfare from available resources.

## THE CORPORATION—AN ENDURING SOCIAL INSTITUTION

The corporation, in the year 2000, will still be a central institution of American society, as well as of the societies of all economically advanced nations. There is simply no promising alternative way of organizing and carrying out most of the tasks of production. Utopians may sigh for the bucolic joys of the simple rural existence. Alienated youth may experiment with life in communes. Social critics may excoriate bureaucracy. But in the long run, society will continue to rely on corporate organizations to carry on most of its work. Even in the Soviet Union and other socialist countries, the determined search for better management has led to the establishment of an increasing number of state-owned corporations in place of government bureaus. This trend will continue strongly into the future.

During the quarter-century after World War II, the corporation expanded the scope of its operations by conglomeration, spread around the world by multinationalization, adopted new methods of rational management, put the computer to work, and proliferated on an unprecedented scale. In the quarter-century to come we may be sure that it will display an equal flexibility in adapting its structure and processes to the needs of a changing environment. For many centuries, the corporate form has been used to organize man's economic drives as well as to satisfy his psychic and social needs. We have every reason to believe that the corporation will survive and flourish as a social institution long into the future.

## NOTES

1. The strong current interest in futurology is demonstrated by the following leading works: Daniel Bell, "Notes on the Post-Industrial Society," Part I, *The Public Interest,* No. 6 (Winter 1967), p. 28. Also Daniel Bell and Irving Kristol, eds., *Capitalism Today* (New York: Basic Books, 1970); Bertrand de Jouvenal, *Futuribles: Studies in Conjecture* (Geneva:Droz, 1963–1965), I (1963), II (1965); Peter Drucker, *The Age of Discontinuity* (New York: Harper and Row, 1969); Paul Ehrlich, *The Population Bomb* (London: Ballantine Books, 1969); Jay W. Forrester, *World Dynamics* (Cambridge: Wright-Allen Press, 1967); Theodore J. Gordon, *The Future* (New York: St. Martin's Press, 1965); Olaf Helmer, *Social Technology* (New York: Basic Books, 1966); Herman Kahn and Anthony Wiener, *The Year 2000* (New York: Macmillan, 1967); Dennis Meadows *et al., The Limits to Growth* (New York: Universe Books, 1972); and Alvin Toffler, *Future Shock* (New York: Random House, 1970). See also Ian Wilson, *The Business Environment of the Seventies* (New York: McGraw-Hill, 1971); Carl H. Madden, *Clash of Culture: Management in an Age of Changing Values* (Washington, D.C.: National Planning Association, October 1972).

2. See G. C. Lamb, "A Framework for Analysis of Societal Change," *Proceedings of the International Congress of Cybernetics, 1969* (London: 1970).

3. Dennis Gabor, *Inventing the Future* (New York: Alfred A. Knopf, 1969); also *The Mature Society* (London: Martin Seckert and Warburg, 1972).

4. John Platt, "How Men Can Shape Their Future," *International Future Research Conference Proceedings* (Kyoto, Japan: April 1970).

5. Ehrlich's forecasts of population growth, and Forrester's and Meadows' prognoses of population, production, and natural resource relationships pertain to the "uncertainty" period. See footnote 1.

6. See Kahn and Wiener, *The Year 2000*, p. 7.

7. *United Nations Statistical Yearbook 1971* (New York: United Nations, 1971).

8. Neil H. Jacoby and James E. Howell, *European Economics: East and West* (New York: World Publishing Company, 1967), p. 93.

9. Paul R. Ehrlich, "The Biological Revolution," *Center Magazine,* Vol. 2, No. 6 (November 1969).

10. Jacoby and Howell, *European Economics: East and West,* Ch. 8.

11. See Toffler, *Future Shock*, p. 168.

12. See B. F. Skinner, *Beyond Freedom and Dignity* (New York: Alfred A. Knopf, 1971).

13. See Emmanuel G. Mesthene, *Technological Change: Its Impact on Man and Society* (New York: Mentor Books, 1970). Among those who predict the replace-

ment of markets by government planning are Daniel Bell. (See his "Notes on the Post-Industrial Society," Parts I and II, *The Public Interest,* Nos. 6 and 7 (Winter 1967 and Spring 1967), pp. 24–35 and 102–118, respectively; and John Kenneth Galbraith, *The New Industrial State* (Boston: Houghton Mifflin, 1967).

14. This is a rounded total of physicians, dentists, lawyers, and engineers in private practice in the United States during recent years. See U.S. Bureau of the Census, *Statistical Abstract of the United States 1971* (Washington, D.C.: U.S. Government Printing Office, 1971).

15. Robert Soldofsky estimated that individual holdings of common stock will grow at the rate of 6.4 percent a year from 1968 to 1980 and at the rate of 4.8 percent a year from 1981 to 2000. See his *Institutional Holdings of Common Stock 1900–2000: History, Projection, and Interpretation* (Bureau of Business Research, Graduate School of Business Administration, University of Michigan, 1971), p. 85.

16. Theodore J. Gordon, *A Study of Potential Changes in Employee Benefits* (Middletown, Conn.: Institute for the Future, April 1969).

17. A survey by *Business Week* of 166 large companies in 31 industries. See *Business Week* (July 1, 1972), p. 41.

18. George Kozmetsky, "Reflections of a 21st Century Manager," *Bell Telephone Magazine* (March–April 1969).

19. Richard Eells, *Global Corporations: The Emerging System of World Economic Power* (New York: Interbook, 1972), p. 231.

20. *Ibid.,* Ch. 8.

21. See Neil H. Jacoby, "Corporate Enterprises in an Ocean Regime," *Columbia Journal of World Business,* Vol. 6, No. 2 (March–April 1971), for a full discussion of this subject.

22. See Richard Eells, "Corporate Sovereignty: A Charter for the Seven Seas," *Columbia Journal of World Business,* Vol. 5, No. 4 (July–August 1970).

23. See Elisabeth Mann Borgese, *The Ocean Regime,* Occasional Paper (Santa Barbara, Calif.: Center for the Study of Democratic Institutions, 1968).

24. Charles L. Schultze *et al., Setting National Priorities in the 1973 Budget* (Washington, D.C.: Brookings Institution, 1972), pp. 417–419.

25. General Electric established five new committees on its twenty-one member board on audit, management development and compensation, public issues, science and technology, and operations, each chaired by an outside director. See *Business Week* (July 8, 1972), p. 53.

26. See Soldofsky, *Institutional Holdings of Common Stock 1900–2000,* pp. 84–85.

27. See *The Future of American Enterprise* (Ann Arbor: Bureau of Business Research, Graduate School of Business Administration, University of Michigan, 1967), p. 16.

28. These four subsystems plus a "core" of basic population and institutional data constitute the modules of the Integrated National Socioeconomic Model System designed by North American Rockwell and a group of well-known social scientists during 1970.

29. See *Fortune* (April 1971).

# ADDENDUM

---

# The World Monetary
# Crisis of Early 1973

$S$ ERIOUS monetary disorder reappeared in the world in February, 1973.
Because American multinational corporate investments abroad had
created many of the $80 billion Eurodollars that were the object of specu-
lative activities, the world monetary crisis was linked to multinational
business. Of course, it was also the product of American military spending
abroad, American tourism, and American inflation.

The United States dollar was devalued by 10 percent on February 12,
1973, following an initial devaluation of more than 8 percent in December,
1971. It was generally expected that a depreciation of the dollar of more
than 18 percent against the strong currencies (notably the German mark,
the Japanese yen, and the Swiss franc) would lay the foundation for a new
set of stable exchange rates. This expectation proved to be unfounded. A
tidal wave of doubt arose among holders of foreign dollar balances, as to
whether the United States really would curb inflation and balance its international trade and payments. President Nixon's premature action of
January 11, 1973, replacing the mandatory wage and price controls—
which were slowing inflation—by voluntary restraints—whose effectiveness
was unknown—triggered a widespread erosion of confidence in the dollar.
(The writer had advocated a tightening of anti-inflation controls in November, 1972, to assure continued progress toward a stable price level.
See "After Phase II—What?," *Center Report,* October, 1972.) European
investors, oil-rich Arabs, multinational corporations, and even some central
banks sought to sell billions of dollars in order to buy gold and hard

currencies. The value of the dollar plummeted. Foreign exchange markets were closed.

During February and March of 1973, finance ministers and central bankers met in urgent efforts to find a key to a new monetary order. Although the outcome of their quest was unknown at the time of this writing, two propositions were clear enough:

1. The basic question was whether the 18 percent devaluation of the dollar had so realigned the cost and price structure of the United States with those of other nations, that reasonably free international trade and payments would bring American accounts back into balance with the rest of the world. *There was persuasive evidence that if this country ended inflation, its international trade and payments could come back into balance.* If foreigners saw American inflation ending, their confidence in the dollar would return; the American trade deficit would shrink; an inflow of long-term foreign investment would eventually take place. Stopping inflation is the key to international monetary stability.

2. Viewed in a longer perspective, the 1973 monetary crisis showed that the nineteenth-century system of multiple national currencies was inconsistent with stable exchange rates in the present era of massive international transfers of funds. Immediately, measures were needed to limit such transfers, and to create a return flow of dollars. Ultimately, a more fundamental solution was needed. *Contemporary multinational business ultimately requires a world currency and a world banking and credit system, in order to avoid disorder in the future.* The International Monetary Fund and the International Bank of Reconstruction and Redevelopment (commonly known as the "World Bank") do not now meet these needs. Until there is a unified world monetary system, speculative drives against *any* national currency can generate monetary disorder and impede world economic development.

The international monetary crisis of 1973 illustrates the principle stated previously in Chapter 5: *multinational business is forcing the evolution of global institutions of trade, investment, and finance.*

# Index

accounting, 63; faults in current system of financial reporting, 90–91; "human-asset," 59; new emphasis on "managerial," 64; teaching of, 61–62

Adams, Walter, 11, 238

advanced technology defense products, 226, 227; alternative sources for, 236–37; cost overruns of, 234; procurement policies for, 237–38; reward/risk ratio for, 238–41

aerospace companies, 225, 227, 228, 229, 230, 231, 233, 234, 257; profits of, 235–36; 240–42; under regime of Secretary McNamara, 239

Aerospace Corporation, 236

AFL-CIO, 157

Agency for International Development (AID), 103, 105, 120

Air Quality Act, 155

Algeria, 116

Aluminium, 98

American Medical Association, 153

American people, consensual goals of, 15–16

American society, 16–17; "corporate state" as model of, 20–21; the corporation within, 21; the emerging, characterized, 255–58; interactions of subsystems within, 189–90; pluralistic nature of, 13, 149–51, 257–58; predictions about, 250–52

Anaconda Copper, 97

anarchists, activist, 9

antimilitarism, 6

antiracism, 7

antitrust laws, 258

Arab nations, 13

Argentina, 104

armaments, reduction of, 230

assets, corporate, 30–33

Atomic Energy Commission (AEC), 226

Australia, 99

automobiles, 209–10; 216–16; internalizing costs of antipollutants, 189–90; safety of, 188, 190, 196, 221

Avco, 74, 227

Bain, J. S., 137

Ball, George W., 119

Bank Holding Company Act, 89

BankAmerica Corporation, 89

banks, and conglomerates, 89

Baran, Paul, 11

Barnard, Chester, 63, 65

Bayer (company), 97

Bell, Daniel, 255

Bell Laboratories, 237

Bendix (company), 74

Berle, A. A., Jr., and Means, G. C., 13, 37, 193

Bethlehem Steel, 141

"big business," as owners of wealth, 35; economies of scale, 137–38; traditional attitude toward, 131–132; see also corporate business

Blair, John M., 11, 130
boards of directors, 165–77, 179–81, 265; compensation of outside members of, 180–81; complaints of restricted social perspective of, 176–77; employee representation on, 175–76; improvement of functioning of, 177; limitation of members from financial institutions, 177, 180; multi-interest, 173–74; nonofficer majorities, 180; "outside" members, 179, 221; survey findings about typical, 169
Boeing (company), 227
Bolivia, 116
Borch, Fred, 229
Borgese, Elisabeth Mann, 263
Brazil, 99
Britain, 97, 98, 99, 100, 101
British Petroleum, 97, 98
Bronfenbrenner, Martin, 8
Brookings Institution, 264, 268
Brown-Boveri, 141
Buchanan, Scott, 173
budgets, 57, 58; variable, 60
business, American: criticisms of, 4–17; critics of, categorized, 7–10; emerging system of, 258–59; increased liabilities of, 156; popular disillusionment with, 154; postwar concentration changes in, 134–36; postwar trend in, 41; programs for systemic reform of, 6–10; proportion done by corporatitons, 23–24; and recent public issues, 155; and social goals, 185, 186; trends in corporate size of, 27–28; unincorporated, life expectancy of, 26; *see also* corporate business
Business Council, 152
business population dynamics, 131

Canada, 97, 98, 99, 100, 113, 114, 115, 116
capital, increased price of, 81
capitalistic system, 7–8
Carnegie Corporation, 63, 66
Casey, William J., 91
*Census of Shareowners,* 36
Centre for the Settlement of Investment Disputes, 120
Chamberlin, Edward S., 193
charitable contributions, 198–99
Chase Manhattan Bank, 177
Chase Manhattan Corp., 89
Chile, 9, 99, 116
China, 109, 113, 114, 254, 255
Chrysler Corporation, 107, 141, 142, 227
civil rights, 154, 158

Clark, J. M., 139
Coca-Cola, 97
Commission on National Goals, 16
Committee for Economic Development, (CED), 6, 7, 152, 197
Common Cause, 160
Common Market, 100, 107, 138, 142, 262
competition, 7, 191; effect of conglomeration on, 85–88; of institutions, 150; model of, 138–40; strengthening of, 142; types of modern, 141
computers, 61, 79; in government policy-making, 269
concentration, of corporations, 134–36
conglomerates: in banking, 89; control within, 74; cross-subsidization by, 86–87; economies of scale, 83–84; financial reporting of, 90–91; further defined, 74; merger boom of 1965–68, 75, 78–81; public policy toward mergers of, 90; risk reduction in, 83; social gain of efficient management in, 84; taxation as factor in mergers, 80–81; theory of centrality, 73–74
conglomeration, 72; antitrust enforcement as factor toward, 81; and competition, 85–88; concern over aggregation of power by, 87; energizes competition, 86; increases macroeconomic concentration, 85, 87; increases potential competition, 141; management science and, 79; potential financial effects of, 88–89; private gains from, 81–82; social gains from, 83–84; restraints on, 90; summing up, 91
Congress, and military spending, 230, 231, 232, 233
Consumer Affairs, Department of, 162
consumerism, 6, 7, 12, 154, 158, 195, 221, 264; interests of, 158–63; legislation on behalf of, 155
consumers, 176; exploitation of, 10, 14; interests of, 137, 158–63, 165–66
Container Corporation, 80
corporate behavior, 7, 203; charitable gifts, 198–99; and the environmental problem, 219, 221–22; rise of political influence on, 195–96; self-interest and, 196–98; theories of, 190–95; "voice" as a reaction to, 195–96
corporate behavior, 7, 203; charitable gifts, 198–99; and the environmental problem, 219, 221–22; rise of political influence on, 195–96; self-interest and, 196–98; theories of, 190–95; "voice" as a reaction to, 195–96

corporate business, 249; assessment of performance, 16–17; charges of critics against, 10–15; decline in power of, 264–65; direct and indirect investors in, 37; exploitation of workers and consumers, 14; future concentration of, 258; popular confidence in, restored, 154; population of, 21–24; "power elite" within, 13–14; and social institutions, 3–4; social predictions about, 250–52; standards for judgment of, 15–17; as a subsystem within U.S. society, 16–17; use of economic power, 10–11, of political power, 12–13

corporate income, taxation of, 82

corporate management, postwar trends in leadership styles, 59

corporate organization, 57–58

"corporate state," 5, 20–21, 40, 249

corporation: as arms maker, 225–43; authoritarian vs. participative styles of management of, 59, 171; defined, 3; an enduring social institution, 269–70; as environmentalist, 206–23; essence of, 21; future of, 249–70; instrument of political action, 151–53; limitations on "social responsibility" pressures, 219; organization of, for environmental action, 221; profit-seeking, 4, 23; as social activist, 185–203; summary assessment of, 249; a uniform law in the U.S. for, 179

corporations, business: abuse of privileges, 153–54; assessment of largeness and concentration of, 144–45; assets statistics, 30–33; basis of corporate political action, 150–51; changes in concentration of, 134–36; concentration of share ownership in, 38–40; "concentric" companies, 73, 74; conglomerate, 72–91; contemporary government of, 168–70; decline in power of, 153–54, 264–65; departments of public affairs in, 221, 260; distribution of dividend income, 39; economic power of, undue, 129–45; as employers, 34; functioning of boards of directors of, 166–68; future roles for, 257, 261–62; as generators of income, 33–34; government of, assessed, 165–68; growth of in U.S., 21–24; growth rate of large, 133–34; growth through merger, 73, 134, through internal investment, 134; incorporation figures for, 24–25; increase in number of small, 33; key to better government of, 177; large, as barriers to entry into business, 136–37; legislation and social action by, 201; life expectancies of, 24–25, 26; limitation of liability in, 23; managers of, seen as "power elite," 167; market power of large, 140–44; military hardware industry, 226–228; models of enterprise behavior of, 190–95; multinationalizing of, 261; need for rapid responses, 170–71; need for revised policies for social and political variables, 201–203; objections to largeness, 87; ocean regime and, 262–64; one social institution among many, 149–151; performance of, in U.S. economy, 40–41; political contributions of, 161–62; political power of, 148–63, vs. unions, 157–58; population figure summaries, 28–29; post-World War II evolution, 55–70; predictions about, 258–67; "professional," 258; profits of, as share of national income, 35–36; proper relationship to state, 267; public policies to promote social action by, 199, 201; rationale for charitable contributions by, 198–99; recommendations for performance improvement by, as source of weapons, 237–42; reduction of competition through concentration of, 130–36; reform proposals for, 167, 171–78, 179–81; response of, to non-market factors, 195, to shifts in public values, 221; restraint of competition on behavior of large, 140–42; role in the U.S. economy, 21–26; shareowner population, 36–37; size-class growth-rate figures, 28–29; size-distribution of, 27–33; "social account" in, 260; social involvement and profits of, 196–98; social responsibilities of, 60–61, 69; and social values, 267; task-oriented, profit-minded, 266–67; theory of the social role of, 186–198; trend in size of, 27–28; wealth of, 35; *see also* big business, conglomerates, corporate behavior, corporate business, enterprises, multinational corporations

Cuba, 104, 105

Czechoslovakia, 9

data processing equipment, 61

Datsun, 141

Davis-Bacon Act, 159

defense expenditures, primary determinant of, 229–30

defense industry, measures for improved performance by, 242–43; profits in, 235–

36, 240–42; reward/risk ratio in, 239–42
defense procurement, 227; alternative sources for, 236–37; need to improve system of, 236; recommendations for, 237–42
Denison, Edward F., 145
Department of Defense, 152, 226, 227, 229, 230, 239
Depression, Great, 5–6, 35, 37, 154, 193
directors: cumulative voting for, 168; legal liabilities of, 169–170; *see also* boards of directors
Doane, Robert R., 23
"dollar diplomacy," 116–17
Dow Chemical, 197
Dunning, John A., 115
duPont, 57

Economic Stabilization Act, 160
economics, 63, 64; teaching of, 61, 62
economy, U.S., 33–36; high concentration in, 135; performance of corporate sector in, 40–41; pluralistic nature of, 41; possibility of noncompetitive behavior, 85; transformed to "service," 80
Eells, Richard, 262, 263
Ehrlich, Paul, 211
Eisenhower, Dwight D., 228
elections, reform of, 160, 161
Employment Act of 1946, 156
English Electric, 141
enterprise(s), 23–24; expansion of, 73; managerial model for American, 193–94
environment, 16; byproducts of an improved, 223; charge of corporate exploitation of, 14–15; cost allocations for improvements in, 217; deterioration of urban, 207–11; ecologists, 176; economics of solutions to problems of, 215–17; improving political and corporate behavior toward, 219–22; instruments for enhancing, 218; instruments of governmental policy toward, 217–19; internalizing costs of, 222; population concentration and, 207–208; problem of improving physical, 206–11; public policy for improving, 215; restraint of actions harmful to, 217; schools of thought about, 211–15; technology and, 208–209
environmental forecasting, 56
Environmental Protection Agency, 222
environmentalists, 6, 7, 15, 154, 158, 160, 264
Epstein, Edwin M., 154–55, 156, 158

Eurodollar market, 117
European Corporation Board, 174
European Economic Community (EED), 100, 113, 119, 179, 254; Proposed Statute for the European Company, 174

Farmers Union, 157
Fayol, Henri, 63, 65
Federal Air Quality Standards Act, 196
Federal Communications Commission (FCC), 154, 156
Federal Election Campaign Act, 161
Federal Pay Board, 157
Federal Power Commission (FPC), 154, 156
Federal Trade Commission (FTC), 134, 135, 156
Fiat, 109, 141
Ford, Henry, II, 221
Ford Foundation, 63, 66
Ford Motor Company, 97, 141, 227
France, 97, 114, 115–16, 174
Friedman, Milton, 197–98
Fuchs, Victor R., 34
futurology, 251

Gabor, Dennis, 250, 255
Galbraith, J. K., 141
Gantt Chart, 57
General Dynamics, 227, 236
General Electric, 73, 107, 115, 141, 142, 227, 229, 266
General Motors, 57, 73, 97, 100, 101, 107, 115, 129, 133, 136, 137, 141, 150, 176, 197, 215–16, 227
Germany, 97, 100
Gini Coefficient, 28, 30
Glover, John D., 10
Goldberg, Arthur J., 166
Goldsmith, R., 35
Goodrich, B. F., Company, 107
Goodyear Tire & Rubber Co., 107
government, U.S., growth of, 133; relationship to corporate business of, 266–67
government sector, of U.S. economy, 33
Gross National Product (GNP), 133, 212, 213, 222, 232, 253, 256, 257
Graduate School of Business, University of Chicago, 61, 62
Graduate School of Business Administration at UCLA, 65
Grumman Corporation, 227
Gulf and Western Industries, 74
Gulick, Luther, 63, 65

Haldane, J. B. S., 253
Harris, Patricia, 177
Hart, Philip A., 143–44
*Harvard Business Review,* 156
Harvard Graduate School of Business Administration, 62
Hippies, 8, 9
Hirschman, Albert O., 195
Hobbes, Thomas, 173
Honduras, 99
Hong Kong, 254
housing, 187, 201
human nature, changes in, 9–10
Hutchins, Robert M., 255

Imperial Chemical Industries, 97
import quotas, 155
incentive compensation, 58
incentives, profit, 266–67
India, 254
Indonesia, 104, 254
inflation, 159–60, 251, 254
institutions, growth of, 131–32
integration, of enterprises, 137–38
Interest Equalization Tax, 110, 115, 120
International Basic Economy Corp., 103
International Business Machines (IBM), 59, 129, 142
International Centre for the Settlement of Investment Disputes, 105
International Monetary Fund, 111, 254
International Nickel, 97
International Petroleum, 117
International Telephone and Telegraph Co. (ITT), 56, 74, 80, 88, 149
Israel, 13, 117

Japan, 97, 98, 102, 254, 261
Japan Economic Research Center, 254
Jet Propulsion Laboratory, 236
Johnson, Lyndon B., 69, 161, 162
Johnstone, Allan, 114

Kaplan, A. D. H., 142
Kennecott Copper, 97
Keynes, J. M., 63
Korea, 254
Kozmetsky, George, 260
Kuhn, Thomas S., 194

labor, 159–60; monopoly power of, 130–31; political contributions of, 162; political power of, 157–58; unions, 118, 153; *see also* workers

Lampman, Robert J., 39
Lange, Oscar, 8
legislation, and socially desirable behavior, 190, 196, 201
leisure time, 256
Lever Brothers, Ltd., *see* Unilever
Libya, 112
Likert, Rensis, 59
Lilienthal, David, 102
Lincoln Electronics Laboratory, 236
Ling-Temco-Vought, 88
Litton Industries, 88
lobbying, 151–52, 264
Lobbying Act of 1946, 162
Lockheed Aircraft Corp., 142, 226, 227, 236; C5A contract, 238, 239; government loan guarantee to, 229
Logistics Management Institute, study of defense industry profits, 235–36
Los Angeles, quality of air in, 209, 216
Los Angeles International Airport, 218

Mace, Myles L., 167, 177
Machines Bull, 107
Madden, Carl H., 260
Malaysia, 104, 254
management, 56–61; advance in, summarized, 259; behavioral sciences and, 64; education in, early, 61–61; executive development programs, 58–59; future of education in, 67–69; future trends in corporate, 259–60; managerial "gap," 108; of multinational corporations, criticized, 114; postwar, 63–65; postwar practices of, 137; schools of, 63–69; "science" of, 56; social gains from superior, 84
management science, 79
managerial theory, on charitable contributions, 198–99
manager(s), 193–94; as controller of a cybernetic system, 60; education of, 56, 61–69; performance evaluation of, 58; programs for practicing, 68; skills of, summarized, 70; of socialist enterprises, 212; styles of leadership, 59; in underdeveloped countries, 69, 70
Marcor, 80
market mechanisms, 7
Marshall, Alfred, 191
Marxism, humanistic, 8, 9–10
Marxists, classical, 6
mass transit, 69
Massey-Ferguson, 98
McCoy, C. B., 188

McDonnell Douglas, 227, 229

McNamara, Robert S., 152, 234, 235, 239; "total package procurement" policy of, 238

Melman, Seymour, 234

Mercedes-Benz, 141

merger(s): among aerospace companies, 236; bans and breakups, 131, 137; conglomerate, 73, 78–81, 86; growth of corporations through, 73, 134; Justice Department guidelines, 143; motives for, 81; private gains from, 81–82; public policy toward conglomerate, 90; social gains from, 83–84; theories about, 76; types of, 73; waves of corporate, reviewed, 72, 74–75, 77–78, 79–81

Mexico, 102, 103, 104

Middle East, 117

military hardware industry, 226–28; costs to U.S. of products of, 233–35; government authority over, 233–34; nationalization of, 237; profits in, 235–36, 239–40; risks of, 233–34

military-industrial complex, 228–29, 234, 242

Mill, John Stuart, 191

Mishan, E. J., 66

Mitsubishi, 141

monopoly, 85, 86, 133

"monopoly capitalism," 12

monopoly profits, 198

Montgomery Ward, 80

multinational corporation(s): as agent of change in a developing country, 105–6; American investments abroad through, 98–99; basic organizational forms of, 101; charges against, 111–17; refined, 95; effects of corporate investment in, on U.S., 110–11; effects of, on developed host countries, 106–8, on international institutions, 117–18, on international relations, 111–17, on less developed countries, 102–6, on socialist countries, 108–10; expansion of business of, recommendations for, 119–21; flowering of, 97–98; foreign investment controls on, 110–11; future of, 121–22, 261–62; geographical diversification of operations of, 100; as instrument of national power, 116–17; joint venture affiliates of, 102; labor union criticism of, 111; management patterns for, 101; nationalism a threat to, 122; penetration of foreign economies by U.S., 98–99; power as agency for global economic unity, 122, as human institution, 262; recommended policies for, 119–21; rise of, 95–98; supranational chartering of, 118–19

multinationalizing, motives toward, advantages of, 99–101; of manufacturing, trading, and banking enterprises, 117–18; of labor unions, 118

Nader, Ralph, 160, 162, 173, 176, 195, 197

National Association of Manufacturers, 152

National Aviation and Space Agency, 226

National General, 74

National Labor Relations Board, 154

National Planning Association, 103

Netherlands, 97

New Deal, 6, 11, 150, 154

New Left, 198

New York Stock Exchange, shareowner census of, 36

Nigeria, 112

Nixon, Richard M., 109, 223, 224, 243

North American Rockwell, 227, 229, 236

Northrop (company), 227

Norton, Simon, 74

Occidental Petroleum, 74, 109

oceans, government of, 262–64

open markets, 7

operations research, 57, 63

organization, of corporations, 57–58

Ornstein, Stanley I., 136

Palmer, H. Bruce, 267

Panama, 99

Pay Board, 160

Pechiney (company), 98

Penn Central, 166, 176

Pentagon, 230–31, 234, 235, 239; *see also* defense procurement

Perlmutter, H. V., 121

Peru, 104, 116, 117

Phillips (company), 97

planning, and control, 60; corporate, 56–57; environmental forecasting, 56; long-term, 56–57

Planning-Programming-Budgeting System (PPBS), 57, 69

Platt, John, 250

pluralism, of U.S. society, 16

policy, public, *see* public policy

political campaigns, reform of, 161–62

political power, of corporations, 148–63

pollution, 7, 69, 188, 201, 208–11, 221, 263;

pollution (*continued*)
by autos, 189–90; determining standards of, 217–18; generated by current production processes, 214; governments as contributors to, 218; internalizing costs of antipollution measures, 215–16, 217, 218; need for government legislation against, 215, 216; rationale for antipollution standards, 216; in socialist countries, 212; *see also* environment

population(s), corporate, 21–33; growth in human, 212, 213, 255, 256

Postal Clerks Union, 157

poverty, 69, 187, 188; allocation of resources to, 268

power, economic, of business, 10–11; of corporations, 129–45

power, political, of corporations, 10, 12–13, 148–63; of corporations vs. unions, 157–58; enhancing citizen and consumer, 160–62

power elite, within business, 10, 13–14

private sector, 7

Program Evaluation and Review Technique (PERT), 57

programming, linear and dynamic, 57

public interest organizations, 264

public policy: on business competition, 142; on corporate political power, 148–49, 160–64; for corporate social action, 199, 201; on the environment, 215, 216, 217–19; on political power of consumer groups, 160; systems analysis and, 267–69

quality of life, 213

Radical Left, 4

Radio Corporation of America (RCA), 142

Rand Corporation, 57, 235

Reich, Charles, 4–5

Remington Rand, 115

Renault (company), 109

rent subsidies, 201

research and development, 79–80

reward/risk ratio, 83

Ricardo, David, 191

Robinson, Joan, 193

Roche, James M., 186

Rockefeller, David, 203

Rockefeller, John D., 153

Rockwell, Willard F., 229

Rolls-Royce (company), 97, 229

Roosevelt, Franklin D., 6, 152, 154

Roosevelt, Theodore, 133

Rumania, 109

Russia, 10, 109, 173, 230, 238, 269

Safarian, A. E., 113, 114, 115

*St. John's Law Review,* 88

Saloutas, Theodore, 5

Scherer, F. M., 144, 145

Schumpeter, Joseph A., 107, 139

Sears, Roebuck (company), 103

Securities and Exchange Commission (SEC), 37, 82, 91, 154, 156, 169, 178

security, national, 229–31

Security Council, United Nations, 254

self-employment, 23–24

"service economy," 80

service sector, 33

Shell Oil Company, 97, 121

Sierra Club, 160

Simons, Henry C., 158

shareowners, 193, 260; boards of directors as representatives of, 164, 171, 173; concentration of ownership, 37–39; direct, 36–37; expanded involvement of, 179; further diffusion of, 258–59; institutional, 266; interests of, 194; new "managerial," 177–79; population figures, 36–37; power of active, 177–78; restoration of control of corporations by, 265–66; weak influence of, charged, 167

shareownership, 40

Skinner, B. F., 256

Smith, Adam, 191

smog, in Los Angeles, 216

"social account," 202, 260, 267

social action, corporate, 196–99; promoted by public policy, 199, 201

"social audit," company, 60–61, 203, 260, 267

social change, 220, 221

"social conscience," 190

social problems, 186–88

social responsibility, 12, 69, 219; classical market model of, 191–93; corporate, 60–61, 185ff; managerial model of, 193–94; social environment model of, 194–95

"social sensors," 202

social values, corporations and, 220, 221, 267

socialism, 7–8, 10

society, *see* American society

Sony, 98

Soviet Union, *see* Russia

Spiro, Herbert, 240

Standard Oil (New Jersey), 58, 97

stockholderism, 6, 7, 12
stockholders, *see* shareowners
stockholding, institutionalization of, 37
Suez Company, 97
Sullivan, Leon, 176
supranational organizations, 261–64
Sweezy, Paul, 11, 12
Switzerland, 97
systems analysis, and public policy, 267–69

Taft-Hartley Act, 155
Taiwan, 104, 254
taxation, relation of, to mergers of 1960's, 80–81
Taylor, Frederick, 62
technological gap, 107–8
technology, and pollution, 209; social policy toward, 213
Temporary National Economic Committee (TNEC), 37, 133, 193
Tenneco, 74, 88
Texaco, 216
Textron, 74, 88
Theobald, Robert, 9
Thompson Ramo Woolridge (TRW), 227, 236
Thyssen (company), 97, 141
Tillman Act, 152, 153
Toffler, Alvin, 255
"total package procurement," 238, 239
Toyota, 98, 141
Trans World Airlines (TWA), 166
Transamerica, 74, 80

unemployed, unemployment, 69, 251; hard-core, 7, 188, 201
Unilever (company), 97, 121
United Aircraft, 227
United Fruit (company), 103
United Mine Workers, 158
United Nations, 118, 119, 122, 253, 254, 262, 263
U.S. Chamber of Commerce, 152
U.S. Steel, 75, 141

Urban Coalition, 160
urban planning, 218
urban rehabilitation, 218–19
urban renewal, 69, 201
urban slums, 188
urbanization, 208
Utopia, Utopians, 8–10, 12, 14, 186, 256, 269

Venezuela, 112
Vernon, Raymond, 104
Vietnam War, 6, 188, 228
violence, and social change, 8
"voice," 195–96
Volkswagen, 141
Vorstrand, 174

Wagon Lits Company, 97
Water Quality Standards Act, 155
Ways, Max, 26, 268
wealth, corporate ownership of, 35
Weisenbaum, Murray, 240
West Germany, 174
Westinghouse Electric, 141
Weston, J. Fred, 141, 145
Wharton School of Accounts and Finance, 61
Wilcox, Clair, 237
Williamson, Oliver E., 137
Wilson, Charles E., 150, 152
Woolworth, F. W. (company), 97
work ethic, 256
workers, exploitation of, charged, 10, 14; boredom of, 59–60; *see* labor
World Corporation Authority, 118–19

Yarmolinsky, Adam, 230, 234
Yippies, 9
Youngstown Steel, 141
Yugoslavia, 9, 10, 109, 110
Yugoslavia Enterprise Board, 175–76

Zero Growth school, 212–13
zoning, 218

## ABOUT THE AUTHOR

NOW A PROFESSOR in the Graduate School of Management of UCLA, of which he was the founding dean, Neil H. Jacoby has combined the careers of scholar, administrator, and corporate director. Born in Canada, he holds a B.A. and an LL.D. degree from the University of Saskatchewan. In 1938 he received the Ph.D. degree in Economics from the University of Chicago, where he later became Professor of Finance and Vice-President. For the past twenty-five years he has been at UCLA. He served on President Eisenhower's Council of Economic Advisers, was U.S. Representative in the Economic and Social Council of the United Nations, headed official missions to India, Laos, and Taiwan, and has been a member of the Pay Board. Jacoby was president of the American Finance Association in 1949 and was on the Executive Committee of the American Economic Association in 1963–66. He has been an organizer or director of several corporations, including one of the largest multinational firms. Author or co-author of more than fifteen books, including *United States Monetary Policy, United States Aid to Taiwan* and *European Economics—East and West,* Jacoby is an Associate of the Center for the Study of Democratic Institutions at Santa Barbara and is a frequent contributor to *The Center Magazine.*

STUDIES OF THE MODERN CORPORATION
*Columbia University Graduate School of Business*

FRANCIS JOSEPH AGUILAR
*Scanning the Business Environment*

HERMAN W. BEVIS
*Corporate Financial Reporting in a Competitive Economy*

COURTNEY C. BROWN, *editor*
*World Business: Promise and Problems*

CHARLES DEHOGHTON, *editor*
*The Company: Law, Structure, and Reform*

RICHARD EELLS
*The Corporation and the Arts*

RICHARD EELLS and CLARENCE WALTON
*Man in the City of the Future*

JAMES C. EMERY
*Organizational Planning and Control Systems:
Theory and Technology*

ALBERT S. GLICKMAN, CLIFFORD P. HAHN,
EDWIN A. FLEISHMAN, and BRENT BAXTER
*Top Management Development and Succession:
An Exploratory Study*

NEIL H. JACOBY
*Corporate Power and Social Responsibility:
A Blueprint for the Future*

JAY W. LORSCH
*Product Innovation and Organization*

KENNETH G. PATRICK
*Perpetual Jeopardy   The Texas Gulf Sulphur Affair:
A Chronicle of Achievement and Misadventure*

KENNETH G. PATRICK AND RICHARD EELLS
*Education and the Business Dollar*

IRVING PFEFFER, *editor*
*The Financing of Small Business: A Current Assessment*

STANLEY SALMEN
*Duties of Administrators in Higher Education*

GEORGE A. STEINER
*Top Management Planning*

GEORGE A. STEINER AND WARREN M. CANNON, *editors*
*Multinational Corporate Planning*

GEORGE A. STEINER AND WILLIAM G. RYAN
*Industrial Project Management*

GUS TYLER
*The Political Imperative: The Corporate Character of Unions*

CLARENCE WALTON AND RICHARD EELLS, *editors*
*The Business System: Readings in Ideas and Concepts*

A000011404019